Policing the Fringe

POLICING THE FRINGE

THE CURIOUS LIFE

OF A SMALL-TOWN MOUNTIE

Charles Scheideman

HARBOUR PUBLISHING

Harbour Publishing Co. Ltd.
P.O. Box 219, Madeira Park, BC, V0N 2H0
www.harbourpublishing.com

Front cover, main image: Charles Scheideman patrolling Chilcotin Highway 20, near Anahim Lake, early summer 1968 (photo courtesy the author). Front cover inserts: Left, grizzly bear, (sjulienphoto/iStockphoto). Centre, Scheideman at N Division Training School, winter 1961/62 (photo courtesy the author). Right, outhouse (mawear/iStockphoto). Back cover: A Freedomite attempts to save his greenhouse from fire while a plain-clothes officer looks on, Krestova, BC, circa 1965 (photo courtesy the author).
To protect the privacy of individuals, some names and details have been changed.
Printed and bound in Canada.
Printed on 100% PCW recycled paper using soy-based ink.

THE CANADA COUNCIL | LE CONSEIL DES ARTS
FOR THE ARTS | DU CANADA
SINCE 1957 | DEPUIS 1957

BRITISH
COLUMBIA
ARTS COUNCIL
Supported by the Province of British Columbia

Harbour Publishing acknowledges financial support from the Government of Canada through the Book Publishing Industry Development Program and the Canada Council for the Arts, and from the Province of British Columbia through the BC Arts Council and the Book Publishing Tax Credit.

Library and Archives Canada Cataloguing in Publication

Scheideman, Charles
    Policing the fringe : the curious life of a small-town Mountie / Charles Scheideman.

ISBN 978-1-55017-482-3

    1. Scheideman, Charles. 2. Royal Canadian Mounted Police—Biography. 3. Royal Canadian Mounted Police—Anecdotes. 4. British Columbia—Biography. I. Title.
HV7911.S34A3 2009   363.2092   C2009-900932-3

To
my wife, Patricia,
children, Howard, Sherry and Chris,
all those with whom I worked,
&
Reg. #18517 Staff Sergeant William Barry Beaulac
(retired),
my mentor and the finest police officer
I had the pleasure of working with.

Without Fear, Favour or Affection.

Contents

Preface

From 1961 to 1989 I was a member of the Royal Canadian Mounted Police patrolling the small and sometimes isolated communities of the interior of British Columbia. For all but a few months I worked in uniform at the street and road level. These years of experience "where the rubber meets the road" generated this collection of stories. All are based on actual happenings, but I have taken some liberty in the telling. Most are from my experiences, but some are from the memories of friends and workmates.

Some are funny, some are very sad, and some are downright gruesome.

I have diligently searched for any contamination by political correctness and have found none.

These stories describe the way I saw things, and I would like to think that in most cases that was the way it actually was. In every case I tried to call a spade a spade, but I have, in some cases, called a spade a #!*!+ shovel.

Car Chase
at Kicking Horse Pass

This story begins on a beautiful summer morning on the highway leading from Revelstoke toward Golden and the summit of Rogers Pass. A small two-seater sports car, a Fiat Spider, had caught the attention of everyone on the highway with extremely erratic driving. The little car was reported to be using the left side of the highway more than the right, cutting corners, passing in unsafe locations, and then slamming on the brakes very close in front of other traffic. The only person in the car, a young man, was constantly waving his arm out the driver's window and flashing the peace sign. Several motorists stated that they thought he favoured large transport trucks for his "cut in and brake" stunts. They felt he was suicidal.

The summer traffic volume did not allow for continued high-speed driving, but it also appeared that this driver was not intent on high speed alone. He drove very fast at times, but he also frequently slowed to speeds that severely restricted the normal flow of traffic. This erratic behaviour created a block-age of eastbound vehicles more than a mile in length. The west-bound traffic was only affected briefly when the offending ve-hicle was in their lane forcing them to take evasive action by braking or swerving to avoid head-on collision.

Reports of the erratic driver began to reach the RCMP in Revelstoke and the Park Warden Service at Glacier National Park headquarters at the summit of the pass. The primitive po-lice radio system that served the Rogers Pass highway corridor at that time only allowed communication between the summit area and the police office in Revelstoke. Police and Parks ra-dio signals went to a location at the summit where they were switched to a telephone link and carried to Revelstoke by wire. This non-system was unreliable in the summer and all but use-less in the winter when heavy snow interfered on a constant ba-sis. There was no permanent police presence on the ninety-two miles between Golden and Revelstoke. Requests for police ser-vices went to the park wardens, who relayed the information to Revelstoke whenever the radio-phone link was operable. When police attendance was required for incidents east of the summit in the Golden RCMP area, the requests were manually put into another radio and telephone link between the Revelstoke police office and the one in Golden.

The mobile offender in this case was eastbound and over the summit of the pass before we in Golden received informa-tion that he was headed in our direction. We later learned that the information had been delayed in the system by about twenty minutes; a delay that could have cost lives.

Our follow-up investigation revealed some strange happen-ings. During one of the frequent slow-driving parts, the small car was caught behind a transport truck and forced to stay there by another transport driver who moved alongside. This hap-pened in one of the double-lane sections of the highway, but the truck drivers were fast running out of room. When they reached the single lane ahead, they would have no choice but to allow the offender out again. Another trucker saw what was developing and he immediately moved his smaller truck in behind the sports car and completed the box. The truckers were able to communicate with their citizen's band radios and they used them to great advantage. The lead truck began to slow, as did the other two. This left the sports car and driver in a very restricted place. He swerved desperately, looking for an escape, but the truckers were in no mood to accommodate him. As the four vehicles came to a stop, the outside truck moved to his right, leaving the little car so tightly positioned between the transport truck and the guard rail that the driver was not able to open either of his doors.

At the moment the citizen's arrest was being executed, one of the park wardens arrived on the scene in an International Travelall four-wheel drive. The event should have been over. However, the arrival of the warden seemed to take the initiative away from the three truckers. They were glad to have the "authority" there to take over. I believe that if it had been left to the drivers for a few minutes longer, the result would have been different.

The warden approached the pinned sports car from the passenger side and spoke to the driver, who was still inside the car. The warden later advised that the driver was calm and in control of himself, and that he apologized to any and all present, saying he did not know why he had acted like that. The warden assisted him out of the car through the passenger window. When the offender was out of the car, he continued his apologies and even thanked the truck drivers for bringing him to his senses and stopping the danger he was creating. No one thought to secure and disable the little car. The driver was able to convince the warden that he was sane and remorseful and that he would make himself available to face any charges resulting from the happenings that morning.

The warden then shifted his attention to the long line of traffic that had built up behind the trucks. He left the offender standing beside the pinned sports car and began directing traffic. Soon he decided to speed up the clearing of the traffic and asked the truck drivers to move their vehicles so they only blocked one of the two uphill lanes. The lead truck had only moved a few feet ahead when the Fiat burst out of the box and sped away with the driver flashing the peace sign from his open window.

The warden ran to his vehicle and slowly set out in the direction the fast little car had gone. The International Travelall four-wheel drive was very useful in some circumstances, but highway travel or pursuit driving was most definitely not its long suit. The offender's Fiat, on the other hand, was right in its element on the open highway. This fact was about to be very clearly demonstrated.

The parks vehicle was able to struggle up to a maximum speed of about forty miles per hour on the mountain grade while the sports car could make eighty or more. The pursuing warden never saw the offending vehicle again.

The forced stop had taken place only a short distance west of the highway summit. The pursuing warden immediately started the message intended for us at Golden, which began the tedious process of being relayed back to Revelstoke. Eventually we received enough information to conclude that the offender must be stopped at the first opportunity and decided to establish a roadblock on the Columbia River bridge between Golden and the east end of Rogers Pass. We needed about ten minutes to reach this ideal roadblock location, but we were about halfway to our planned destination when we met the little car and saw the driver waving the peace sign as he streaked past us. I was in the passenger seat of the police car; the driver was an experienced police constable and an excellent driver. We executed a skid turn and immediately pursued the Fiat, which was travelling at about eighty miles per hour. We immediately radioed this information back to Golden. There was only one policeman left at the Golden office and he made a desperate attempt to get to the highway with his police vehicle. We saw him near the highway as we flashed past on the main road.

The police car I was in was an extremely powerful Ford sedan with an engine that Ford designated The Interceptor. If this car was pushed for maximum go, it would shift out of low gear at sixty miles per hour and out of second gear at one hundred miles per hour. The man in the Fiat Spider had now met something to be reckoned with.

After we turned, we were in close pursuit of the Fiat within about one mile. We then saw firsthand how this person was performing. He drove on the left into blind corners and passed other vehicles with no regard for oncoming traffic. In the first mile that we were in close pursuit he came close to four or five very serious crashes. It was only the quick evasive actions of other drivers that prevented a catastrophe. We allowed a gap to open between us in the hope that he would use a little caution, but that seemed to make no difference to him. We were aware that the lone remaining RCMP member in Golden was trying to get to the highway junction before we did. However, the highway was more than four lanes wide at the junction and we knew there was little he could do even if he did get there. This guy was not going to stop for a flashing red light on a single police car.

As we entered the congested area of the highway near Golden, the Fiat was forced to slow and swerve through the traffic. The driver braked into a skid to avoid a crash and then geared down and immediately accelerated as hard as the little car could. We came behind with our lights flashing and the siren howling, expecting to see a crash at every intersection. We cleared the first business area along the highway and approached the main highway junction just in time to see our last chance for assistance still a quarter of a mile from where he may have been able to help. We shot by the intersection and started into Kicking Horse Pass, the section of the Trans-Canada Highway that was known as the worst ten miles of driving from one coast of Canada to the other.

We now felt that we had a small advantage. The highway was so winding that traffic was much slower than in the area we had just covered west of Golden. The pursued car had out-of-province license plates, so we were quite sure the driver was not familiar with the road and thought we would be able to push him into overdriving one of the many curves. At that point we would have welcomed the sight of him running off the highway rather than crashing into some other unit of traffic.

We held a small meeting to decide if I should try to shoot a tire off the car. The meeting was called to order. The secretary was absent. A question arose from the floor. SHOOT?? YES! TRY IT! All in favour? Carried. New business? None! I asked my driver to yell "clear" if there was no visible oncoming traffic and "hold" if there was. This motion was also carried by a unanimous vote.

I removed my seat belt and leaned out the passenger window of the big Ford. I had never fired a shot from a car but I was amazed how the car door and the flared fender supported my attempt. As we entered the second mile of very winding road we were in close pursuit. The little car had to slow greatly to get around the curves and it was very short of acceleration compared to our unit. At times we were so close behind the Fiat that I could not see the right rear wheel, which I had chosen as my target. I fired three shots over the next mile, each of which I felt could have done the job, but there was no visible effect. We then entered another very sharp uphill curve to the right. The little car braked hard to reduce his speed for the curve and as he came out of it he presented the side of the car to my vantage point. I could clearly see the right front wheel and I had the "clear" call from my driver. I shifted my point of aim to lead the front wheel and fired. Once more there was no visible result, but we were again tight behind the little car.

After the fourth shot we met oncoming traffic and I held fire. We pursued uphill for nearly half a mile with constant oncoming traffic until the next opening. I was about to take aim again when I saw smoke from the front of the little car. The thin wisp quickly became a cloud and we began to feel we had won. The Fiat was now in obvious trouble. It could no longer accelerate as it had in the previous miles and we could see chunks of smoking rubber flying up from the right front wheel. The driver continued to give it all he had over the next two miles, but his efforts were now futile. He was only able to generate twenty miles per hour or less. Suddenly the little car nearly disappeared in a cloud of steam as a hose burst and the contents of the overheated cooling system vaporized in an instant. This phase was over.

We bounded out of our car and pulled the screaming driver out of the Fiat. He now presented a very different attitude than he had when he was stopped one hundred miles earlier. He appeared to be terrified, and he pleaded with us not to kill him, all the while fighting us with all he had. He had lost control of his bladder. We were easily able to overpower him and we placed him face down and cuffed his hands behind his back. The moment we released our hold on him he rolled over and tried to kick us, but this was of no danger to either of us.

The other police car, which had overtaken us near the slow end of the chase, took the prisoner and returned to Golden. We waited for a tow truck to remove the car to secure storage. I examined the little car to see where my bullets had struck and found three bullet holes in a close group just below the right rear tail light. The bullets had penetrated the outer skin of the car, but then had hit the heavier metal of the inner fender and had not gone through. The right front tire was gone and the wheel was worn down until it would no longer turn on the axle. I examined the right side of the car from end to end but I was unable to find any indication of a bullet impact. We assumed my last shot must have penetrated the side wall of the tire. The flat tire then caused heavy resistance for the little car and the engine boiled and seized.

Any one of the first three shots could have flattened the right rear tire had I been in possession of a better firearm. Neither the issue handgun nor ammunition of that time was effective, and combined they were a bad joke. There were many superior firearm and ammunition combinations available but at that time the upper echelons of the Mounted Police were still looking for a nicer way to shoot someone.

Our prisoner had somewhat regained his composure by the time the car reached our lock-up in Golden. By then he was reciting the standard suspect line of, "I refuse to say anything until I have talked to a lawyer." One of the members who had not been involved in the chase took him aside and advised him he would be held in custody until we were able to take him before a court the next day. He was offered the use of the telephone, but declined. Judging by our observations of his driving and his actions at the arrest, we were all of the opinion that we should have his marbles counted. We warned our civilian prisoner guard to be extremely careful with this man and to watch for a possible suicide. He was not to be let out of the cell unless there was a policeman present.

During the day that he was in our cells, his mood varied from hour to hour. He frequently screamed and ranted and rocked the cell cage like a madman. At other times he would engage in calm conversations with some of us or our cell guard. Apparently, he had been a student at a large U.S. university until he decided to drive home to eastern Canada. We were not able to learn when his psychosis began or what, if anything, may have contributed to it.

Court in Golden in those days was normally held on Saturday mornings and Wednesday evenings. Our lay judge who presided at the scheduled court was a school principal, which necessitated the unusual hours. Most of our local clients appreciated the somewhat unusual court hours because they did not have to take time away from their work to deal with relatively routine brushes with the law.

Our prisoner ranted and visited and yelled and slept and rocked the cell cage over the hours until the evening of the next day when we arranged for him to appear before the local court. The usual Wednesday evening court started at seven. I did not have a long list that evening so I asked two of the constables to very cautiously move the prisoner to court after I had dealt with the few routine matters. By arranging his court appearance that way we would not have an audience in the event our client lost control of himself, as I suspected he would. The court location was about one mile from the police building, so the prisoner had to be moved in a police car.

The magistrate and I dealt with the routine matters and had everyone out of the court building before seven thirty. The two constables brought the prisoner in and we presented him to the court. Our client became very rational and calm. He asked to have the handcuffs removed so that he could write notes. I raised an objection to this but the magistrate decided to grant his request after cautioning the prisoner that there were three relatively large police officers there who would without doubt put the cuffs on again by whatever means were necessary. The prisoner promised to behave.

The hearing began with me reading the charges and requesting the accused be remanded in custody for psychiatric assessment due to the serious nature of the charges and because he was transient. I then tried to briefly outline the circumstances of the chase and capture. I was only able to start the narrative of the event when our prisoner lost his carefully demonstrated control. In an instant he went totally wild. He screamed and kicked and fought with the three of us briefly until we were again able to cuff his hands together. We sat him on a chair and held him there while the magistrate tried, without success, to ask him a few questions about the recent happenings. Communication with the man was now impossible and the magistrate soon gave up and granted the requested adjournment in custody.

We now had our prisoner cuffed with his hands in front rather than the more effective placement behind his back. The two constables escorted him out of the courtroom and down a flight of stairs to the back door where the police car was parked just outside. Just as the three of them went through the doors I heard a scuffle, and one of the policemen yelled something about a gun. I bounded down the stairs and through the doors in time to see the prisoner kneeling on the landing with a holstered police handgun in his handcuffed hands, intent on opening the holster.

This vision was very brief because one of the constables came down across the prisoner like a football tackle. This constable weighed around two hundred and fifty pounds and had tried out for the Saskatchewan Roughriders before joining the Mounted Police. The prisoner was quite flat and the still-holstered handgun squirted out from under the two bodies. I later learned that the prisoner had lunged at one of the members as they went through the door, grabbed the holstered handgun on his belt, and heaved on it with all his weight. The swivel attachment to the waist belt gave way and the prisoner then had the holstered firearm in his hands. The safety catch on the holster slowed him just long enough to save someone from being shot.

I assisted the two constables with changing the cuff position so the prisoner's hands were behind him, and he was soon safely into the back of the police vehicle. They drove back to the cells and I returned to the courtroom to wrap up the last paperwork of the evening. I stayed at the court for a while and then the magistrate and I stopped at a local coffee shop for a short time. I returned to the police office about eight thirty to find an ambulance there. When I went in, the prisoner was lying dead on the floor in the cellblock. The ambulance crew had been unable to revive him and had just given up their efforts.

The prisoner had once again collected his wits during the short ride from the court to the cells. He spoke civilly to the two officers and even joked about being able to grab the revolver from one of them. He ventured the opinion that there were no rules for the game they were playing and that they had clearly won that round, even though it had been close. He had a large drink of water from the fountain in the cellblock and asked if someone could get him a sandwich. He offered to pay for the sandwich with money from his effects since it was not a regular meal time.

The prisoner was returned to the horrible cage that we had for a cell. The standard cages were fabricated from sturdy steel straps about one inch wide which were riveted at every intersection to form square openings of about four inches. The frame of the cage was made from heavy angle iron; the floor was sheet steel, welded and riveted to create an almost watertight bottom. Fluid, mainly urine, would seep under the cages, which were far too heavy to be moved for cleaning. Each cage had an upper and lower bunk, again of sheet steel and angle iron. A thin, plastic-covered mattress and a blanket were provided if the prisoner did not vandalize them.

The prisoner chatted with the constables and the guard as he was again booked into the cell, not objecting to the routine search of his person and clothing. He removed his shoes and belt when requested. Before the guard left the cell room, the prisoner was lying on the bottom bunk as though he intended to go to sleep.

Twenty minutes later, when the guard looked through the small observation window in the cell room door, he could see that something was not as it should be. The guard yelled for assistance and ran to get one key to access the room and another to open the large padlock on the cage door. Another constable was in the office at the time and he attended at the cell with the guard. They found the prisoner hanging from the lattice top of the cage. He had removed his trousers and run a leg over one of the steel straps of the cage roof so that one leg of the pants hung down on each side of the strap. He then sat on the top bunk and pressed the back of his neck tightly under the point where the pant legs hung down and tied a very solid square knot under his chin. He slid his buttocks off the edge of the bunk and hung by his throat.

The guard and the constable struggled to take the prisoner down, but they were unable to raise his limp body enough to untie the tight knot in the pant legs. The constable ran to another part of the office and got a knife; however, he could not work with the knife inside the cage because he could not cut the trousers without also cutting the hanging body. There was about a ten-inch space between the top of the cage and the ceiling of the room. The constable managed to squeeze himself into that space and he began to hack at the cloth of the trousers. Finally the body was lowered to the floor and taken out of the cage. An ambulance had been called for by a radio message to a car patrolling in the town. The ambulance arrived about the time the body was cut down, but there were no indications of pulse or breathing in the body and none was restored by attempts at cardiopulmonary resuscitation.

The coroner's inquest ruled that the death was suicide and attached no blame to anyone other than the deceased.

If this event were played out today, the final storyline would probably be: Scheideman has recently obtained employment at the local mill where the reluctant employer has agreed to hire him for a probationary period of six months. He has agreed to undergo counselling and other therapy until he is thought to be able to control his aggressive behaviour. The community is still reeling and has plunged into a campaign to eliminate all firearms, particularly those formerly used by the police.

When this incident happened in 1974, the community of Golden was very appreciative of what we had done. The local newspaper ran the story with a headline very much in support of the armed pursuit and eventual removal of the dangerous driver from the public road. My daughter, who was in grade three, was assisted by one of her teachers in making a small wooden trophy with a sports car at the top. The words "Sharp Shot Scheideman" were printed on the side of the trophy and "To Dad, Love Sherry" on the base.

I still have that trophy.

The Mysterious Charred Man of Rogers Pass

The Rogers Pass section of the Trans-Canada Highway cuts through some of the most rugged mountain terrain in Canada. A large part of the highway route lies in Glacier and Revelstoke National Parks and has not been impacted by logging. Much of the eastern slope of the Selkirk Mountains along the highway is outside the park system. Every creek valley outside the park has a logging road into the upper reaches and the scars of modern clearcut logging are very evident. It was on one of these logging roads that this story begins.

Two young men were driving along the highway toward Golden from Revelstoke in the very early hours of the morning. They had just crossed the boundary out of Glacier Park and were talking about switching drivers when they saw the headlights of a car facing them. They were still some distance away when they realized that it was not moving. They could see that there was something or someone moving around on the highway in front of the parked car. They slowed and moved to the right, thinking the car may have hit an animal and that the animal might get into their path as well. They watched closely to determine what was happening, unable to see clearly because of the glare from the light beams of the stationary car.

As they came almost alongside the car and were partly out of the direct beam of the headlights, they saw that what they had thought was an animal was in fact a man on his hands and knees a few feet from the front of the car. They stopped to find out what was happening and to offer assistance. Nothing could have prepared them for what they met on the dark road that night. The lights from the car revealed a person who would have been unrecognizable even to his best friend. The person was black from head to toe, burned so badly that his ears and nose were gone. His eyelids and mouth would no longer move, and all his clothing was burned away except for the partial remains of a pair of jockey shorts and his ankle high boots. He was wringing his hands, begging for help, and pleading for a drink of water. As he wrung his hands, the skin peeled away up to his wrists and complete tubes of skin pulled off his fingers.

The two young men found a bottle of pop in their car and gave it to the man, but he was unable to get the bottle to his mouth. One of the helpers held the bottle and tried to get some of the liquid into the unmoving mouth. The man was over six feet tall and he had gotten to his feet when the helpers approached, which made the providing of a drink almost impossible. They helped the burned man into the back seat of their car, moved the other car to the shoulder of the highway, and sped toward Golden. Enroute, the burned man began to wail and scream whenever he was not begging for water. The smell of burned flesh filled the car and before long both of the helpers had vomited until they could bring up nothing more. The twenty miles to Golden were, and will always remain, the longest piece of road those two had ever travelled.

At last the lights of the community could be seen ahead. It was two thirty in the morning when they pulled into the first service station that was open. There happened to be a small café attached to the gasoline station and both sides of the business remained open twenty-four hours a day.

Golden is situated at the confluence of the Kicking Horse River and the Columbia River. There are no all-night services for almost one hundred miles to the east and ninety miles to the west. Everyone who travels that route at night will stop in Golden for fuel and food, resulting in the all-night places being continually busy.

There were twenty-five or thirty people sitting around having snacks or coffee when the burned man lurched into the bright lights of the café and asked for water. He was followed by the young men who had found him on the highway, who had now partially recovered from the initial shock of what they had found. They got the burned man onto a chair and began to pour glass after glass of water into the charred hole that had been his mouth. Someone called for an ambulance and the police. The café emptied.

One of the young constables from Golden arrived and was told the story by the two helpers. He was able to converse with the burned man in a very limited way; however, it was obvious that the man did not wish to tell him how he had been burned. The man said he had been camping alone in the mountains when it happened. An ambulance soon arrived and took him to the hospital in Golden.

One of the few doctors in the small community happened to be at the hospital when the ambulance arrived. No one, including the doctor, had ever seen a living person that badly burned. The doctor was amazed that the man had not lost consciousness.

The doctor determined that there was little that could be done for him. He tried, without success, to find a vein to inject pain medication, and he attempted to give pain killers by mouth and by intra-muscular injection but these things appeared to have little if any effect.

The man had totally lost control by the time he arrived at the hospital. He would not respond to questions or requests and he frantically thrashed about, moaning and screaming and trying to get up from the emergency-room bed. Restraint straps were placed over his pelvic area and legs. His continual movement made the spectacle that much more gruesome.

The doctor told the constable that the man would soon drown and that there was no way to delay or prevent it. He said that the lungs are very dependent on the skin, and that in severe burn cases involving large portions of the skin, the most common complication is a rapid fluid build-up in the lungs. The fluid build-up increases in proportion to the amount of skin that has been burned, and drowning is the actual cause of death in most severe burn cases.

The man died about four long hours after he arrived at the hospital. The staff from the little hospital went home totally exhausted that morning.

Meanwhile, the night shift officer had driven out and found the abandoned car, which was towed to secure storage. It had been parked near a logging road that branched off the highway and went up a creek valley into the mountains. The side road appeared to be a good place to start looking for clues about the mysterious burned man. This incident happened in the late fall and there was snow on the ground in the higher areas of the Rogers Pass. There was no snow where the car had been found, but as the constable drove up the road in the darkness he reached an elevation where the recent snowfall still covered the ground. There were tire tracks visible in the snow. Close

27

examination of these tracks indicated that only one vehicle had been up and down the road since the snow; the tire impressions were similar to the tires on the car where the burned man had been found. The constable followed the tracks up the logging road in the snow. After about three miles, the road came into a clearing where forestry operations had gathered logs prior to hauling them out. The leveled area of the clearing was at the point where the creek valley split, and a road went into each of the branches of the valley. The same tire tracks were visible on both roads leading further into the mountains.

The constable picked the road to the left from the landing area and followed the tracks. The snow on the ground was getting deeper with the increased elevation and he could see that the vehicle had been having some difficulty due to the lack of traction. The police vehicle was equipped with four-wheel drive and had no trouble in the snow. The tracks showed where the suspect car had lost traction on a steep part of the road and had to back down and get a better run to get over that area. The driver of the car showed a considerable degree of driving skill to maintain control and to force the car through the adverse conditions.

After about another two miles on the left fork of the logging road, the policeman came onto another cleared and leveled area, called a landing, where logs were gathered. This landing was smaller than the previous one at the first fork and was covered with nearly three inches of snow. The tracks of the suspect vehicle circled the landing and indicated the vehicle had parked by some scrap logs on a level area at one side. The heat from the engine of the parked vehicle had melted the snow to the ground, indicating that it had been there for some time. The scrap logs had been rolled around so that they formed a rough half circle about five feet in diameter; a small fire had burned out in the centre of the circle. The fire site was about ten feet from where the car had been parked. A stick was propped across one of the logs so that one end extended over the fire and a small metal pot with a wire handle was sitting on one of the logs at the side of the fire pit; the pot was blackened from fire.

The person who camped had heated some water or prepared food over the fire. Cut marks on a log near the fire were from an axe being used to break up and split wood. The snow was packed by foot prints all around the fire area and between there and the vehicle; tracks wandered around the landing as the camper had gathered wood for the fire. Tracks led a few yards away from the car and the fire to where a man had urinated in the snow on two or possibly three occasions. The foot tracks on the landing all appeared to be from the same pair of shoes; they were about a size eleven man's boot very similar to the charred remains of the boots worn by the burned man.

A three-gallon plastic gasoline can was lying in the snow a few yards from the fire. The can smelled of gasoline but there was no liquid left in it. The threaded cap was hanging from a plastic strap around the neck of the can. The can sat in the snow with the opening toward the top; had there been fuel remaining in the container when it was placed there, it would not have spilled. The packed snow between the car and the fire showed traces of colour where small splashes of gasoline had been spilled. Traces of partially burned and melted clothing were in and around the ashes of the fire, and similar particles were in the snow all around where the vehicle had been parked. The snow beside the vehicle, on the side away from the fire, was flattened in about a ten-foot circle where a person had been rolling and thrashing around. Burned and melted pieces of clothing were mixed in the snow throughout this rolled area. A melted nylon zipper, possibly from a jacket, was the largest and about the only piece that could be identified.

The evidence at the camp site seemed to indicate the man

had been there for a few hours and that he had been alone. It appeared he had opened the gasoline container and poured the contents over himself, then tossed the empty container to one side and walked into the fire. He caught fire from head to foot, moved around the parked car at least one full circle, and then began to fight the fire by rolling and thrashing around in the snow. The extensive burning to his head and face indicated that he had remained standing for some time during the fire.

The fire on the man and his clothing burned itself out or was extinguished by his rolling in the snow. By the time the fire was extinguished, the man was nearly nude; his waist belt, part of his trousers and most of his underwear were all that remained, along with most of his boots and the portion of his socks that was inside the boots.

After the fire had burned out, the man got into his car, started it and drove toward the highway. He spun the wheels in the snow for the first few yards but then controlled the car and drove it with the caution necessary to traverse the slippery and steep road. When he reached the large landing below where he had been camped, he became lost and started up the other fork of the road, away from the highway. He drove up the narrow road for nearly a mile to the first place where he could safely turn the car around, and then he turned the car by moving it back and forth and steering to the extreme right and left. He then returned to the log landing and found the road to the highway.

After daylight that morning the area where the car had been parked on the highway was searched. Patches of skin from his hands were located, along with the complete skin from several fingers. The fingers still had the details of fingerprints and were later used to establish positive identity of the dead man.

The contents of the car were viewed and listed in detail. The car was packed full of personal effects, camping gear and books. We concluded that the man had been living in the car or camping from the car for a considerable time prior to his death. Many of the books in the car were textbooks and manuals dealing with engineering. We asked a civil engineer to have a look at the books. He felt that the owner of a collection of books like that was either an engineer or was in the advanced stages of becoming one.

The car also contained three thick volumes about devil worship. These books were worn and dirty. Each one had several bookmarks at pages which were noticeably more worn and dog-eared than the other pages of the books.

News of the person who had burned to death at Golden spread rapidly. Within a day of the incident, people from the construction camp at Mica Creek, where a hydro dam was being built on the Columbia River, contacted us saying they thought they knew who the dead person was. Although we could only give a vague description of the man—his height and weight, but very little more—our description of the car and that it was packed full of effects left little room for doubt.

The mystery man had worked at the Mica Creek construction site on several occasions since the project had started, and most recently during the past ten days. He was a very well-qualified civil engineer who had first come onto the site in the beginning stages of construction, and had convinced the engineering staff to let him demonstrate his skill at planning and drawing some portions of the project. His work was excellent; the management people at the project would have been pleased to have him as part of their team, but he would finish a small project and then disappear. He had returned to the site for the third time on this last occasion and, like each time before, there was a project for him and he tackled it with determination and skill.

The man was described as a social misfit who was a loner

to the extreme; he would write notes to others at the site when he could have turned his chair and spoken with them. He would eat his meals in the camp dining hall, but he would always go there at quiet times and sit in an area away from everyone else. Some had approached him in the dining hall, but they found that he was so ill-at-ease with them that he would get up and leave before he finished his meal.

We obtained a name, address, birth date, and next of kin from the employment records at the construction site. This information matched with the registration records of the car and was later confirmed by the fingerprints we had picked up on the highway. He had been fingerprinted years earlier when he was employed in a high security project in eastern Canada.

His family was traumatized, but not surprised, by the news of his death. He had been an ideal child, an excellent student, and a very promising young adult. He graduated with honors as a civil engineer and had undertaken additional studies to gain further qualifications. It was during his later studies that his personality changed and he withdrew from all others. He shunned everyone; his family had not heard from him for about five years.

The coroner's inquiry ruled that the death was suicide, and attached no blame to any living person.

Domestic Violence

Throughout most of my service in the police business, domestic violence was swept aside by advising the victim to come to the police office on the next business day to start the process by the swearing of information, charging the perpetrator with assault. The victims chose not to, or were too terrified to start a court action in nearly every instance. In the few cases where the process was started, only a very small number actually went to court.

The threat of prosecution and its ensuing publicity could make a teetotaling, gentle and loving, generous and providing husband-of-the-year out of the most brutal wife-beating bastard in the community. Unfortunately, these amazing metamorphoses usually only lasted long enough to convince the victim to drop the court action.

Many of us were shocked by the first few domestic incidents we attended under the guidance of a more senior policeman. We witnessed assaults, or the result of assaults, which left us sickened and wishing that somehow the victim would gather the courage to take revenge in some form, or at least get out of the abusive relationship. This rarely happened, though. In most cases, the abuse just went on and the recipient somehow managed to survive for another day and another beating. Most, but not all.

We were frequently called to a particular home to deal with severe assaults on the wife. The husband was often drunk; he seemed to believe that his behaviour was a normal part of family life. He was always extremely abusive to us and we used extra caution in dealing with him. After one particularly severe incident we removed the beaten woman and her children from the house.

There were no facilities to temporarily house such victims in that community, so we took them to the hospital emergency room. After her injuries were treated, she called her sister to pick her up. The sister's husband was a huge but gentle man who worked as a logger. When the sisters arrived at the logger's home and he saw what had been done to her, he called one of his co-worker friends. The two loggers paid a visit to the perpetrator. During the course of this visit the perpetrator learned the finer points of being on the receiving end of extreme violence. At times during the visit he was afraid he would die, and at other times he was afraid he would not. He recovered as a changed man and his family life was greatly improved. He had not only developed a great respect for his brother-in-law, but he would often thank him for showing him the error of his ways.

The majority of domestic violence incidents involved the woman taking the brunt of the abuse. However, I recall a few cases where this was not true. We had frequent contact with a Native couple, Ernie and Mimi, where the husband was a very thin, smaller-than-average man while the wife was a very strong, much-larger-than-average woman. These two shared an

insatiable thirst and their constant efforts to quench this problem led to frequent disagreements between them. Their disagreements always became physical and little Ernie always got
the worst of it.

One summer evening they came to the police office in their
usual drunken condition. As they entered the front door, Ernie
showed us his black eye and swollen mouth and announced that
he wanted a divorce. One of the constables got up from his desk
and as he walked to meet them at the front counter he said, "We
do have a couple of those left over, so you have come at the right
time." He asked them to take a seat while the divorce papers
were prepared.

They sat down and the constable rolled a piece of blue legal
paper into the typewriter and typed "Decree of Divorce" across
the top. In the next five minutes the document was composed,
with several "wherefores" and "hereafters," and provisions for
the signatures of the combatants and witnesses. At the constable's request, Ernie and Mimi both signed the paper and it was
duly witnessed. As the pair left the office, the little man turned
to the left and the big woman went off to the right.

Later, they must have forgotten about the divorce or chosen
to disregard it, because the couple remained as much a part of
the fabric of the town as they had ever been.

On rare occasions we found humour in an incident of domestic violence. This was partly due to the twisted view of cal-
loused veteran police officers, and partly to the tendency in all
of us to see a little humour in the misfortunes of others.

One such instance unfolded near a small interior community where I was working. My partner and I were the only two
on duty for the afternoon shift of a midsummer Saturday. The
day shift had been on the run all day; they were several calls behind when Dave and I came to work at four o'clock. Dave and
I became responsible for all calls after four, while the day shift

would work until they had cleared all the calls received before that time. The most memorable call of our shift came in at about four p.m.

The person who took the call was a very experienced worker at our office. She was often able to resolve problems over the telephone by applying a wealth of common sense and diplomacy. This lady had been hired to guard prisoners in our cells, but the volume of our work demanded that the guard also take telephone messages and attend the front counter. Our guards were carefully chosen because a competent guard was as good as having another uniformed policeman on the job.

When the call came in, our guard knew immediately who it was. She completed the name and address section of the complaint form from memory as she listened to the details from the inebriated caller. Our guard also noted that she could hear, in the background, an adult female crying like a child in a temper tantrum.

The call was from one of our regular clients, advising that her husband had assaulted her friend who was visiting from a residence nearby. Our guard tried to get more information about the nature of the assault but the caller was reluctant to provide details. She insisted that the police attend immediately to see for themselves what he had done. She did say that immediately after the assault her husband had walked away into the bush.

The caller lived in an area about four miles from town at the end of a dirt road. People chose to live there because it was inexpensive. The dwellings were either run-down mobile homes or shacks thrown together from salvaged material. Electricity was the only service they had. The land around the community was covered in thick bush.

The caller and her common-law husband had lived in one of the weathered mobile homes for several years. The greatest common bond between these two was a lust for drink. Their drinking resulted in numerous calls to our office wherein they complained about assaults on each other or the theft of liquor. The complaints to the police were always received when their supply of booze was running low and they were faced with the ugly fact that the party and the weekend were over.

This call, however, had an unusual twist: the husband was sober. On Friday there was a mechanical problem at the mill where he worked and he had promised to go in on Saturday to help in getting the mill operational again. He spent Friday night at a bar in town with his wife, and at the end of the night they picked up two dozen beer to take home. The husband planned that they would drink that beer together when he got home from the mill the next afternoon.

Saturday morning the husband was up early and off to work. The wife stayed home with the beer. It was around ten o'clock when she met her friend from a few doors away. They chatted for a while until the wife invited her friend over to have a beer. The friend eagerly accepted the invitation. One beer at ten o'clock on a Saturday morning will always lead to another. Four o'clock in the afternoon saw the last of the twenty-four beer and the husband due home at any time. I do not think the two women fully appreciated the gravity of their situation because of the effects of the liquor.

The husband finished his work a little early and he hurried toward home and the beer he had so thoughtfully laid in the night before. He coaxed his tired old truck as fast as it could to make it up the hill to the beer. He slid to a stop in a cloud of dust in front of the trailer. Before the dust had blown away he was inside looking for a beer. The smell in the trailer and a quick look at the two women told him what had happened. He had been very thirsty, but now he was thirsty and very angry.

The two women could be politely described as "abundant."

They both wore brightly coloured pants of a new-to-that-era stretchy material. Perhaps they dressed in that way only because they did not have access to a mirror that provided a rear view. The wife had red stretch pants and her friend's were fluorescent yellow-green.

When Dave and I arrived at the scene of the crime we were immediately informed that the husband had struck the friend with a board. The two women showed us a piece of one-by-four lumber about four feet long and confirmed that this had been the weapon. The wife urged her friend to "show them what he did." The friend lurched to her feet as she pulled down her stretch pants and panties and turned to present us with the "full moon." This presentation left no doubt in our minds that the assault had taken place as the two described it. A bright red welt ran across the full expanse of the crime scene; it was the same width as the board and was continuous except for a break near the centre. The welt was approximately three feet long.

Dave and I left the trailer to regain our composure and to discuss the possibility of recording the crime scene on film. We decided that photographs would not be necessary.

Through inquiries with neighbours we learned that the husband had requested and gotten a ride to town and would not likely be back until the next day.

We returned to the trailer and advised the two women that the perpetrator had left the area. We also told them to think it over and if they wished to pursue charges to contact our office on the following Monday morning. We heard no more of that incident.

Accident on
Adamant Glacier

Before the great BC road-building boom of the early sixties, the road from Golden to Revelstoke followed the Columbia River valley along a route known as the Big Bend. The river
found a way around the Selkirk range by travelling about ninety
miles northwest from Golden and then another ninety miles
southwest to Revelstoke. The road was gravel-surfaced, narrow,
twisting, and in places very high above the river. The Big Bend
was an adventure when conditions were ideal. In any other circumstances it was pure hell. The positive thing along the route
was the scenery; on one side was the vast canyon of the upper Columbia River and on the other, the Selkirk Mountains
rose from the edge of the road to glacier covered peaks. Across
the Columbia River to the east were the awe inspiring Rocky
Mountains. Parts of the Columbia Icefield were visible from a
few vantage points.

The Selkirk Range is a favourite with mountain climbers

from all over the world; it is the reason that Swiss mountaineers were brought to Golden and Revelstoke by the Canadian Pacific Railway. These people came to Canada in the late 1800s to apply their skills as mountain guides and provide a service that the CPR believed would encourage tourist traffic on their newly completed cross-Canada rail line. Their descendants still live in the area today.

The north end of the Selkirks, which lies inside the Big Bend, is a very popular area for hikers and climbers; so much so, that the Alpine Club of Canada has established several permanent camps there. One of these camps is in the headwaters of a beautiful creek just below the base of an icefield known as the Adamant Glacier. The glacier fills the upper end of the creek valley where ragged mountain peaks form a three-quarter circle that is about eight miles in diameter. The Alpine Club hut is a rustic structure which provides shelter and a meeting place for the many climbers who gather there for part of the short high-country summers.

There is no road to the camp. Hikers are dropped off where the creek crosses the Big Bend road, and they walk up a steep trail for about fifteen miles. Everything needed for their stay at the camp must be carried in on their backs, along with their climbing gear. Most of the visitors to the camp make two or more trips to get their supplies in. The people who choose to holiday at this location are prepared to expend a lot of energy and they are true lovers of the wilderness. I have seen the area from the vantage point of a helicopter seat and from that brief encounter I fully understand why people go there and return again.

In the early part of one summer while I was working at the Golden RCMP office, we received a call that there had been a climbing accident on the Adamant Glacier. The information was that three climbers had been caught in a slide; there had been serious injuries and at least one was dead. The report came to us from a young woman who had run from the camp to the road where she contacted a passing vehicle equipped with a two-way radio. The fall had happened nearly twenty-four hours before we received the report.

We were fortunate that the only helicopter in the community was at the hangar when the report came in. The pilot, a very skilled and dedicated man, prepared to leave at once. He suggested that we call for a stretcher-equipped machine from Calgary, about two hours' flying time from the accident location. The second helicopter was requested just before the pilot and I set out for the glacier.

As we turned into the creek valley below the glacier and started to climb sharply, the pilot told me that we would be operating near the maximum elevations that the little helicopter was capable of. The sketchy information we had been given indicated that the injured people were on the glacier at an elevation of 8,500 feet above sea level, which was about the maximum for our machine. The pilot did some calculations, considering the amount of fuel we would have burned by the time we reached the glacier and the approximate air temperature at that elevation; he concluded that we could reach a maximum of 8,700 feet. If the injured people were above that, we would have decisions to make. We could hope there were suitable containers at the camp to allow us to drain off fuel to lighten the craft, or we could wait for the larger machine to arrive from Calgary.

When we arrived at the Alpine Hut, we were met by a group of very concerned people. We learned that two were dead and one severely injured. The injured man and the bodies were on the margin of the glacier just below the 8,500-foot level. There had been a snow and rock slide, which caught them as they were making a descent onto the glacier from one of the surrounding peaks. The three were from the Washington, DC area of the

USA. The survivor was a medical doctor who taught at a university; the two deceased were instructors at the same university, one in the mathematics faculty and the other in nuclear physics.

We were now fairly certain that our machine could reach the scene with both of us on board. We rose out of the camp and in a few minutes we were able to see the awesome scene of the glacier and the surrounding mountain peaks. We flew over the ice in a constant climb, staying to the right margin of the glacier. To our left we could see only the undulating white surface of the glacier to the horizon. Our altimeter indicated about 8,400 feet when we saw where a large section of very thick snow had broken away from a near vertical mountainside and fallen onto the glacier. The snow slide had crossed three narrow bands of bare rock along its course and had then spread out in a fan shape as the mountain tapered out to the relatively flat surface of the glacier.

We continued to climb over the scene so I could obtain photographs and gather evidence for the coroner's inquiry. With some favourable winds, the pilot coaxed the little helicopter to just over 8,800 feet; from there, we were able to see three sets of boot tracks coming from the bare rock of the mountain onto the edge of the snow patch just above where the slide had started. The three tracks ran parallel and straight down the snow-covered mountainside for several hundred yards, then two of the tracks came together. After another one hundred yards, the three tracks came together. The single track continued straight down to the point where the snow had broken loose and taken the track with it. The slide had run down the mountain for half to three quarters of a mile as it crossed three bands of bare rock and tumbled over some near vertical sections of the slope before finally fanning out onto the glacier. The snow was extremely heavy from the summer melt and as it slid, it picked up rocks and mixed them into itself. Some of the rocks were the size of motor vehicles.

As we got closer, we could see people on the snow near the centre of the slide fan. We landed nearby and met the people who had been assisting the injured man. He was conscious and fully aware of everything that had gone on in the twenty-four hours since the slide. He told me of having hiked out of the camp at dawn the previous morning with his two companions; they had stayed along the right rim of the glacier bowl and at about midday decided to go down onto the glacier. The survivor had not been in favour of the glacier route because, in his experience, travel was very slow on the ice. He explained to me that to traverse the glacier surface they would have to be roped together at all times and they would have to keep to the end of their rope in case one of the party fell into a crevasse. A group moving on the glacier surface would be continually searching for the least hazardous route. To travel down the length of a ridge would be very reckless because that is the most common course of a crevasse.

The two dead climbers, being the least experienced of the three, had looked at the snowfield as an easier route back to the camp, and they were tired due to the exertion of the climb and the high altitude. Because they had all done a considerable amount of Alpine hiking, each had a vote in such decisions. Two out of three, the majority, chose to go down. Having made that decision, they next chose to go directly down from where they were rather than seek out a better route. They roped themselves together and discussed the need to stay at the end of their rope and to descend parallel to each other. The tracks above the slide showed that they had started out in this manner but one had drifted into the track of another and then all three had been in a line when the snow broke loose.

The survivor told of the terrifying ride in the tumbling snow and how they had yelled to each other and kept their arms and legs spread in the hope that they would stay on the surface of the falling snow and rocks. Their plan to try and swim over the fall was partly successful, but they were all under the snow for part of the trip down. The doctor told of his going under, and the horrible sound of the snow and rocks crashing down around him; just before he was thrown back onto the surface he felt both his feet getting caught between two huge rocks. He knew at once that his feet were crushed inside his climbing boots, but he felt no pain until after he found himself on the glacier at the leading edge of the snowfall.

The other two were within a few yards of him in spite of their ropes having been cut in several places by the grinding rocks in the snow. His male companion had died before the slide stopped, having received a crushing head injury. The female member of the group had come to rest near the other two, but still partly beneath the fallen snow. The trunk of her body and her head were under the snow. She struggled for some time, but was unable to free herself from the heavy, and now rock-solid, snow. She suffocated in a few minutes while the doctor was unable to do anything but watch.

The doctor found himself in extreme pain and started doing whatever he could to avoid going into shock. It was now after noon and he knew of no others who had chosen to go into the area he was in; without help, death was only a matter of time. He thought, briefly, that perhaps his companions were more fortunate to have gone so quickly. He chose to do whatever he could. He knew he had to get assistance. Sound will carry beyond belief in some circumstances; here, the air was relatively still, clean and silent. The doctor began to yell as loudly as he could, and tried to yodel along with his yelling for help. He called in short bursts and then gathered his strength for the next call.

Another party from the camp had set out at about the same time as the doctor and his companions. This group had stayed to the left rim of the glacier bowl. Near midday, the group on the left had also chosen to go onto the glacier. Their route down was entirely over bare rock, and comparatively easy. After arriving on the glacier, they were sitting around in a group enjoying the experience. Suddenly one of the group alerted the others to what sounded like a call for help; they all listened with concentration and clearly heard the calls. No doubt someone was in trouble and there was also no doubt that the calls were coming from out on the glacier. It did not occur to any of them, at that time, that the voice could be coming from all the way across the icefield. The two groups were later calculated to have been six miles apart when they first heard the calls.

The rescue group prepared to go farther out onto the ice. They roped themselves together and moved in single file, the lead climber watching closely and using all his experience to keep the direction of travel so they would cross a crevasse rather than walk along the length of it. This situation left them no choice but to constantly angle to the left and then right of their intended course, much like a sailboat running against the wind. Their progress was slow, but they did not expect to have to go far to the source of the distress call. After travelling about one and a half miles, they expected to be near the voice they had heard. Some time was spent in careful listening and finally the call was heard again. The voice was now almost impossible to make out. The group of rescuers was familiar with the mysterious ways that sound will travel and echo in glacier and mountain environments, so they decided to stay in the direction the sound seemed to be coming from.

When they reached about the middle of the glacier, they listened again but were unable to hear anything. Several of the group tried yelling and yodelling to see if they could get some response, but all they could hear was silence. There was a small hill of ice nearby. Three of the group made their way up, scanned with binoculars, and made further calls and yodels. They heard nothing, but they were able to see where a bordering snowfield had broken and fallen onto the glacier. The last calls seemed to have been from the direction of the snow slide. They hurried toward the slide site as quickly as the dangerous terrain would allow.

Meanwhile, the injured man was weakening and the pain from his feet was all but unbearable. He had been calling on five and ten minute intervals for about four hours. His hope was fading fast and he expected that he would soon go into shock and lose consciousness. He was searching in his pockets and pack for something to write a farewell letter when the air was filled with yodeling and people calling out, asking if anyone could hear them. The voices were so clear that he thought they must be in sight of him. He yelled as loudly as he could and tried to see where they were, but no one was in sight. His calls received no acknowledgement; however, he received a great boost from hearing the calls. He was now aware that someone had heard him and he was confident they would be there soon.

The sight of the snow slide raised fears among the rescue group that climbers had been involved in it. This and the fact that they did not hear any reply to their calls caused them to use less caution in the remainder of their crossing of the glacier. In just over an hour, they arrived at the accident scene. They started the action that finally got word out to Golden, and the helicopters on their way.

Some of the rescue group started toward the main camp to get help while others stayed at the scene. They used all clothing that could be spared to protect the injured man from contact with the snow. A small tent was set up over him and a shift rotation was implemented to monitor his condition. Hot food and drink was prepared. The arrival of the rescue group allowed the injured man to rest for the first time since the fall.

The group from the accident scene arrived in the main camp well after dark. They were greeted by the entire camp population. During the afternoon another party of climbers had been near the lower face of the glacier when they heard cries for help. The direction of the sound could not be determined from their location, except that it originated somewhere up on the icefield. They had listened in frustration, not knowing how to help. They tried to find a vantage point to better hear the sound, but nothing they tried made any improvement. They returned to camp with the news that someone was in trouble on the glacier. The only positive information they had was that some of them were quite sure they had heard voices from two locations. The one call seemed to be a single voice while there were several in the other. This left them hoping that some assistance effort was underway.

A daughter of the injured doctor was at the camp. She would have been the fourth member of the fallen group, but she had felt ill that morning and decided not to join them. There were no family members of the two deceased climbers in the camp.

At first light the daughter started for the Big Bend highway to summon help. She ran most of the fifteen miles down the creek valley, uncomfortably aware that once she got there she might have to wait several hours for a vehicle to drive by. At that time the new Rogers Pass highway had reduced traffic on the Big Bend to almost nil. Fortunately, as she staggered out onto the road, a radio-equipped BC Forest Service truck happened along. The rescue effort began to move swiftly from then on.

The helicopter from Calgary arrived about an hour after we did. The injured doctor was moved onto a stretcher and loaded into the machine; he requested that they go directly to Calgary University Hospital where he reasoned he would have the best chance of surviving and saving his feet.

The helicopter from Calgary had brought two body bags.

We placed the bodies in the bags and lashed them, one at a time, onto the skid of the little helicopter. I waited on the glacier while the bodies were taken down to a vehicle on the Big Bend road. The helicopter was refueled and returned to take me home to Golden.

The doctor recovered, but lost one foot at the ankle and most of the other except the ankle joint. We received very little information about him but there was an indication that he would be quite capable of walking again with prostheses. Judging by the way he dealt with the situation on the glacier, I expect that he was probably jogging after about a year.

At the time I found it hard to understand why there was no radio communication from the Alpine Camp to the outside world. Over the years my view has changed; the technology was certainly available at that time, but they evidently preferred to experience that pristine wilderness without the distraction of modern technology. I would not be surprised to find that there is still no radio at that camp.

Landslide on Lillooet Road

The Fraser River cuts through the heart of British Columbia from Prince George to Hope, and then through the more open Fraser Valley to tidewater near Vancouver. The walls of the upper end of the river canyon are a combination of clay and rock that is continuously sloughing into the river; this is particularly evident in the canyon between Lytton and Lillooet. The clay of that region is very water soluble and becomes almost liquid during the spring and fall rainy seasons.

In the early seventies, the road from Lytton to Lillooet was forty-two miles of winding two-lane asphalt surface with a few sections of gravel where the soil was too unstable to be paved. One of the gravel areas, known locally as the Big Slide, was about half a mile long, only one lane wide in parts, and was chiseled into a clay cliff about four hundred feet above the churning water of the river. The Big Slide was very well known by the locals. It was near the midpoint of the road between the two towns and when travellers had crossed it, they felt that the trip was as good as done.

I was working at the Lytton detachment and soon became familiar with, but a little afraid of, the road to Lillooet. There was very little traffic on that road but it was a common location for traffic crashes. Vehicles met head-on in the sharp curves or they were struck by falling rocks from the canyon walls above.

The Breathalyzer, a tool for measuring a person's blood alcohol content, was a relatively new addition to the Mounted Police equipment at that time. There was a shortage of both instruments and trained operators due to chronic budget shortfalls for training and the sometimes questionable placement of the equipment that was available. Lytton detachment was issued a Breathalyzer because it was on the Trans-Canada Highway and had a qualified Breathalyzer operator stationed there—me. Lytton was also considered close enough to three other detachments that drinking driver suspects could be transported there for tests. Lillooet was one of the locations required to haul their impaired driving suspects to Lytton, in spite of the forty-two mile trail between the two villages.

Placement of the available Breathalyzers was also influenced by the fact that the Mounted Police had still not started to pay overtime. There was no cost involved for rolling me out of bed three or four nights a week to do the tests.

It was about one thirty in the morning when I got a call that an impaired driver had been arrested at Lillooet and the patrol was enroute to Lytton for a Breathalyzer test. I dressed and went to the Lytton police office to prepare for the test. About an hour had passed since the call came in and the patrol had not arrived. I called on the radio to check on their progress. The radio response was almost inaudible; a muffled voice advised there had been an accident. The patrol car had fallen into a hole and there were other cars in there with it. The police driver did not think he had any serious injuries, but he was concerned about his intoxicated passenger. The policeman had not been able to get to the other vehicles that he could see in the hole. From what he was able to see of the other cars, he felt there would be severe injuries or fatalities.

Radio contact was very poor but I did learn that the hole they were in was on the Lytton side of the Big Slide and that our driver thought he was nearing Lytton when it happened. He advised that he was going to try to get back up to the roadway to prevent the next vehicle from going in on top of those already there. I called for an ambulance and other detachment members to assist, and I advised the remaining policeman at Lillooet and our dispatch centre at Kamloops of what I knew. They called the highways maintenance crew to provide barricades and to close the roadway immediately; meanwhile, I drove out to find the scene.

About fourteen miles from Lytton, I came around a curve to see a flashlight waving frantically across the roadway. As I got closer in the total darkness my headlights revealed a mud-covered person with a flashlight standing by a huge crater where the roadway had been. About forty feet of the entire road was gone, including the ditch and some of the bank from the uphill side. Where there had been a two-lane paved highway, there was now a hole with vertical walls of about fifteen feet on three sides. The mud bottom of the hole sloped sharply toward the open side in the direction of the river.

The bottom of the hole was sloppy mud with a small stream running through the middle of the still slowly moving mass. The police car was standing on its front end, which was pushed into the mud nearly up to the windshield. The rear bumper was below the level of the road. The rear wheels of the police car were resting against the wall of the hole.

The mud-covered officer was badly bruised, but had no cuts

or broken bones. He told me there were at least two other cars down there on the Lytton side of the hole. One was on its roof, and the other was upright with severe front end damage. Several people were badly hurt, and one was dead.

We set flares and barricades on each side of the missing section of roadway and then went into the hole to assess the situation. I walked over the edge on the downhill side of the highway and went to the area where the roadway had fallen out. The debris field from the slide had crashed into the trees below and had caused a small clearing in the forest. The entire mass was sloppy mud, just a little too thick to continue flowing down the hill toward the river. The mud in the middle of the hole was more than knee deep and almost impossible to move through; as I struggled to pull one foot free, the other would sink deeper, forcing me to move on my hands and knees. I knew then why I had not been able to recognize the policeman with the flashlight.

The ambulance arrived and we struggled to get stretchers into the hole and back out with five injured men and a dead woman. In the darkness, mud, and confusion, we thought that we had accounted for all the people who had been in the vehicles, but we were wrong. We soon realized that one of the men from the second vehicle was missing.

About this time, a tow truck arrived on the Lillooet side of the hole and began the task of lifting the police car out.

Daylight arrived and we were able to examine the scene more thoroughly. We searched the mud and debris below the hole for the missing man but failed to find any trace of him. He was familiar with the area but no tracks could be seen below the highway where he might have walked out. A patrol to his home learned that he had not been seen for a few days and his family believed he was still in Lillooet. One of the crash victims said he thought he had seen him crawling away into the darkness toward the Lillooet side of the hole. This information caused us to closely examine the hole where the police car had just been lifted out. The body of the missing man was pressed into the mud at the bottom of this hole. In the total darkness and confusion he had crawled through the mud until he was at the base of the wall of the hole on the Lillooet side. He had probably just managed to struggle to that location when the police car fell into the hole on top of him.

In the days after the slide, when talking with the three drivers, we pieced together the events of that evening. The occupants of the first car had been visiting with friends in Lillooet and they were late getting on the road for the drive home. They came around a bend in the road and saw the blackness of the hole; the driver at first mistook it as a new section of asphalt. He took no evasive action and suddenly fell into the hole at about fifty miles per hour. His car flew across most of the very loose mud and crashed into the relatively solid opposite side wall of the hole. The heavy front end of the car left the road first and therefore fell farther than the rear, leaving the car at a downward angle when it crashed. This caused the passengers to be thrown toward the upper edge of the windshield, and resulted in fatal head and neck injuries to the woman who had been seated in the middle of the front seat.

The driver of the second car had been in bed at his home near Lillooet when he was awakened by two Native men who asked him to give them a ride to Lytton. The two were quite drunk and the driver was new to the area; against his better judgement, and partly out of fear of the two, he agreed to do as they asked. He came around the curve and saw what he thought was a new patch of asphalt but, realizing what it was an instant later, he slammed on the brakes and steered left. This car went over the edge at a lower speed than the first and it landed on its front end in the mud with just enough momentum to go end over end to where it stopped close beside the first car, upside down and facing back in the direction it had come from. The driver had a broken femur and was in severe pain. He had suggested to his two passengers that they stay in his car, but they chose to crawl out. One of them crawled to the wall on the Lillooet side of the hole.

The police driver came around the curve and saw the black area. He was familiar with the road and braked very hard, locking all four wheels. The police car screeched toward the hole, slowing rapidly; the front wheels went over the edge and it seemed for an instant that the car would stop, but it continued to slide forward on its frame and it dropped straight down into the mud, killing the man who had crawled to the wall of the hole. The impaired driving suspect in the rear of the police car fell forward against the security screen and broke his collar bone.

The police car driver had only enough time to assess the situation in his car and look around with his flashlight when I called him on the radio. He then left the car and fought his way through the mud up to the highway, to prevent any further mayhem.

The cause of the slide was a faulty drainage culvert under the roadway. The pipe was of minimal size, only required to handle the small amounts of water from the hillside above the highway. The water ran down to the highway ditch and then along the ditch to the culvert. The unstable ground had shifted over the years to the extent that the uphill end of the culvert had become lower than the other; the shifting clay had then built up inside the culvert until it was completely clogged. The water had accumulated in the ditch and permeated into the road and the ground under it, finally resulting in the slide.

The highway hole was filled and repaved, and additional drainage culverts were installed. The highway maintenance people were cautioned to keep a close watch for water pooling in the ditches. Within a few months, funds were made available to provide a Breathalyzer and a trained operator for Lillooet detachment.

The Nelson Axe Murders

The city of Nelson is a beautiful place with a rich history of mining and forestry. The mountains throughout the West Kootenay area have abundant mineral deposits, many of which have been mined over the years. Signs of mining can be seen along any roadway in the region, ranging from small shafts driven into the rock with hand drills and explosives, to large ventures where ore was taken out on underground narrow gauge railway tracks. Some of the mineral veins were still being worked in the early 1960s, and a few are still active today. Most of the mining activity was for lead zinc ore, known as galena, which was fed into the smelter operations in Trail. Nelson had a population of about ten thousand in the year 1900, and this census remained almost unchanged right up to the 1960s. As one mining venture petered out, another would be opened and the workers would drift around the district, nearly always able to find work. Local wags explained the unchanging population numbers by saying that each time a baby was born, some guy left town.

The mining areas of the world always attract a few pros-
pector-promoters who prey on each other and on anyone else
whom they can con into believing in their latest fabulously
rich find. These types do most of their prospecting in bars and
lounges, looking for victims with a few dollars from which they
can be parted. There was an abundance of these barroom prospectors in Nelson in the early sixties. Conversations one would
overhear in Nelson watering holes were nearly always about
the latest strike that had been made on some mountain not far
away. Most of these finds were claimed to be galena ore so rich
that a man could not lift a water-bucket full. When interest was
shown from a bystander (victim), the conversation became very
secretive and furtive glances were cast about the room as bits of
disinformation were carefully leaked out. Numbers were whis-
pered about the percentage of silver in the ore sample and the
potential tonnage of the new find. After a great deal of probing
to see if the mark could be trusted, a chunk of very heavy, shiny
black ore would be produced from a pocket or briefcase. The
ore samples were very guarded, usually kept under the table,
and the mark was only allowed to hold them for a few seconds.
Most of these very rich ore samples had found their way out of
a commercial mine in a worker's pocket and had been traded in
the bar for a few drinks.

Three promoters had been working as a team during the
summers of the early sixties. They favoured the Kootenay region and centred their activities in Nelson. In the winter they
drifted away to sponge room and board with relatives or others
who did not realize their friends were such shady characters.

During their promoting/conning activity in the later part
of one summer they became acquainted with a man who had
immigrated to Canada from Czechoslovakia. Petre came here
shortly after the Second World War and settled in Nelson for
reasons that we were unable to determine; he had no family

there or anywhere outside Czechoslovakia. He had kept himself employed at a variety of labour jobs and he was a skilled stonemason who took great pride in his work. Those who were fortunate enough to learn of his skills and to find and hire him were rewarded with an everlasting example of fine European craftsmanship. His work was remarkable, with perfect fitting and immaculate pointing. Stonemasonry was not in great demand at that time, however, and Petre was unable to communicate in English beyond the most basic requirements; these combined problems left him to seek work at whatever hard labour he could find.

Petre was a willing worker. Those who hired him were often amazed at how he would work from dawn to dark with only short breaks for meals or rest. He kept track of his hours and requested payment only for each full hour that he had worked. His attention to detail was as obvious in menial tasks as it was in his masonry. He was a very proud man.

Petre lived an exceedingly frugal existence. Home was a shack on a narrow wedge of property between the highway and a creek. The shack consisted of one room with a lean-to extension on the side where he parked his old car. The size and location of the property ensured that no others lived near him. Over the years he had closed the back end of the lean-to and put on a pair of hinged doors at the front, allowing him to get his old car in and out with some difficulty. The shack was heated by a light metal air-tight stove which also served for any cooking that he did. The wood for the stove was piled on the creek side of the shack, where it was handy to the door and kept out of the rain by the overhang of the metal roof. Every piece of wood was fitted into the pile perfectly; each square-sawn end was not more or less than one quarter of an inch different from the next. There was no electrical service to the shack; the only source of artificial light was a glass kerosene lamp. After about twenty years of this frugal living, Petre had saved some money. His bank records showed that he had a balance of nearly seven thousand dollars around the time he first met the three prospectors.

Petre corresponded with a niece in his homeland and occasionally received newspapers or clippings from there, which he stacked neatly on a stand beside his army-cot bed. The letters from his niece indicated that he had a dream of returning to Czechoslovakia for an extended visit. He wanted to entertain her and her friends and travel with them to all the places he remembered as a young man. It seemed the only thing delaying this dream trip was that costs were constantly increasing at a greater rate than his savings. If he could somehow double those savings, he would be able to travel and enjoy himself before old age left him unable to do so.

The three promoters became close friends with Petre almost immediately. One or more of them was always with him when he was not working. They introduced him to prospecting and helped him get a free miner's license, which entitled him to stake and register a mining claim in the province. No doubt they told him how easy it would be to find the ore vein of all their dreams and become wealthy almost overnight. They helped him locate, stake and register a mineral claim. Petre's claim lay only a few yards off the main highway just outside Nelson. They took him on their travels around the region, showed him claims they had registered and told him of the great potential of these properties—given the necessary investment for development. Petre was made to feel very fortunate to have met this trio of kindly and generous men.

It was just before the onset of winter that the three conmen made their final pitch to Petre and made off with his savings. The three drifted away for winter as they always had, leaving Petre to brood about his foolish error. Petre sat quietly in his shack by the creek and worried about his loss. His anger grew with each passing day, and he gradually formulated a plan to even the score.

In the early spring of the following year, Petre contacted one of the three promoters. They had an amiable conversation. Petre pretended to be understanding about the money having been used in the business of promoting mining ventures and that things did not always work out in spite of people's best intentions. He went on to indicate that while things had not gone well with the mining investment, he had been very fortunate and had come into a sizable amount of money. He said he was looking forward to the return of the three to Nelson so that they could work together on some new projects.

During this early spring conversation Petre learned that one of the three promoters had indulged in excessive drinking, as he always did, but that that winter, the booze had killed him. This news was another great disappointment for Petre; he had had some plans for this man and now he had cheated him again. Petre waited for the snow to melt and for the remaining two conmen to return to Nelson. While he waited, he travelled to an area near Nelson and staked another claim. This claim was another part of Petre's plan to even the score with the promoters.

Claims are often marked by cutting off a small tree at each corner of the selected property. The trees are cut leaving a stump about four feet tall, which is squared at the top with an axe. A soft aluminum tag is attached with a nail, and the claim information is then scratched into the aluminum tag with another nail. A typical claim tag will have the name of the prospector, the date, and the free miner's license number. Petre had learned the proper procedure to mark his new claim, and applied it correctly.

At last the two surviving promoters returned to Nelson and Petre met them like long lost friends. They talked about their plans for the summer and Petre made it very clear that he wanted to be involved in their activities: he had faith in their knowledge and skills, and he was sure that some day they would be rewarded.

About six weeks after the promoters returned to Nelson, a citizen came to the police with a concern that all was not normal at Petre's shack. He had been walking along the creek near the shack when he became aware of an overpowering stench. Having served on the battlefields in the Second World War, he could tell us with certainty that what he smelled was a dead body in an advanced stage of decomposition. Before he came to us he had found that the odour was coming from the lean-to garage on the side of the shack. Peering through the crack between the doors, he was able to see a car. He also saw that there was a hose attached to the car's exhaust pipe.

We drove the few miles to Petre's place, wondering what was in store for us there. I was new to police work and had not yet encountered a decomposing body. I grew up on a farm and had been in contact with rotting animal carcasses, but that experience did not leave me fully prepared for what we found that day. We parked the police car by the garage doors. It was a bright warm early summer day and our windows were wide open. Before the car had come to a stop we were assaulted by an odour like none I had ever experienced. I suddenly understood how the former soldier was sure that there was a rotting body there.

We were able to see through the crack between the doors that there was an old Buick in the garage and that there was a hose from the exhaust pipe along the side of the car. The building had no windows and no other door. We called for the Identification Section to photograph the area before we moved anything. The delay while we waited for the identification man would give us time to stand well back and formulate some kind of a plan. We very soon found that there was a slight breeze flowing down the creek valley and that the place to be was on the upwind side.

A police car on the side of a road with two uniformed police standing nearby always arouses a little curiosity from passing motorists. Most slow down to see what they can see and many stop to inquire and offer assistance. Almost everyone drove with their car windows open in those days, before air conditioning. While we waited for the second police car to arrive we watched the people in their cars. Those who approached from the downwind side would slow and move to the right and look with interest to learn what we were doing. When they caught wind of why we were there, their change of expression was startling; none stayed to inquire or offer assistance. The upwind vehicles, on the other hand, would stop, and in some cases people would get out before they got the rude message from the air. Then they all made a hasty departure.

The photography expert arrived and recorded the outside of the scene on film. There was no reason to delay any longer. We opened the double doors to reveal the horror inside. The odour in the lean-to garage was beyond description. Fortunately the open doors allowed a change of air and it became just a little thinner. Also fortunate is that the human sense of smell partly shuts down under a severe overload. Once this shutdown had occurred, the task was more manageable.

The car windows were closed, except for the one on the right rear where a vacuum cleaner hose had been placed through and the window turned up to hold the hose in place. The insides of all the windows were black from a carbon deposit left by the exhaust. The car must have been nearly full of fuel, because it had run for a long time after the occupant was dead. The body lay in the front as though the person had been sitting in the driver's position and then fallen away from the door so that his head was on the passenger's seat. The entire interior of the car was crawling with maggots, and adult flies filled the air of both the car and the garage. The body was fully clothed in what appeared to be work clothes of the kind worn by men in the construction or labour trades. The maggots were nearly finished their work. The body had been reduced to less than half of its original weight; only bones and some of the tougher skin tissue remained. Positive identification of this body would have to be done by dental records or through medical records of bone fractures.

Three pages of handwritten information in Petre's native language was lying on the dash between the windshield and the steering wheel. Petre had started this writing in his shack some time before he moved to the garage to end his life. The first two pages were neatly done with straight lines of words and uniform penmanship; the final page had been written in the car while he waited for the exhaust gas to do its work. Petre had taken a small square of plywood into the car to hold on the steering wheel and support his paper while he wrote. The final page was uneven in both line and penmanship; toward the end of the writing it was obvious that he was having difficulty with coordination and thought. We were fortunate that Petre was so attentive to detail; even in a near-death state he had folded the pages together and placed them where they would surely be found. Had the notes come in direct contact with the body during decomposition there would have been very little, if anything, left of them.

Finally, the photographs had all been taken and the necessary records had been carefully made in our notebooks. All that was left to do was to remove the wriggling remains. I suggested to the others that I could hear my mother calling and that I would have to leave immediately. They did not believe me and they were very blunt about it. We wrapped the upper part of the body in disposable blankets and slowly moved it toward the passenger door of the car. As we did this the legs and feet followed; mainly because the trousers were holding them together. More blankets were added as the move progressed until the body was wrapped like an Egyptian mummy. The cold storage at the morgue would eventually stop even the most determined of the maggots.

The remains of Petre were identified from dental records and he was buried by the public administrator. His niece in Czechoslovakia was unable to attend and she knew of no other living family members. Petre's old car was towed away by a very reluctant auto wrecker and it was burned as soon as we were certain that it could provide no further evidence. The shack was also burned because it had been illegally constructed on Crown Land.

The three pages of writings were translated for us. In them, Petre told of his first meeting with the three promoters, and how they had convinced him that he would receive great returns by investing his savings with them. He told of the great friendship that rapidly developed between the four of them, and how they had included him in all their prospecting activities. He told of withdrawing cash from his bank and turning it over to these men, and how they disappeared as soon as they were sure they had the last of his money. Petre said that the actions of these three men had ruined him and that his life was now "not worth a pipeful of tobacco." Our translator told us that the reference to a pipeful of tobacco was a Czechoslovakian colloquialism.

The writings described an intense hatred for the three promoters and talked about the one of them who cheated Petre again by dying. There was no direct confession of having harmed the two con-men; however, the translator felt that neither of them had been alive at the time of the writing.

Our investigation moved to trying to find either of the promoters. They were well known among the regular bar patrons in town. Their return without their third partner had been noted, but no one could recall seeing either of them for over a month.

Obviously no one had missed them. The government records of mine claims showed several hundred claims registered over the years by the three promoters, and three by Petre. Two of Petre's claims had been registered about the time he first met the con-men; the third was made just before the two promoters returned that spring.

The most recent claims by the three promoters had been registered late the previous summer and were all in the Creston area. We had our office in Creston make inquiries about the con-men. The records at an old hotel in Creston showed that Petre and one of the promoters had stayed for one night nearly seven weeks earlier. They were driving Petre's old Buick, and he had paid for the room. The hotel staff felt quite sure that there had been only two of them, but they were not positive.

There were a total of fourteen claims along the Goat River near Creston; it was decided to start by searching the most recently recorded claim and work back, by date, through all of them. The police service dog and his master were called to assist. On the second claim to be searched, the dog found some bone fragments and a pair of false teeth. The teeth were identical to a dental impression of one of the missing men. The bone fragments were identified as part of a human skull. Nothing further was found in a search of the claim and surrounding area but it was obvious that someone had died violently at that claim site. We were quite sure that the false teeth told us who that person had been. Wild animals had eaten and scattered the remains; the area was common range to bear and wolverine.

The police dog team returned to Nelson and started a search of Petre's most recent claim. The search ended at the first corner marker of the claim. The aluminum tag was inscribed with Petre's full name and free miner's information as required. Face down at the base of the claim post lay the third promoter. He had been there for at least a month and the maggots were nearly finished their work there as well. A starfish-shaped wound was clearly visible in the mummified scalp over the crown of the head. This appeared to have been caused by a blow that had crushed the scalp between the flat of an axe and the momentary resistance of the skull beneath it. The blow was delivered from behind; the man would not likely have been aware of his impending death. The man wielding the axe did not stop at that: he stood over the body and chopped through the neck, leaving only the tissue of the throat area to hold the head to the body. He then stepped back slightly and with a final overhand swing, buried the axe head between his victim's shoulder blades and left the handle standing up from the wound. Petre was a very angry man.

The exact date of the killings and suicide were never determined. It did appear that Petre went home after killing the second promoter and contemplated what he had done for several days before he gassed himself.

The Greatest Goal

There are times and events that are so overwhelming that we always remember where we were and who we were with when they happened.

One of these occurred while I was working at the Golden RCMP detachment. We were in the middle of a routine day, with lots of files scattered around. Some people were calling with serious problems; some with trivial matters only they felt were worthy of police attention.

Canada was playing Russia for the Canada Cup and we had moved a television set into the office. We were busy at Golden, but not to the extent that we could not find time for important events like that game.

Several of the single members were living at room-and-board arrangements around town, and as the game began most of them drifted into the office to watch. There was a crowd around the television and most police functions had come to a stop. The game was all that we had anticipated: the Russians

67

skated and passed as only they could; and the Canadians played the game the way they had taught it to the world, fast and rough, with great team spirit and extreme individual effort. A cheer went up each time one of the Russian players was caught concentrating too much on his precision passing and he found himself airborne. It was anyone's game, from the opening face-off until the final seconds ticked off the clock.

Golden was a training detachment, where new recruits were teamed with more experienced constables for the first important months of their field training. This training function resulted in a lot of young single police officers living in Golden, and a lot of attention being focused on the RCMP office by the young ladies of the town. The town didn't have a great variety of entertainment facilities, but the young guys managed to keep themselves quite busy in the social network of their adopted community.

In small, isolated towns like Golden, a portion of the needed entertainment comes in the form of practical jokes. Great effort is put into planning these stunts and setting them in motion. A complicated plan may involve half the community, and it then becomes a challenge for the planners to pull it off.

A rather nasty plot had been hatched a few days before the big game. One of the more popular single guys was identified as the target, partly because of some awful joke he had pulled on someone and partly because he was such a perfect target for this plan.

The two plotters approached one of the doctors from the little clinic across the street and asked if they could have a sheet of the clinic letterhead. The doctor knew immediately that they were up to no good and he demanded to be let in on it. Once he was briefed on the plan he was fully supportive and made constructive suggestions for the wording of the missive. A letter was prepared on the official paper and posted with the outgoing mail from the clinic that day. All the mail for the police members came to the same post office box in Golden and was distributed through a pigeonhole system in the police office.

Because the victim had worked the graveyard shift the night before the big game, he didn't get to the office until partway into the third period. Excitement was at a peak—Canada was down by one but then managed to tie it up. Our victim came in and was immediately caught up in the excitement of the game. During a break in the play, he reached over and picked up his mail. During following game breaks he began to open the envelopes and scan the various contents. Everyone watched through the corner of one eye. He finally got to the one we all knew about, and he opened it. A Russian shot hit our goal post and we all thought it was over. Everyone was very disappointed until we realized it had bounced to the outside of the goal. There was great excitement clearly visible in all our faces—all except our victim, who was pale and drawn and had lost interest in the game. He quietly got up and walked down the hall to the bathroom. He emerged from there to make a brief telephone call from a side office away from the noise of the game.

Canada was putting heavy pressure on the Russian goal— shots from the circle, shots from the blue line—the Russians tried desperately to clear the zone, but were blocked each time. There was a scramble in front of their net. Paul Henderson was knocked to the ice but he sprang to his feet and took a wild swing at the puck and scored the winning goal. Only seconds remained. There was little if any chance for the Russians to come back. Canada had the cup.

Our victim left the office in the midst of all the celebration. He walked across the street toward the clinic as though he were carrying the world on his shoulders.

The letter from the doctor stated that a patient had come to the clinic infected with a very communicable disease. He explained that the law required him to question her about contacts where the infection may have spread, and that the name of our victim had been mentioned. He was requested to attend the clinic at his first opportunity, and that was exactly what he was doing. The victim's first clue that he had been had was when he realized that the doctor was laughing, and he recognized about seven faces peering around the door frame of the examining room.

Watch for Falling Rock

The canyon of the Fraser River cuts a great ditch through the interior plateau of British Columbia from Prince George to Hope. The northern part, from Prince George to Lillooet, passes through the clay soils of the Cariboo. Here, the river water becomes loaded with clay and takes on a pale brown colour. At Lillooet, the river enters more rocky terrain, the canyon becomes narrower, and the river runs faster in its restricted bed. The best-known area of the Fraser Canyon is from Lytton to Hope, because it is on the Trans-Canada Highway. The Trans-Canada Highway and both major railways enter the Fraser Canyon from the Thompson River canyon at Lytton and all three follow the Fraser Canyon to Hope.

The lower end of the Fraser Canyon is a very unstable place. This is the area where the railways and the highway share the fragile canyon walls. The canyon is a relatively recent development, geologically speaking, and it is still growing with every season—particularly with each spring flood of the river. The walls of the canyon continuously drop rocks, which range from insignificant pebbles to huge sections that peel away from the upper edges of the walls.

As the rainy season progresses through the autumn, the rocks come down in direct proportion to the rainfall. As the rainy autumn season gives way to winter, the wind from the interior brings a sharp drop in temperature and all the rain-filled cracks in the rocks become ice. The newly formed ice can create enough pressure in the cracks to split a clean break through previously solid rock. These wet or cold seasons are always memorable times for the railway and highway workers as they try to keep the rockfalls clear of their routes.

From 1969 to 1972, I worked from the RCMP detachment at Lytton. One evening in the early part of the winter we were called to a motor vehicle incident on the south slope of Jackass Mountain. There were no injuries reported, so we drove out to investigate at a rather relaxed pace. The information we had was that a vehicle had hit some rocks. That side of Jackass Mountain was one of the few three-lane sections of the canyon highway in those days. One lane was for downhill traffic, two for uphill. This allowed most traffic to pass the transport trucks that were very slow on the steep grade.

When we arrived, we found that a pickup truck with a camper had somehow made its way onto the top of a rock in the middle of the highway. The rock was so large that the frame rails of the truck were eight feet above and parallel to the surface of the highway. The truck had relatively light damage to the front bumper and undercarriage.

The driver told us that he had been going down the mountain in total darkness, except for the lights of his vehicle, when his headlights had suddenly picked up a moving mass directly in his path. At first he thought that the movement was a flash flood and that water was rushing across the road. Before he could react, he was into the moving mass and he knew then that it was not water. His truck slammed into something so hard that he and his two passengers were thrown forward into their seatbelts. At the same moment, the truck was lifted straight up with such force that the three were forced downward into the bottom of the seat. They then realized that they were at a full stop. The headlights of the truck were still on and were shining out into empty space. The lights of an approaching vehicle gave them a reference point, and they realized that they were high above the highway surface. The driver checked with his passengers, his wife and daughter, and determined that they were not hurt. He found a flashlight in the cab and began to assess their situation. People from the other vehicle assisted, and the three were able to get down from the stranded truck to the road surface.

The truck's spare tire was on a bracket on the front bumper. An eight-foot rock had fallen onto the highway and was rolling down the hill away from the truck when they hit it. The spare wheel and tire had gripped the rock and lifted the front of the truck. The truck and the rock had rolled as a unit for a little less than a half a turn of the rock to where they had both stopped. Had the rock rolled another small part of a turn, the truck would have been slammed down onto the highway, causing severe injuries and probably death to its occupants.

The big rock that the truck hit was accompanied by a few hundred cubic yards of rock, most of it in smaller pieces. The two uphill lanes of the highway were completely covered, and smaller fragments covered the downhill lane so that traffic was unable to get through.

A very skilful and well-equipped tow-truck operator was called from Boston Bar. He looked at the truck sitting high on the rock, laughed, and said he had never seen one quite like that. He rigged two lines to the front of the truck and a third line over a triangular frame on the back of his tow truck. He then gently slid the truck forward and put it down on the highway as though it were a toy truck in his hand. He checked the truck for damage and found none that would affect its temporary operation, so the driver and his family drove away toward their destination.

While we were at the scene, more rock was continually falling from the fresh break just above the highway. This was normal after a rockfall. We did not like to be there, but it was considered part of the job hazard. The highway had been closed from the time of the rockfall, and traffic was being re-routed at Spences Bridge and at Hope. We knew we could look forward to a quiet night because the road would not be cleared until heavy equipment was brought in to lift or break up the big rocks. The highway maintenance crew from Lytton brought their small front-end loader and a small dump truck to the scene and started to clean up the pieces that they could handle.

Two men from Lytton had been working around the edges of the rockfall in the two machines for several hours. More rock continued to fall, making them nervous and extremely cautious. The regulations of the Worker's Compensation Board required that a truck driver be out of the cab of his truck while it was being loaded. The driver at this site would back the little truck into position and then stand alongside it where he could watch and listen for more falling rock. He positioned himself so that he could signal the loader operator if it became necessary to move away.

At about midnight the truck driver was in position, watching the loader operator. The loader was turning away from the truck to go back to the rockfall when the truck driver heard a sound like a dynamite blast. The sound came from the mountainside directly above them. The driver gave a frantic signal to the loader operator to get away and he started to run up the highway away from the rockfall area. The loader operator was facing toward the slide with his machine; he slammed the machine into reverse and threw the throttle wide open. He had just started moving backwards when the first pieces of rock began to hit the machine. Both the truck driver and the machine operator knew they were about to die. A chunk of flying rock hit the bucket of the loader and shoved it sideways, almost causing the machine to roll onto its side. However, the operator was able to steer it enough to prevent a roll-over. The truck driver was able to run much faster than the loader could go in reverse gear, but he wished he had the winged feet of Mercury.

The truck driver was wearing a waist-length leather jacket, and running like he had never run before. He heard the rocks hitting the loader behind him and the overpowering roar of a tremendous force being released. The earth was trembling so hard that both the running man and the machine operator could feel it. The running driver was hit by a blast of wind that picked him off the ground and threw him several yards; he found himself on the ground with his leather jacket inverted over his head and arms as though it were a pullover sweater that he was in the process of taking off.

The explosive sound had been generated when a huge slab of the mountainside suddenly broke away and opened a crack. The air rushing into the vacuum in the crack created the explosion-like sound. The wind that hit and picked up the running driver was caused by the mass of falling rock displacing air between it and the highway surface; the air rushed out with an amazing force.

About the same time that the loader operator had regained control of his machine, he realized that he had escaped the rockfall and that he was still alive. He turned his machine to move it farther up the highway. In the lights of the machine, he saw the truck driver sitting on the road. The driver was struggling with his leather coat, which was turned inside out over his head and arms. The loader operator had to help him remove the garment.

The small dump truck had been twisted and flattened by the falling rock. It was lying on the highway surface at the edge of the rockfall as though it had been crushed and then tossed aside.

The scene was amazing in the light of the following morning. The place where we had stood around the pickup truck on the rock was now seventy to eighty feet below the top of the rockfall. All three lanes of the highway and a wide shoulder on the outside were under the rock pile. About half of the total rockfall had gone over the highway and down the mountainside toward the Fraser River and the Canadian Pacific Railway. Fortunately there was a bench of land a few hundred feet below the highway where the rock had come to rest without involving the rail line.

Had the two men and their machines been working at the preliminary rockfall from the downhill side, they would have had no chance of escape and no chance of survival. The largest part of the main rockfall landed on the highway just below where the first small one had hit. From the uphill side they escaped by moving fifty to one hundred feet. On the lower side, they would have had to move at least four hundred feet.

The bench land below the highway was privately owned. The Provincial Government negotiated with the owner and bought a ten-acre piece of the land. The newly acquired land was used as a disposal site for the rock. Three large bulldozers were then brought in to push the slide material over the edge of the highway. Much of the rock on the road surface was in such large pieces that it had to be drilled and broken with explosives before even the largest bulldozers could move it. Crews worked around the clock for the next seven days before traffic resumed on that section of the Trans-Canada Highway.

The next time you pass through the Fraser Canyon and are about midway between Boston Bar and Lytton, watch for the scar above the highway on the side of Jackass Mountain, and the pile of broken rock below. You will be amazed that people who were there at the time of the rockfall survived it.

Airplane in the Canyon Wind

On hot summer days in the Fraser Canyon, the wind pushes up the canyon with a tremendous force. Trees and rocky formations along the canyon walls do provide some sheltered areas on the ground, but in the open centre of the canyon there is no relief. The same trees and rocky formations that provide shelter on the ground create a frightening turbulence in the main channel.

A young man from Washington State had recently obtained his pilot's license and was eager to try his new skills. After a lot of talking he convinced his young wife to join him on a flying trip into the interior of British Columbia. He obtained the use of a rental airplane for a few days of travel and made plans to fly into the Cariboo area for some sightseeing and fishing.

The little airplane had just enough power to fly with two people under fairly good conditions. The two travellers had packed some camping gear and a few groceries, which did not help the little plane in its struggle with gravity and air currents. In spite of the limitations of their flying machine the two set out enthusiastically—although I suspect there was more enthusiasm on the part of the pilot than the passenger.

The weather reports were excellent through the area where they planned to fly. They enjoyed clear skies and warm temperatures as they made their way from the Seattle area to their first stop at the airport near Abbotsford, British Columbia, where they made their required report to Canada Customs.

The next leg of their trip was to take them along the Trans-Canada Highway to Cache Creek, and then along Highway 97 to Clinton. Their flight plan was filed from Abbotsford, but no one made them aware of the extreme winds of the Fraser Canyon. By the time the little airplane reached Hope, at the lower end of the canyon, the pilot had noticed that he was being tossed around by wind. However, it did not seem serious at that time. They passed over the little town of Hope and turned into the canyon, using the highway as their route marker.

As soon as the little craft passed Hope, the walls of the canyon closed from both sides and the wind took over most of the control of the plane. As the town of Yale flashed by below, terror took hold of the two travellers. The little plane was going at about twice the speed it would have under calm conditions. Things were happening way too fast. There went the highway bridge, and then the walls closed in even more as they shot through the narrow section of the canyon known as Hell's Gate. The new pilot was experiencing a test of his skills that would be a challenge to even the most experienced of flyers.

The little craft was being tossed from side to side, forcing the pilot to use all his resources to avoid the trees and rocks on his right and left. He tried to gain altitude, but it seemed the aircraft could not lift itself out of the funnel of wind that had a stranglehold on it. He was aware of a small grass landing strip beside the highway just north of Boston Bar, and his mind raced trying to formulate a plan to get the plane onto that little patch of grass. He so desperately wanted to feel ground under his feet again, but he was beginning to think this was not to be. On the positive side, his wife was not screaming as much as she had been earlier.

The little grass strip flashed by under the plane and the pilot knew there was no hope of reaching it. He was quite certain that if he tried to turn and go back to the landing strip he would lose control or wind up travelling backwards in the wind. He wisely chose to stay with the horrible predicament he had survived since he left Hope. The next possibility of landing was now at Lytton, where the Thompson River joins the Fraser. The Thompson meets the Fraser at about ninety degrees, both in deep, narrow canyons. A gravel airstrip lies on a bench about 1,000 feet above the rivers and at a forty-five degree angle to both rivers. The pilot planned to dive down into the Thompson canyon in the hope that there was some calmer air down there. He would then turn and climb up to the level of the airstrip.

The first part of the plan went well. There was a sheltered area deep in the Thompson canyon and he was able to control the plane and turn toward the airstrip, which was now slightly above him. The little plane struggled upward until the airstrip was suddenly visible just ahead. At that moment the airplane became exposed again to the full force of the wind. The wind tossed the plane up and backwards, forcing it to do a complete loop so it was then headed straight down, nose first toward the river.

The pilot was sure this was the end. However, he managed to regain control before he reached the river. His wife was not screaming at all now. They thought they were brushing the trees and rocks as they struggled to find some room to fly. The little craft was now about fifteen miles into the Thompson canyon.

The wind was much less punishing, but the pilot was so unnerved that this did not even occur to him. The next time the pilot took note of any details outside the plane, he could see a straight section of the Trans-Canada Highway directly ahead. At that moment there was no traffic visible, so he landed right there.

A transport truck was heading along the highway at that moment, a long experienced driver at the wheel. The driver was enjoying the nice weather and thinking of his next stop, where he would enjoy some fresh coffee and a bit of a walk. Suddenly an airplane dropped onto the highway right in front of him. Fortunately, they were both going the same direction and he braked to a stop and ran to assist the people in the plane.

It took a few minutes for the couple from the plane to realize that their ordeal was over. They had both been convinced that they were going to die, and it seemed possible to them that the feeling of standing on the ground again was part of the death process.

The wife made arrangements to return home by bus. The trucker carried on with a hell of a story to tell at the next few stops. The next morning we blocked the highway traffic for a few minutes and the pilot flew away, completely convinced to never again fly the Fraser Canyon route.

Runaway Truck

During the 1960s, British Columbia was in a road building boom. The projects included Rogers Pass, from Golden to Revelstoke; the Blueberry Paulson from Castlegar to Christina Lake; the Salmo–Creston Highway; and the link from Prince George to McBride. These roads were all through mountainous terrain that had defeated earlier construction plans. Much was said about the sections of the Rogers Pass where snowsheds were required and the road cost more than a million dollars a mile. At that time my net paycheck was $128 twice a month.

The first of the projects to be completed was the Castlegar to Christina Lake road. Prior to the completion of this link, traffic had to go through the US or by the old Cascade Highway, both of which were steep and winding routes involving excessive travel time. The second link to be completed was the Salmo to Creston Highway. This road greatly improved the access between the East and West Kootenay; prior to this road the highway ran along Kootenay Lake, which had to be crossed on ferries. The one hundred and forty mile drive from Nelson to Cranbrook took the best part of a day on the old route.

The new highway greatly reduced the travel time, but it also brought added dangers and maintenance problems. The Salmo–Creston Highway crossed the spine of the Selkirk Mountains. It is one of the highest-altitude highway passes in Canada. To reach the summit of this pass from the west, the highway rises sharply from a point near Salmo. The last stretch to the summit has a constant grade of seven percent, rising nearly five thousand feet in thirteen miles.

The new roads brought fresh opportunities to many people. The travelling public could enjoy the previously isolated areas, and new businesses would be required to meet their needs. The hauling of goods and resources had been largely done by the railway, but now the trucking industry was able to provide faster and more efficient service. Highway trucks of that era struggled to drag themselves up to the summit and they had to ease themselves down the other side very slowly to maintain control. The weight of these units combined with the steep down-grade created a runaway danger, not fully appreciated by some of the inexperienced drivers who found themselves making deliveries into areas previously served only by the railway.

The highway plan included runaway lanes, wherever it was possible to build them, for vehicles that had lost control. These escape lanes consisted of crude roadways that branched away from the highway at a very steep upward pitch. They were narrow, rough and short. A driver would have to be very cool headed to try to put a runaway truck into one, considering that the ninety-thousand-pound machine might be going eighty miles per hour or more. What the inexperienced drivers could see was that the escape lanes would result in a sure crash, albeit one where the driver might survive. What they did not realize was that the alternative was certain death.

In the early fall of the first year of the new highway, a truck from Alberta was westbound, destined for the city of Trail, BC. The truck was carrying a flat-deck trailer loaded with four tiers of bagged Portland cement. The driver was quite experienced, having logged over two hundred thousand miles; the unfortunate thing was that nearly every one of those miles had been driven on the Canadian prairies. This trip was his first one into BC, and the first time he had encountered a mountain pass. Most highway transport trucks, in those times, carried a device called a tachometer card that recorded the activity of the truck over a twenty-four hour period. A trained analyst could determine the speed of the unit, which gear it was in, and the rpm of the engine at any given time. Many drivers disliked these tracking devices in the extreme. They had been a free roving group and the tach cards were the beginning of a very sophisticated system of accountability. Today many long haul trucks are on global positioning systems which can tell their head office their exact location at any given moment.

The tachometer card from this truck showed it had stopped at Creston for about thirty minutes before entering into the pass. The card from the cab showed the truck struggling up the east side of the pass, where it was only able to manage fifteen to twenty miles per hour. As the truck approached the crest of the pass, it accelerated past a series of signs cautioning it about the severe down grade ahead and compelling all trucks to pull over and adjust their brakes. The truck picked up more speed as it passed the large parking areas that are provided on each side of the highway at the summit to accommodate truckers in doing their mandatory checks and adjustments. The truck entered the top of the thirteen miles of downgrade at about forty-five miles per hour, and accelerating.

It was impossible to determine from the tachometer card the exact location where the driver first realized his error. He did, at some point in the first few miles, attempt a full brake application. However, the brakes on both the truck and trailer were not in good condition and they were badly in need of adjustment. Had the brakes been in new condition on both the truck and trailer, and had they been correctly adjusted, the driver might have been able to make one full stop, at that speed, on that grade, with the load he was carrying. The attempted brake application at first caused some slowing of the truck, but that was all. Truck brakes generate tremendous heat at that weight and speed, and the hotter they get the less they hold. This, combined with the lack of maintenance and adjustment, caused the air brake system on this driver's truck to fail.

There is no doubt that the truck was in a full runaway by the end of the fourth mile of the downgrade. Nine miles remained to the point where the grade would lessen slightly and the highway would take a sharp turn to the right. The highway is carved into the side of the mountain along this steep grade; it follows a long arc to the left, for downhill traffic, and then makes a sharp turn to the right. The long bend to the left tightens as it approaches the sharp right turn. If the runaway truck had been able to negotiate the tightening left turn at the end of the steep grade, it would then have entered the sharp right turn. With the load the truck was carrying it may have been able to take the right bend at about sixty-five miles per hour. It was going over ninety, however, two miles before that point, and still picking up speed. Had the truck reached the sharp right turn at the speed it was then travelling it would have been forced across the oncoming lane and over the side of the mountain, taking with it any traffic it happened to meet in crossing the oncoming lane. It would then have fallen about one thousand five hundred feet to the creek bed below.

After the trucker lost control of his rig, he passed four escape lanes, each of which was marked by signs in advance of the point where they left the road. The incident happened in daylight, so he had an instant to look at the escape routes as he sped toward them. The runaway lanes were anything but inviting in appearance; however, I can only guess why he chose not to attempt one. The questionable circumstances of his passenger would no doubt have had some bearing on his decisions. The driver was accompanied by a woman from his home area. They were both married, but not to each other.

A witness was travelling down the pass in his car when he saw and heard the truck overtaking him at an unbelievable speed. He estimated its speed at one hundred miles per hour as it passed him; the truck engine was making a screaming sound. As the truck passed, the witness noted that the brakes on both the truck and the trailer were glowing white. He watched the truck race away into the tightening left curve to the point where it disappeared into a cloud of grey dust.

The speed, weight, and the tightening curve caused the truck to go over the right edge of the roadway into a shallow ditch, on the outside of which was the almost vertical side of the mountain. As the truck dropped into the ditch and crashed into the mountain, the trailer sheared away from the truck frame and crushed the cab. Bags of powdered cement burst on the rocks above and around the wreckage. When the dust had settled, everything was blanketed in cement. The dismembered bodies were caked in cement; even the fuel and radiator fluid from the truck had been absorbed into the tons of powder.

The call to police was received at the Salmo detachment, which consisted of two officers, one very experienced and one with a total of three months in the field. The senior man was away for the day, leaving the new member to rush to the scene alone, radioing for assistance. I was called by our dispatcher in Nelson and advised that the new member was alone in the crash area. I was about one very high-speed hour away; in about forty-five minutes I was close enough to radio the new member at the scene. During the brief radio call it was quite obvious that things were not going well for him. He repeated himself and talked about things not relevant to what he was doing. He informed me that the driver was dead and that the truck had been driven by a woman.

When I rounded the sharp curve to my left, just below the scene, I saw the twisted wreck beside the road and the cement spread over the whole area. Some of the cement powder had flowed down the ditch for several hundred feet. The young constable was standing near the wreck, waving traffic around the scene. He was covered in cement dust from head to foot, which added somewhat to the high colour of his face. In the hand he wasn't using to wave he held a human foot and ankle encased in a nylon stocking. He tried to wave me by, failing to recognize the marked police cruiser. He was vomiting continuously. His policing career was not getting off to a good start.

I took the nylon stocking and its contents from the grey policeman and had him sit in his car to gather his composure. He told me he had found the foot in the flowing cement powder just below the wreckage but did not know what to do with it.

The removal of the wreckage was a very slow process. None of the machine could be moved on its own wheels because of the extensive damage. Trucks were brought in and pieces were loaded with a portable crane. As each piece was removed, we all worked with shovels to search for body parts. We knew early in the job that there were at least two bodies, but we had to determine if there were more. A temporary morgue consisting of emergency blankets was prepared at the edge of the cement. As body parts were found we cleaned away some of the cement, tried to identify them as male or female, and placed them in one of the two blankets. Clothing and foot wear was also collected to confirm the number and identity of the victims. The job went on well into the night until the last of the truck had been removed and we were fairly certain that we had all the major parts of two bodies.

The damage to the truck was the most severe that I saw in all my years of police work. The ten wheels and tires had all burst during the impact, and pieces of inner tube and tire casings were scattered in a half circle away from the mountainside. The engine block and transmission were crushed, separated from the frame and from each other. At the moment of impact there would normally have been a huge fireball which could have ignited the diesel fuel that sprayed into the air as the tanks were shredded. Fire was probably prevented by the cloud of cement dust that instantly blanketed the entire scene.

The driver and his friend died needlessly. A knowledgeable mountain driver would have stopped at the summit and carefully inspected and adjusted his brakes. Then he would have started down the mountain at a greatly reduced speed, using the engine to hold back the load. A truck driven in that manner would be capable of stopping in any sort of emergency it happened to encounter. The downside of such cautious driving is the time it takes to make the descent. The driver and his friend thought they did not have the time to follow these rules, but as so often happens, trying to save a few minutes cost them the rest of their days.

Transferring Trouble

The RCMP system of moving members regularly had many positive features, but it often created situations that were either comical or tragic. Your view of whether a given situation was comical or tragic depended on whether you were directly affected or were just far enough away to observe without getting splashed.

The transfer of staff was, and still is, used to deal with all types of personnel problems. Discipline is a difficult exercise: it most often results in bad publicity, the exposure of everyone to scrutiny, and waves of fear throughout the organization. The Royal Canadian Mounted Police learned long ago that it was less damaging to simply transfer the problematic people and hope that the situation would resolve itself somewhere else in a different mix of personalities.

This transfer method was effective in a surprisingly high number of situations. Young members who had been identified as a problem by one supervisor were often developed into well-rounded constables by a more adept man at their next posting. The member subjected to the transfer was not always the root of the problem. Many good young constables found themselves branded as a problem only because they used their mind and asked questions. A more sure method of becoming a problem was to formulate a good plan of their own and achieve positive results; such actions were often viewed as a threat.

Of course, this method also had its failings. The practice of transferring trouble led to a free ride for many who could not or would not do their duty in any semblance of an acceptable manner. I had brief encounters with some people during my service who had experienced more transfers than they had years of service. The comical aspect of this would be evident in the service record of such people, if one was privy to this classified material. These service files would contain many highly generalized positive statements of the member's great potential, and how it could be realized by moving from a small unit to a larger one, from a populated area to an isolated one, from general policing to a specialized unit, and so on.

Common phrases in these reports would include "to broaden his horizons," "to round out his experience" and "to enhance his latent abilities." Anyone who had gained an understanding of the inner workings of the organization would know that these writings were done with only one purpose in mind: "Get this son-of-a-bitch out of my hair." One of the tragic features of these highly mobile people was that they were often promoted because of their broad geographical experience and the sheer volume of complimentary sendoffs in their personnel files.

When an unsuspecting group of policemen had their supervisor replaced by one of these mobile miracles the day-to-day satisfactions and disappointments of a policing career were made meaningless in an instant. Working became a matter of survival until they or the new supervisor were transferred.

I recall hearing of a senior member who was in charge of a prairie detachment. This member had a reputation as a good instructor, and he had successfully guided many young constables in the early parts of their careers. He also had a reputation as a very hard-nosed policeman who did his duty by the book and dealt with the public "Without Fear, Favour or Affection," as the old police motto went. The public respected and admired him, but they all knew that one did not approach this man to fix a ticket or grant a favour just because they felt themselves to be too important to be subjected to the trivialities of law enforcement.

This man was in charge of a busy detachment where he and one constable had their hands full dealing with everyday occurrences. The administrative people at the Subdivision were aware of the demanding load, but they were faced with a problem. A young member had been identified as difficult. He had been transferred to three units by that time and each supervisor had found him to be "a very suitable candidate for a transfer." The Subdivision people wanted to see what the hardnosed supervisor could do with this one.

A telephone call was made to the busy detachment commander and the problem was outlined. The commander stated that he would not be able to deal with such a problem unless he was granted an additional experienced constable so that some of his time would be available to deal with the problem member. In those days, such a statement by a subordinate was considered near mutiny. The telephone call ended abruptly with the Subdivision officer informing the detachment commander that the problem would arrive by bus the next morning and that he would deal with it without additional manpower.

The problem constable arrived as promised. He was given a stern lecture and told that he would be expected to carry his share of the load while at that detachment. The supervisor spent many hours in addition to his regular shifts trying to guide this new constable. It soon became apparent to him that this person did not have the basic requirements to perform police duties. In less than one month, the detachment commander sent the young man back to Subdivision on the bus. The young man was given an envelope that he was to deliver to the Officer Commanding. The envelope contained a memorandum from the detachment commander advising that he was sending the problem member back to Subdivision. He briefly referred to the earlier telephone conversation wherein he had pointed out that he would be unable to deal with the supervision of the difficult member because of the demands of his work.

The arrival of the constable and the letter caused great turmoil around the Subdivision building. How dare this man challenge authority in such a blatant manner! No doubt the continued employment of the detachment commander was in question at that point. The matter was temporarily resolved by a heated telephone call advising the detachment commander that the recruit would be returning on the next bus and that no further insubordination would be tolerated.

Several weeks passed with no communication between Subdivision and the detachment. The folks at Subdivision were concerned at first, but by the end of the fifth week they could contain themselves no longer. The detachment commander was contacted by telephone and advised that the patrol sergeant would be visiting the next week for a routine audit. The call seemed to go on for an inordinate time, but the detachment commander made no mention of the problem member. The caller from the Subdivision headquarters tried in vain to tactfully open the touchy subject, but at last he gave up, knowing that the audit would solve the riddle.

The appointed day arrived and the patrol sergeant started his routine inspection. The detachment was without fault. Every item that was examined proved beyond reproach. There was no indication in any file or document that the problem member had been involved in any way. Finally the patrol sergeant asked how the new member was performing. The detachment commander stated that he had sent the problem member home to his mother shortly after he had returned from Subdivision. The old patrol sergeant was apoplectic. He walked in a tight circle within the office, then gathered his things and left without a word.

I would like to have been a fly on the wall at Subdivision when the old patrol sergeant arrived there. No doubt there was unbridled rage from the Officer Commanding, but this obviously gave way to some soul searching and then to the realization that their bluff had been called. They had not had what it took to deal with the first problem and now they had another that made the first seem like a walk in the park. Their problem was exacerbated by the knowledge that if they fired the detachment commander they would have to answer some very difficult questions.

The young constable was called at his mother's home and told to return to the Subdivision immediately. He was dismissed from the service.

The detachment commander was transferred with a glowing recommendation that did not include a single reference to this incident.

The Great Fernie Bank Heist

Winter still had a firm grip on the mountains and valleys of the East Kootenay as this story began. We were past the shortest day of the winter and the days were getting just long enough that the change could be noticed. The winter snow still lay thick and each storm that passed through added a little more in the valley bottoms and a lot more to the mountaintops.

The previous summer seven members from the East and West Kootenay regions had been trained to operate as an emergency response team. We had done a few practice exercises, but we were still waiting for the first actual call. The call finally came about mid-January: something requiring our team was happening in Fernie. For security reasons we were told only to meet for briefing in Cranbrook as soon as possible. Cranbrook was chosen because we would have been too obvious had we suddenly appeared in the smaller community of Fernie. In a few hours, six of our number arrived in

Cranbrook in an assortment of unmarked police vehicles and private cars.

The story we heard in Cranbrook was almost unbelievable. Two young men who lived in Fernie had teamed up with an old criminal from the United States and were planning to rob a bank. The one young man, Mike, had lived all his life in Fernie; he had a girlfriend there and his family had been part of the community long before he was born. The second young man, Eddie, had lived all his life in the Kootenay region but was only on his second winter in Fernie. He had no family there and had been in trouble with the law for break and enter, theft, and assault offences. The older man was an American citizen who was nearly sixty years old and had spent more than half of his life in prison. His record was mainly for theft and fraud, but he had also been convicted for robberies where he had carried firearms.

The "old boy" from the States seemed to be the leader. He was armed and had to be considered very dangerous. He was a career criminal, well past the age when many of his type give up the trade and settle down, but here he was in the midst of a bizarre plan involving robbery and kidnapping. From our point of view, if there was a confrontation involving firearms he would be the one to neutralize at the first opportunity.

Eddie was also to be considered dangerous. He had quite an extensive record for his age and he had shown a penchant for violence in several of the offences he had committed. Police members who had had dealings with him believed he was mentally unstable when sober, and explosive when under the influence of drugs or alcohol. Eddie and the old criminal made a team that would be capable of trying almost anything prohibited by the Canadian Criminal Code.

Mike had worked with Eddie during the last two years and had come to consider him a friend. They had often gone on day outings in the mountains around Fernie on snowmobiles. Mike's family owned an assortment of snowmobiles and there was usually a machine available for Eddie to borrow. Mike described Eddie as an okay guy as long as he was sober, but a complete idiot if he was drinking. Mike had no criminal record and had seldom if ever come to the attention of the police.

Mike and his family had many years of experience with snowmobiles. They had been into every mountain valley within a hundred miles of Fernie; they had visited most valleys many times. It was Mike's experience with snowmobiles and his knowledge of the local mountains that led to him being invited into this criminal conspiracy. Eddie had frequently talked to Mike about his old friend and the great times they had had at the bar; he was determined that Mike should meet this man. Early that winter, Mike finally agreed to join them at a coffee shop.

At first the older man claimed to be a prospector and asked Mike a lot of questions about the mountain valleys around Fernie. He was very interested in the possibility of leaving Fernie on a snowmobile and crossing a mountain pass where there was no road. He wanted a way out of town that would not require using the only highway or the parallel railway. The old criminal became very interested when Mike told him the possibilities of crossing mountain passes into the United States, Alberta, or into another part of British Columbia near the town of Canal Flats. When he asked if Mike would be interested in guiding him and some others through one of these routes for a share of a few hundred thousand dollars, Mike also became very interested. The conversation did not go into the source of the money at that first meeting.

Over the following weeks there were several more meetings between the three men; they looked at maps and plotted the time required to traverse a variety of snowmobile routes. Mike tried to find out more about the source of the money, but was not given any more than that he would be told about it when the time was right. At that point Mike began to realize that the other two were plotting a major theft or robbery.

During one of their meetings, Mike was taken up to the old boy's room on the third and top floor of the Fernie Hotel. The accommodation was very basic, with a bed, a dresser, and a washroom at the far end of the hall that was shared with every other occupant on that floor. The most impressive thing about the trip to the room was a Ruger .44 Magnum revolver that Mike was shown. The old man had a hundred rounds of ammunition for the big hand gun and bragged about how a round from that weapon would go through an engine block.

Mike had been having a lot of sleepless nights since he was introduced to Eddie's friend. He had been curious about their plan at first and their talk about all the money had kept him excited. His curiosity and excitement had gradually changed toward fear and suddenly became full-fledged terror when they showed him that big revolver. Up to that point, Mike had felt in the back of his mind that this whole thing was a fantasy. Seeing the gun changed that. Mike left the Fernie Hotel with his head spinning; he went straight home and told his father everything.

Later that night, Mike and his father met with the Fernie detachment commander and Mike revealed his very strange story. The plan was to storm into the police office and force everyone into the cellblock. They would steal RCMP uniforms and police cars. They would destroy the police radio and then go to the bank dressed as police officers. The bank staff would be forced into the vault and the three would then have time to gather all the cash and make their way to the edge of town, where they would have their snowmobiles sitting ready to go. The snowmobiles would carry them through a mountain pass to a place where they could divide the money and go their separate ways as wealthy men. The plan was so poorly thought out that it was more like comic theatre than a criminal conspiracy.

However, when all the information had been considered from the police point of view, there was no alternative but to consider it genuine.

Mike was asked by the police if he would consider continuing with his part in the plan and assist with gathering evidence against the other two. He considered this, and discussed it with his father. They knew that there was very little to support charges against Eddie and the old boy. They also knew that without their assistance, Eddie would be on the street knowing that Mike had gone to the police. They agreed to assist the police by remaining a part of the plot.

The technical assistance people of the RCMP were called in. They rented the room in the Fernie Hotel across the hall from the old boy and began their surveillance. A thin wire with a microphone was pushed under the hall carpet between the two rooms. The carpet in the hall had seen many years of traffic, leaving it so thin that a ridge was visible where the wire crossed the hall. I believe that the ridge was much more obvious to us because we knew it was there; it was not noticed by the suspects.

Mike was now having regular meetings with the police. A plan was hatched to buy some time. Mike claimed that he needed parts for the snowmobiles and that the only source of these parts was in Calgary. Mike told the other two that he was broke and that they would have to come up with the money to get the parts. Neither of them was working so this presented a considerable obstacle.

The public pay phone in the lobby of the hotel and another near the hotel had been tapped by the technical assistance team. Several calls from Eddie and the old criminal were intercepted. Eddie called the parts supplier in Calgary and pleaded with them to send the needed parts for the snowmobiles. His pleas were not taken seriously because he was asking them to send the parts on credit. The old criminal made calls to Eddie and Mike, arranging meetings to work on their plan. He was very cautious in his use of the phone and would not discuss any part of their plans even when Mike asked direct questions.

The investigation dragged on for nearly two weeks with very little progress. The bugged phone calls confirmed the information from Mike but very little else; the microphone under the carpet picked up bits of conversation in the old criminal's room but nothing of any significance. The costs to the police budget were spiralling and soon became the topic of daily telephone discussions between Fernie detachment and British Columbia RCMP headquarters in Vancouver.

Meanwhile, we were holed up in a small motel outside Fernie with instructions to be invisible. Days were spent lying around the motel listening to CBC radio interviews with apiarists or people who had developed an improved barley crop through cross-pollination. The high point of our days came after dark when we tried to find an inconspicuous place for the evening meal. We drove across the border into Alberta on several occasions to have dinner as a group without drawing attention. We needed to see the end of this operation.

The decision was finally made to arrest the three conspirators and go with the limited evidence we had. There had been nothing new for several days. Eddie was still trying to get the machine parts on credit and the old criminal had called fewer meetings with the three of them. We formed a plan that would let us take them into custody with a minimum of risk.

Mike had told us that the old criminal would often carry his big handgun when he ventured out of the hotel or went to the bar downstairs. The gun was always loaded and was carried in a holster inside a small backpack. The backpack hung from his shoulder when he was walking on the street and when it contained the gun he kept it in his lap when he sat in the bar. If the gun was not in it, he would put it on the floor under his chair.

The day of reckoning arrived. Our first break came when the old criminal called Mike and Eddie to meet him for beer at about two o'clock. Well before two, a couple of policemen who looked like prospectors were in the Fernie Hotel pub dawdling over some flat beer. Just before two o'clock, the old criminal came in and took his favourite seat with his back to a corner; he was carrying his backpack and placed it in his lap when he sat down. He signalled the waiter and a glass of beer was delivered. He took a long pull and relaxed. After a few minutes, he put the backpack under his chair. He signalled for another glass and was nearly finished drinking it when Mike and Eddie came in and joined him.

The information was passed to the rest of us that the three were in the bar and it appeared the gun was not in the back-pack. We crashed the door to the room and confirmed that the handgun was there. Within a few seconds of us finding the gun, the three suspects found themselves with their hands pressed against the wall and their feet too far from the wall to be comfortable. The jig was up.

The three appeared in court the following day, all apparently charged with conspiracy to commit criminal offences. The old criminal was also charged under the Immigration Act and with possession of the big handgun.

Mike was not officially charged but it was made to appear that he was for the benefit of the other two. To explain why he wasn't held, they were told that he had been granted bail because he had no previous record and had roots in the community.

Eddie and the old criminal were remanded in custody to await trial. When the Crown case was fully prepared, the old criminal pleaded guilty to all charges and testified that he had been the instigator of the whole plot and that Eddie and Mike had only gone along with it because they were young and foolish. This testimony made it appear that the old criminal had some sense of fairness and decency about him in spite of his lifetime of crime. Eddie was released without charges after having spent a few months doing dead time in the provincial jail. He left Fernie to start anew somewhere else.

The old criminal was sentenced to five years. After serving a small part of his sentence he was ordered deported to the United States. On his return to the United States he was arrested on a parole violation and numerous theft, fraud and firearms offences. Beyond that, I have no knowledge of what became of him, but I suspect he was on the inside for a long time.

The Eye of the Storm

The biggest annual event in the Cariboo is the Williams Lake Stampede. People come from far and wide to take in the events that happen every July First weekend. This annual rodeo is the last of the truly Wild West events. The competition and prizes are big enough to attract cowboys from the professional circuit, but small enough to allow anyone who wants to give it a try. The little town rocks and rolls with the festivities and the local police call for additional bodies from all their neighbouring units. Liquor consumption, per capita, is the highest in the world during these weekends.

The stampede has become a time for family reunions for the old families of the area and a time for various groups to come together just for the celebration of the event. Two members of one of the informal groups were a couple from the Vancouver area, who had happened into a group at the stampede a few years prior to this event and had returned every year since that first time. They had such wonderful experiences and memories that they planned to be there every year.

This couple had a small camper unit that they carried on their pickup truck and they used it for the stampede each year. Their camper was small, but it was equipped with a kitchen and lamps that used propane fuel. These people did not feel entirely comfortable with propane fuel, but they enjoyed the convenience of making meals and having the handy light that did not drain their battery. Their discomfort with compressed fuel had resulted in the habit of shutting off the fuel at the tank valve every night just before they went to bed.

On this occasion, their third or fourth trip to the stampede, they had been delayed in starting out from the Vancouver area. They arrived at Williams Lake about nine p.m., found the camping spot they had reserved, levelled the camper and set out to find their friends. They located their friends and partied until about one a.m.

They were tired and a little inebriated when they returned to the camper, so they hurried into the bunk and fell asleep in a very short time. They both forgot their routine of shutting off the propane valve before retiring for the night.

It was about two a.m. when they awoke feeling sick. They told us later of feeling nauseous and light-headed. The husband stepped out of the camper and walked a few steps away to urinate. He was thus occupied when his wife decided to have a smoke. She had gotten down from the camper bed and was sitting at the little breakfast nook near the centre of the camper. She located her cigarettes and lighter. When she struck the lighter, she saw a very bright flash and felt a huge shock.

The camper had filled with an explosive mixture of propane and air from a small leak in one of the fuel lines. When the mixture was ignited by the cigarette lighter it blew all the windows out. The door flew out, along with its complete frame, and landed on the ground beside the husband. The entire roof of the camper separated from the sides and the rear end and rose some distance over the blown-out walls. The shock of the blast was over in an instant and the roof of the camper fell back inside the walls, where it came to rest on debris from the furniture and fixtures.

The lady in the centre of it all found herself caught under the camper roof and unable to move. She had no idea what had happened. The blast had blown every stitch of clothing off her body and her skin was very lightly singed by the instantaneous flame. The husband was sure he was a widower; he walked around the wreck in a daze. A neighbouring camp resident came out with a flashlight and tried to figure out what had happened. The husband borrowed the light and was trying to locate his wife under the fallen roof when she asked him to help her get out of there. When the police and ambulance arrived, the lady had been helped out of the wreckage and someone had provided her with a blanket.

The woman was taken to the hospital emergency room, where she was examined by a doctor and released. She and her husband were given a spare bunk at a friend's camp and they stayed to enjoy the stampede.

The lady's narrow escape was talked about for years. She had no damage to hearing or sight, she had no cuts or bruises, only a very slight singe on her skin. The firefighters had heard of similar happenings, where a person had survived right in the centre of an explosion. They believed that there was a relatively calm area at the centre. They must be right, but I do not wish to test their theory.

The explosion was the result of a very small leak in the

propane lines near one of the lamps. The leak appeared to have been there since this couple had bought the unit new, a few years before. The fault had not been discovered because of their habit of shutting the gas off every night.

Pot Cowboys

In the early spring of 1974, we received a call at Golden detachment from the RCMP at Banff, Alberta. We were advised that the national park wardens had observed two men in an old pickup truck near Lake Louise. The two men had driven from the highway into one of the restricted areas where the snow-clearing machines were parked, and they had allowed two large dogs to run at large.

Dogs must be on a leash or caged at all times in a national park. Therefore, the wardens had approached to speak to the violators. The two had been extremely nervous. They had apologized profusely, tied the dogs in the open truck box and driven away immediately. The two wardens were convinced that these two men were involved in something illegal. In addition to describing the two young men, the truck and the two dogs, the wardens advised that when they had first approached the truck, one of the men had the passenger door open and had placed something behind a speaker in the door panel. After the encounter with the park wardens, the truck returned to the highway and turned west toward British Columbia.

One of our highway patrol units was working in Yoho National Park, ten or fifteen miles east of Golden, and they were advised of the report from Banff. Within thirty minutes the patrol met the truck and interviewed the two men.

The two were dressed in well-worn cowboy costumes, complete with ten gallon hats and vests with fringes hanging from every seam. Their dogs, a German shepherd and a Doberman pinscher, were in the truck box along with a large red fuel tank and two very used western saddles. The dogs were very aggressive, barking and growling and giving the clear impression that anyone who got within their reach would be bitten. The two cowboys said they had been to Calgary to visit some friends. They had also met with some people in connection with their plan to provide rodeo animals for the next Calgary Stampede. They cursed at the dogs, which increased their aggressiveness, and said they had only brought them along because they could not find anyone to care for them. They said their home was in the south Okanagan and that they had both lived there for several years.

The fuel tank was across the front of the truck box and was large enough that the dogs could not reach anyone who was getting into or out of the cab. One of the policemen had made a note of the information about the passenger door and radio speaker. He scanned through the junk inside the cab and looked under the seat with his flashlight. He then turned his attention to the doors. There were radio speakers mounted through the inside panels of both doors. He grasped the outer ring of the speaker in the passenger door and the entire unit came away in his hand. There were no wires attached to the speaker. In the hollow of the door, directly under the speaker opening, was a small brown paper bag which contained sixteen thousand eight hundred dollars in cash. The money was in one hundred, fifty, and twenty dollar bills; about half of the total was in twenties. It was a very impressive wad.

The discovery of the brown bag in the door brought about a remarkable change in the two cowboys. They were no longer slow talking, "ah shucks" good old boys. Suddenly, neither of them would answer a question unless they were pressed to do so, and they both demanded their right to speak to their lawyers. One of them did say that they were antique dealers and that the cash was there in case they found some good buys.

The identification documents that the cowboys had presented were put through the police computer system. One came up completely clean. The second had been convicted for trafficking in marijuana about three years prior. The combined circumstances were enough to take them into custody for further investigation. The cowboys were arrested, advised of their rights, and placed in the police vehicle. With the consent of the cowboys, one of the investigators drove their truck into Golden behind the police car. The two dogs remained in the truck box for the ride to Golden.

I met them when they arrived at the police office in Golden, and I assisted with placing the cowboys in our cells. We wanted to have a really good look at their truck, but the dogs would not let us near it. I approached the prisoners and asked that one of them remove the dogs from the truck. They refused. I told them that it was my duty to search the truck and that the dogs were keeping me from doing so; I was prepared to do whatever was necessary to facilitate the search and that would include eliminating the dogs. After a brief conference between the two prisoners, one of them volunteered to come with me and take the dogs out of the truck. We found a suitable place to tie the dogs, who were provided with food, water and shelter.

After I returned the prisoner to the cells, I went back to the truck. The two policemen who had intercepted the truck were thrilled to have discovered that the fuel tank had a false bottom and that it contained two kilograms of Mexican marijuana. The marijuana was in the typical one-kilogram blocks, about four inches thick, twelve inches long and six inches wide. The blocks were wrapped in translucent red cellophane. We now had more than enough to support the arrest and detention of the cowboys.

The fuel tank was the common type and design used by loggers and contractors to haul fuel; it was half-round on the top with short vertical sides and just long enough to fit across the front of a pickup truck box. The tank appeared, at first glance, to be bolted to the floor of the truck box. However, a firm lift on the tank allowed it to easily come up from the truck floor. A square hole had been cut in the bottom of the tank allowing the kilogram blocks of marijuana to be placed into the tank or taken from there. The main bung on the top of the tank was fitted with a hand-crank operated fuel pump, complete with a hose to carry fuel to another vehicle or to the tank of the host truck. The intake pipe from the pump reached into a fuel can inside the tank. The fuel can contained motor oil, so if anyone had tried the pump, it would have produced light oil.

Over the following weeks, many hours were put into the investigation. The marijuana appeared to be part of a huge shipment that had come from Mexico into the American Northwest. Marijuana, at that time, had a street value of three hundred and fifty dollars a kilogram. The money in the paper bag and the two remaining blocks indicated that the cowboys may have started their travels with fifty kilograms. The description of the truck, dogs, and cowboys was recognized by both the American and Canadian Customs officers at the south Okanagan border crossings. They were remembered as the two good old boys who nearly always stopped at the border to visit a while.

The cowboy with the clean record was fingerprinted and

the prints were forwarded for identification. The fingerprints were searched through the system and were found to belong to a very active criminal. A photograph we received along with the record was identical to our cowboy with the clean record so we now had a different name for him. Most of his criminal record had been accumulated in the province of Alberta. We made many inquiries with our counterparts in Alberta and gradually pieced together a history of the man.

The name he was using had come from a grave marker. He had found the grave of a boy who was born about the same time as himself and adopted the identity of the deceased, who had died about fifteen years earlier. He had applied for a birth certificate and the document was issued in spite of the overlooked fact that there was a death certificate on the file. Through the use of the fraudulent birth certificate, he obtained a social insurance number, a driver's license with his photograph, and several credit cards from oil companies and other retail outlets. Information from sources in the criminal element indicated that this man was developing several other identification files by similar means.

At the time of the arrest, both criminals were advised of their right to contact counsel and their right to remain silent. Before they were placed in the cells they were both asked if they wished to make a phone call, but both declined, saying they would place calls later in the day. It was about two hours after the arrests when we received a call from the senior partner of a very well-known Vancouver law firm. He was aware of the arrest and he asked to speak to the cowboy with the clear record. The cowboy was brought from the cells and had a brief conversation with the lawyer.

We were now positive that we had found some key operators in the marijuana industry. This lawyer had a reputation as a very effective defense counsel. He was very expensive and he did not make phone calls or talk to people until he had received a large deposit. We concluded that there had been a second vehicle with some associates of the two cowboys and that the people in the other vehicle had seen the arrest and reported it to the lawyer.

A criminal with any experience and a little finesse will have a lawyer on a retainer; getting caught is simply a cost of doing business. A good or, more accurately, an effective lawyer is a necessity when the inevitable happens.

I have always been puzzled by the fact that lawyers, who are officers of Her Majesty's court, are so willing to accept payments in such obviously dirty money. In this case, I took the opportunity at the trial to ask the lawyer if he ever engaged in barter with his clients or if it was necessary for them to convert their product to cash in every case. He curtly replied that everyone was entitled to counsel. I replied that I was well aware of that, but that he had not answered my question. He walked away.

The cowboys appeared before the court within twenty-four hours and they were released on the condition that they would appear for trial in due course. They appeared at that first hearing without counsel but I suspect that the Vancouver lawyer had been in touch with the judge, who was a former lawyer, and that they had discussed the merits of the case.

When the cowboys eventually came to trial, the Vancouver lawyer attacked every aspect of our case with great vigour. He shouted and frequently jumped up from his chair to object to points of evidence against his clients. It was very obvious that he was there not only to ensure that his clients got a fair trial, but also to do whatever he could to obstruct the presentation of the Crown evidence. He put great effort into the trial. Undoubtedly, he came away from the trial with a great deal more of his clients' ill-gotten money than what we found in their truck on the day of the arrest.

The outstanding performance by the expensive lawyer was not enough on that occasion. The cowboys were convicted and sentenced to eighteen months in the provincial jail at Kamloops.

From the first day after the arrest, the brown paper bag we had recovered from the truck door and its contents had been the subject of much interest and correspondence from the Vancouver lawyer. It took a considerable effort, but eventually the funds were ordered deposited to his trust account. We must bear in mind that this gentleman was an officer of the court. Who could possibly be trusted with these funds, if not this honourable man?

Wolverine

Spring comes late in the high mountain passes of British Columbia. It was about the middle of May when some road maintenance men were walking along the edge of the Trans-Canada Highway on the east slope of the Rogers Pass. The snow had melted away in most of the areas that were exposed to the full power of the spring sun. The area where the two men were walking had been under a thick covering of snow that had been pushed up by the snow-clearing machines over the past winter. Even this heavy snow cover had started to give way to the power of the coming spring and summer.

The two men were able to see most of the steel guardrail along the area where they walked. Part of their reason for walking that area was to inspect the guardrail for any damage from the snow-clearing work of the previous winter. The two workers found a section of the steel rail with some slight distortion; they were puzzled by the nature of the damage. What the men expected to see was damage caused by the heavy crawler tractors and blades used to shove snow over the edge of the mountain. When one of these units came into contact with the guardrail, the rail was often cut or torn through like tissue paper.

What the men found instead was a warped section of guardrail that suggested it had been struck by something much lighter than a crawler tractor. Closer examination of the damaged rail indicated that a motor vehicle had collided with it and that the vehicle had gone over the top of the railing. A vehicle crashing over the guardrail at that point would be at the beginning of a crash and roll which would carry on for about one thousand five hundred feet to the valley bottom.

The two workers contacted their office and reported what they had found. They had looked over the side of the mountain below where the rail had been damaged and sighted a shiny object near the valley bottom. The shiny object was near the Beaver River and was estimated to be one thousand feet below the level of the highway.

One of the workers decided to make his way down the treacherous slope to determine what the shiny object was.

The call came to our office in Golden. The caller outlined what the men had observed and that when the worker had made his way to the shiny object he had found the front bumper of a vehicle with a license plate attached to it. The license plate was from the province of Alberta. The worker had walked over the compressed snow below where he found the bumper and license plate, but was unable to find anything more. He reported that there was still a very thick layer of snow in that area and that it was entirely possible that a vehicle could be under the snow.

The license number was entered into our computer system and was linked to missing person who had not been heard of since early in November of the previous year.

The missing man had been involved in an argument with his wife and had left home in his car. He had a history of this type of behaviour. However, he had returned within a few days on all previous occasions.

The missing man had used a credit card to buy fuel for his car. The credit card bills showed that he had travelled from his home to Edmonton, Peace River, Prince George and Kamloops. The last gasoline purchase had been at Revelstoke, at the west end of the Rogers pass. The purchase in Revelstoke had been made two days after he left his residence in Alberta. It appeared he was on his way home.

Many of the daylight hours of the following days were spent on the mountainside where the car had crashed. Each day the snow melted and revealed more about the final moments of the man's life. The crushed windshield and the glass from the sides and rear of the car were in the area where the vehicle first came into contact with the rocks. The crushed glass indicated that the car had gone end-over-end after it vaulted the guardrail, and was upside-down when it first hit the rocks. That first impact was huge and would most likely have killed anyone in the vehicle. At that point, however, the vehicle had only begun the total distance it would plunge, crash, and roll, until it came to rest in the valley bottom.

Vehicle seat belts were not in common use at that time. The use of a seat belt in that crash would not have made any difference in the fatal result; however, it might have made the body stay with the vehicle until it came to rest near the river. Later examination of the wreckage showed that the seat belt was not broken, and therefore was likely not in use before the crash. We were not able to determine where, or if, the body had been ejected from the vehicle.

Metal detecting equipment was used to scan the field of compacted snow in the valley bottom where the car would most likely be. The electronic search indicated a vehicle-sized metal object under ten to twelve feet of snow. The area was probed with avalanche search rods, which confirmed there was a vehicle there and that the whole area was made up of rocks the size of motor vehicles and bigger.

The next day was spent shovelling down to and around the wrecked car. The serial numbers showed that the wreckage was the vehicle that had been registered to the missing man from Alberta. There was no trace of a body or any identification documents to be found.

The warm spring rains came and the snow melted quickly. The hole to the car almost disappeared over the next few days and the scene changed rapidly. The vehicle was lying near the river channel beside a pile of driftwood; the wood had been carried by the river and piled up there by the high water in previous years.

As the snow receded we learned more about the scene. The interior mouldings and upholstery of the car had been chewed and torn. The extent of the damage indicated a powerful and aggressive animal or animals.

One of my neighbors in Golden was a man who had made his living for many years as a trapper. I called him and discussed what we had found in the mountain pass. He was quite certain that the animals involved would be wolverines, but he came to the crash scene with me the following day to check. A quick look at the tooth marks in the car and the droppings around the area were all he needed to confirm his suspicions.

The old trapper told us that a wolverine is capable of breaking up the bones of an adult moose to get at the bone marrow. He speculated that if we were to find any remains of a body it would be in the tangle of sticks and logs that made up the driftwood pile near the wrecked car. His experience with these animals had taught him much about their behaviour. He knew them as quite intelligent and extremely aggressive, even among their own kind. If wolverines were feeding on something, they would fight over each portion and they would try to drag their feed into a protected spot where others could not attack them from every side. For that reason he felt the pile of driftwood would be where the wolverines may have sought cover from others while feeding on the missing body.

During the next day the driftwood pile was taken apart, piece by piece. In the lower areas of the log pile we found excrement from the wolverines but nothing more. Bone fragments and unidentifiable fibers were evident in the excrement. Samples were collected to determine if the bone fragments could be identified.

Several visits were made to the area until the last of the snow was gone, but no additional material was ever located. We knew that the man had credit cards and a wallet; however, no trace of these items was found.

The laboratory processes in those days were far less sophisticated than those available today. A report from the analysis indicated that the bone fragments in the animal excrement were of human origin, but there were no methods available then to identify a specific person.

All the information that we had been able to gather was provided to the local coroner to facilitate an inquiry. The coroner examined all the available information and issued a document stating that the missing man from Alberta had met his death at the crash scene.

Canoeing the Quesnel Canyon

In June of 1978 I was transferred to Quesnel from Golden. I was new to the community and to my duties there as a watch commander. Quesnel was a busy spot during those years so my introduction to the job consisted of being told where the washroom was and where to find the car keys. I was on my first evening shift and was in the office just as the sun was going down. At that time of year in the central part of British Columbia there is reasonable daylight until about ten o'clock at night.

An anxious young man came to the office to report that he had dropped off two of his friends up the Quesnel River along the Hydraulic Road, south of town. They had put their canoe into the river with the intention of paddling downstream to Quesnel, where this lad was to wait at the highway bridge to pick them up. The three friends were newcomers to the Quesnel area, having just arrived there for summer jobs. They had estimated that it would take the two paddlers about an hour to reach the pick-up location, but it was then nearly three hours since they had set out.

The route out of Quesnel to the drop-off location followed the main highway south for the first two miles and then turned onto the Hydraulic Road, which eventually came alongside the river about eight miles from town. The river could be seen from the highway bridge in town and again in the area along the Hydraulic Road where the canoe had been put in, but between those two viewing places was not easily accessible or visible. The river at that time of year was just past the spring rush; the water was quite clear and it moved along smoothly at a fairly quick pace but betrayed no sign of turbulence.

I found a number for the local Search and Rescue group and called one of the contact people. As I outlined the situation to the man, his first question was, "Do they know about the canyon?" I turned from the phone to the young man at the counter and repeated the question. The expression of alarm on his face gave the answer. The Search and Rescue people were asked to assist immediately. The young man left to continue his watch at the bridge, having been told we would look for him there if any reports were received. The Search and Rescue people arrived at the office to organize their efforts and told me about the river canyon. The Quesnel River has its origin about seventy-five miles from the town, where it leaves Quesnel Lake to make its way to the Fraser River. The river has a few rapid sections shortly after leaving the lake, and then it rambles across the plateau until near Quesnel, where it plunges into the deep valley of the Fraser River. This plunge takes place a few miles downstream from where the canoeists had started their adventure

The river provides a warning in the form of a small waterfall just where the rock walls close in from both sides and the river bends sharply to the left. The current then surges up against a series of rocks as it bends to head into the main plunge through the gorge to Quesnel. The water condition ahead is now very obvious; the roar is overwhelming and the air is filled with a fine spray which will soak a person in a very short time. The rock walls close in on both sides, giving the appearance that the river passes through a hole in the wall ahead. The search and rescue people assured me that if the canoeists did not manage to abort their trip before entering this section, only a miracle could save them.

Just before we left the office two local women came to the counter to report that they had been walking across the highway bridge when they saw a crushed and mostly submerged canoe pass underneath. The colour was the same as the one just reported missing. A power boat was put into the river and a search of the area below the canyon was carried out until well after dark; nothing was found.

The search was suspended for the night, but before it could resume word came that the two missing adventurers had been found on the Barkerville Highway some ten miles on the other side of Quesnel.

We got the full details of their brush with disaster the next day.

The first waterfall had scared the hell out of them and when the current pushed the canoe against the series of rocks they made the most of their chance to get their feet on solid ground. In their haste they overturned the canoe and it filled with water. Before they could right it, the current took over and away it went. They had both gotten wet and any remaining dry clothing on their bodies was rapidly being soaked by the mist from the river gorge.

They were now on the other side of the river from where they had entered. The only escape was to climb the steep bank away from the river and hope for a road when they reached the top. Darkness would not be long in coming. They walked through the bush for about four miles after reaching the rim of the canyon. They were able to guide themselves out by lights visible on the distant hills and by the sounds from the highway. A motorist brought the two into Quesnel, very tired and much wiser about the ways of rivers.

Death at Kootenay Pass

The Salmo-Creston section of Highway 3 was one of many very large projects undertaken in British Columbia in the early part of the 1960s. The new roadway cut across a mountain range that had been considered impassable by all previous generations. The advent of monster crawler tractors and high-speed rock drilling machines had brought about a re-thinking process.

The government of British Columbia made a decision to open the province by improving access to the communities of the interior and to the rest of Canada. The government commitment, new engineering technology, and powerful machinery brought new roads to many previously isolated places.

I remember the first time I saw a Caterpillar tractor ripping what appeared to be solid rock. The monster tractor crawled along a steep mountainside pulling a steel tooth that was cutting into the rock to a depth of several feet. The machine struggled with its task but it was doing work in a few hours that would have required months of chipping away with the less powerful equipment used in earlier days. Following a few passes by the rock-ripping tractor, the loose rock was loaded into trucks and moved away, or simply shoved over the side by a bulldozer.

The ripper tractor did encounter some areas where the rock was so hard that it could not break it. In these places, drilling machines were used to drive a line of holes, and explosives were set to break up the rock. The drilling machines were powered by compressed air and could punch holes into solid rock at an amazing speed. The explosives-men would place the blasting materials with such skill that very little rock would fly, yet every part of it would be broken loose, ready for the loading machines or the bulldozer.

I thought of the men who had built the mountain railways and the first road in the Fraser Canyon only a century before. These men had drilled into the rock with hand tools and placed explosives to move each piece of rock; the rock that did not fly from the force of the blasts was moved with shovels and wheelbarrows. I would like to have seen the look on their faces if they could have been brought back to see what I was watching that day.

The breaking of the rock and the construction of bridges brought the new roads to reality. The next struggle was to keep the roads open through the winter season. Heavy snowfall is normal in all the high mountain passes; the Salmo to Creston route over Kootenay Pass is second in snowfall only to the Rogers Pass on the Trans-Canada route between Golden and Revelstoke. The total annual snowfall on these passes will often be forty feet. Snow in such volume causes major problems in keeping a roadway open, even without the inevitable slides and avalanches. The conventional method of plowing the snow to the side of the road is limited because the ridges of snow at the edges of the road become so high that no more can be pushed over. The snowbanks must then be pushed away by machines or thrown away with snow blowers.

The first winters on the new mountain passes were challenging for the maintenance crews. There were no records to assist them, and no one who had experienced the conditions they met on a daily basis. The snow would frequently break loose from a mountain peak miles above the roadway and become an avalanche. The energy of an avalanche concentrates its snow to the weight of water, and as the weight increases, so does the speed of the moving mass. An avalanche can attain a speed of about two hundred miles per hour, and generates an unearthly sound. Wind at the sides and in front of an avalanche is deadly and has been known to overturn a railroad locomotive. When the avalanche snow stops moving, it freezes solid in an instant and is nearly impossible to penetrate with a shovel. A person or a machine caught in the path of an avalanche is doomed: if the wind or the crushing power of the snow does not kill them, they will certainly be unable to breathe in the airtight solid mass when it stops.

People have survived being buried in snow that has sloughed down a short distance. Snow retains its characteristic fluffy and porous texture if it has not slid over great distances as it does in a full avalanche.

It was early spring on the new Salmo-Creston highway, and an overnight storm had dropped nearly a foot of fluffy snow. Daylight came and the storm had moved away; the sun came up over a breathtaking scene. The changing shadows of trees and mountains on the perfect white carpet caused even those who worked there every day to stop and stare for a while.

The snow-clearing crews had been working steadily since the snow started the evening before, and by daylight they had the highway clear and sanded. At about mid-morning a young man was driving through Kootenay Pass on a business trip; he stopped briefly at the summit of the pass to look at the scenery before continuing on his way. A short distance from the summit, his car was suddenly buried by a small snow slide. The overnight snow had sloughed from a steep slope above the highway. This slope held only enough snow to cover the road and bury the car. The slide covered the highway for less than half a mile, and the car was near the middle.

The man in the car soon realized that he could see light through the snow over his windows; he could tell that there was only a thin layer of snow over the top of his car. He was unable to open the car doors but he could turn the window down. In a short time he was able to open a hole to the surface of the snow.

The snow-clearing crew had started to work on the slide almost before the last of it had fallen. The crew was aware that a car was covered because one of them had seen the slide come down. A worker saw the young man stick his head out of the snow and wave to him. The worker waved back to the man, who was sitting in the open window of the car with his head and neck above the snow, and signalled that the machines would reach the car in a short time. After the signals between the two men, the driver of the car disappeared into the snow. The crew assumed he had chosen to wait for them in the car rather than fight his way to the edge of the snow.

The crew worked as quickly as they could to free the man and his car, but it took between thirty and forty-five minutes to reach their objective. The last scoop of snow came away from the back of the car to reveal that the engine was running. A feeling of panic spread through the workmen. A tow-line was attached to the rear and the car was yanked out of the snow; the doors were opened to reveal that the driver was dead from carbon monoxide poisoning.

The young man was obviously unaware of the dangers of trapped exhaust fumes from an internal combustion engine. He had left the engine running to have the comfort of the car heater, and it had cost him his life.

The Birth of BC Bud

In the early sixties I was stationed at Lytton, a small town in the Fraser Canyon, and came to appreciate the geological and botanical diversity of the region. The steep, undulating canyon walls are relieved at intervals by flat benchlands that jut out like giant steps. Apparently these were deposited when the water level in the canyon was much higher, then left high and dry when it subsided. Some of these benches appear in midsummer to be desert-like, but others display vegetation of surprising richness and variety. This lush growth is the result of two factors. One is, the surface soil is fed by a constant underground water source because the relatively recent erosion of the canyon wall cut across former underground streams.

The second factor is the thin clay soil itself, another of the canyon's mysteries. Wherever a source of water is provided, the combination of the canyon soil and the hot sun, which frequently gives Lytton the highest summer temperatures in Canada, will produce amazing growth from almost any vegetation. The pioneer British Columbia marijuana growers became aware of these little oases and their potential for record growing in the early 1960s. These pioneers would go to work every spring with seeds or started plants and would set them into the fertile soil with loving care. One of the benefits of this cropping method was that the pot farmer did not have to risk being arrested should he be caught at the tedious work of tending and watering. The plants were simply set out in these little self-watering gardens and left to nature. The canyon soil and the sun worked together to produce some marvelous marijuana; many of the plants grew to over ten feet in height and were over two inches in diameter at the ground.

It seemed the only plague to inhibit the crop was the local police, who would pull the plants and leave them to die in the sun. The police, however, were always busy with their day-to-day duties and seldom found time to get into any but the most accessible locations. The pot farmers continued to plant these accessible locations in the valid belief that once the police had pulled a few hundred plants, the novelty would wear off, and the bulk of the crop would be left to mature and be harvested as intended. On a rare occasion, one or two of us would borrow saddle horses and spend a day riding and pulling plants until we were saddle sore and our hands were blistered. A late summer ride through some of the more productive areas of the canyon would yield hundreds of plants.

The reputation of Fraser Canyon pot spread far and wide. The product became known for its quality and high content of the active ingredient. The local potheads spoke in hushed tones about the wonders of the canyon harvest. They had cute names for their product, most indicating the area where it was grown. They staged heated debates over the merits of "Fraser Funk" as compared to "Thompson Green" or "Stein Stun." The one point they all agreed on was that any of the local product was at least equal to or better than "West Kootenay Thunder Fuck," which was famous across the North American continent.

West Kootenay Thunder Fuck was rumoured to have been developed by a group of American draft dodgers who had gathered in the Slocan River valley to wait out the war in Vietnam. Among these people was a very knowledgeable botanist who guided the others in plant husbandry and led to the beginnings of the present day high-potency marijuana plants. The modern-day marijuana grow operations all use plants that are the results of early research done in the West Kootenay. Today, "BC Bud" is held in high regard by marijuana connoisseurs around the world.

All this came about because some enterprising pothead set out a few plants in the fertile soil and hot sun of British Columbia and learned that it could thrive. I do not know where the first plant was set in the soil of British Columbia, but I would make a small bet that it was in the Fraser Canyon within sight of the Trans-Canada Highway.

The Highwaymen
of Hixon

The small isolated communities in the interior of British Columbia have their share of colourful characters. Hixon, a settlement in the Woodpecker area south of Prince George, was particularly blessed in this regard.

This story begins on a clear and warm fall evening. Walter and Wilbur, two Hixon residents, had begun their party at several of the bars in Prince George in the early part of the afternoon. Eventually they decided to pick up a large quantity of beer and move the party to one of their homes in Hixon. Though this decision was made about suppertime they did not find time to have their evening meal, choosing rather to take their nourishment in liquid form.

By nine o'clock they were well into their cache of beer; rational thoughts and actions were becoming increasingly difficult. Fate could have done them both a favour if it had allowed them to pass out from the excess of alcohol. Unfortunately, this did not happen.

The two drinking companions were known for their inability to stop once they embarked on a binge. They were also known to do some really bizarre stunts while under the influence.

Walter and Wilbur had reached what is known as the excitement stage in their drinking binge. I have seen this condition in many alcohol abusers over the years. A drinker will suddenly change in appearance and actions: his face may become pale and his eyes go blank. While he may have been staggering and falling just before, he will suddenly regain most of his coordination. His emotions may run wild. One minute he will cry and the next he will be in fits of laughter. If anything is certain about a person in this state, it is that they are totally unpredictable and dangerous to themselves and everyone around them.

Walter and Wilbur must have reached the excitement stage about the time they left the house and got into their old pickup truck. The truck was in very poor condition. One headlight was the only light on the whole vehicle, the muffler was missing, and one door was held shut by wire. Like almost every pickup truck in the region at that time, it had a rifle hanging on a rack in the rear window of the cab. The rifle in this case was a .308 Winchester.

The two found themselves on the main highway, where they watched a few cars pass by. One of them suggested that they should rob a few of these people. The other immediately grabbed the loaded rifle and walked out onto the highway. Their truck on the highway slowed the traffic and they were able to stop the first car by waving as though they needed assistance. The couple in the first car found themselves looking down the barrel of the rifle at two men demanding money. The driver of the car immediately gave them twenty-five dollars and said that was all he had. The new highwaymen thanked the couple most graciously and allowed them to go on their way.

Over the next short time, four more vehicles were stopped and the process was repeated. Three of the victims gave a few dollars to the highwaymen, who thanked them and sent them on their way. The fifth vehicle was driven by a man who did not appreciate the gravity of the situation. He told the two drunks to get out of his way and he drove off. As he drove away he could hear the two cursing and shouting at him, but no shots were fired.

The highway robbers chose to stop only the vehicles travelling south from their location. About a mile south from the robbery site was a telephone booth in a well-lit spot at the side of the highway. The phone booth now had a lineup of customers who wished to speak to the police. The first victim had made contact with the police dispatcher in Prince George and was telling his story when the second arrived; before the first caller was off the phone all five were together at the phone booth.

The highwaymen may have been startled by the man who told them to get out of his way and drove off, or by any number of other events, but they got back into the old truck and drove north toward Prince George. It seems they felt that some additional threat was necessary for them to be more convincing to their next victim.

The two pulled off the highway into a rest area a short distance north of Hixon. Here they found only one vehicle: a large motorhome with Alaskan licence plates. American tourists frequently carried a rifle or a shotgun and could do so legally; vehicles from Alaska all carried firearms. The Hixon Highwaymen were not aware of this fact, or perhaps they just didn't care at that moment.

The old truck made a hell of a ruckus as it lurched off the

highway and slid to a stop on a grass strip across from the big motorhome. The couple in the motorhome was awakened by the commotion. As the man in the motorhome swung his feet over the edge of the high bunk in the front of the unit, he grabbed his short-barreled twelve gauge shotgun and peered out the small window near the bunk.

The moon provided enough light for the man to see the truck and the two men now moving toward his motorhome. He could see that one of them was carrying a rifle and pointing it in a menacing way. The two highwaymen were yelling for the people in the motorhome to come out and give them all their money. When the two were within a few feet of the motorhome, the man saw the flame from the rifle muzzle and heard the blast of the shot; he also heard a bullet rip through the door and out the opposite wall of his vehicle. The shooter now worked the action to re-load as he stood right in front of the door, still yelling for the people to come out and give him their money. He was less than ten feet from the muzzle of the twelve gauge shotgun.

The blast of the shotgun cut through the small window and a charge of buckshot struck the rifleman in the upper area of his body; he was slammed to the ground by the impact, but he was likely dead before he got there.

The former partner of the dead man was now having serious doubts about their new endeavour. Drunk or whatever, he now had an overwhelming desire to be somewhere else. Without thought of his dead friend, he ran to the truck and raced away as fast as he could make it go. The noise of the old truck was horrendous, but it sounded good to the couple in the motorhome.

The Alaskan couple immediately called for assistance on their citizen's band radio. They were able to contact a vehicle near Prince George, and the information reached the police very quickly. The police units who were responding to the armed robbery calls were now redirected to the homicide at the rest area and additional investigators were called from their homes.

The first police unit to the scene was driven by a constable who had worked the Prince George area for several years. He recognized the dead man and knew immediately who the other would be. Before daylight the surviving highwayman was in police custody and was relating the story as best he could in his drunken condition.

The couple from Alaska were interviewed and detailed statements were recorded; they were released by noon the next day.

Blood tests on the dead man and his partner showed alcohol levels that would surely be fatal to any but the most conditioned of drinkers. The survivor was charged with several counts of armed robbery and was sentenced to three years in prison.

Little Home in the Woods

During my police experience, I found that the smaller and more isolated a community was, the more colourful were the local characters. This little community deep in the British Columbia interior was no exception.

The resident RCMP members in these remote places always introduced a visiting policeman to the local colour. On one of my visits to this community, which was policed by one corporal and one constable, I was introduced to Ralph and his mother. Both Ralph and his mother seemed quite personable and they visited with me politely for a few minutes at the time of our initial introduction. The mother appeared to be in possession of all her faculties, but not so for Ralph; during a conversation he would perform odd gestures and contort his body, and he seemed unable to control the level of his voice. At times one would have to listen very closely to Ralph while at the next moment he could be heard all over the village.

During subsequent visits to the community over a few years, I spoke to Ralph on many occasions and to his mother on a few. Ralph nearly always had a few flattened cardboard boxes with him, and sometimes he would have more than he could carry. He was known to stash boxes in various places around town, but he eventually came back and collected them and was often seen carrying boxes along the road toward home. Ralph was often a little evasive when asked why he collected the cardboard.

Mother was generally nearby when I met Ralph but she usually stood back and let Ralph be the extrovert. An encounter with Ralph was always a puzzle; his disjointed conversations covered a range of topics. It seemed that a few words of agreement or questions were what he wanted to hear and he always left with a big sparsely toothed smile. I estimated Ralph to be past forty and Mother to be on the downhill side of sixty.

All the people of the community knew Ralph and his mom. One of the storekeepers told me that they had been around as long as he could remember, and he had lived there for over twenty years. The storekeeper knew that they lived somewhere between the road and the lake about three miles north of town. They came into the village about once every week but they would be there without fail on the day that the social assistance cheques were distributed every second week. Their routine was known to everyone: they would pick up their cheque, cash it, buy some basic groceries and begin the walk to the north. They divided the weight of their groceries between them as they walked along the little-used road. Most of the local citizens would give them a ride if they saw them on the road; they always gladly accepted a ride and would ask to be let out of the car at a place where there was only a footpath intersecting the roadway. No locals that I met had ever been to the actual home of Ralph and his mom.

Their clothing all came from the local secondhand store or

from other citizens who wanted to assist them. Ralph and his mom were not fashion statements but they always seemed to have clothing and footwear suitable to the weather and the season. Many of the local citizens felt sorry for these two but I did not get the impression that Ralph and his mom felt sorry for themselves. They appeared to have found a degree of acceptance in the little community and they had accepted their meagre way of life.

On one of my visits to the village I learned that Ralph had come to town that morning alone. It was the first time that anyone could recall him showing up without his mother. Ralph was an emotional wreck, sobbing loudly but unable to tell anyone what was wrong. He finally confided to the village RCMP corporal that his mother was sick and lying on the ground.

We called an ambulance and told them the general location of the patient. The ambulance people were told to watch for a police car on the side of the road and to come down the footpath near the police car. We took Ralph with us and drove north of the village until he told us to stop. The ambulance arrived within a few minutes and we followed Ralph down a steep and muddy path into the bush below the roadway. The ambulance attendants had a struggle with their stretcher and were mud from head to foot in a very short time. The three of us in police uniform were no better off; each of us had lost our footing on at least one occasion. Ralph's stress level grew worse with each step of the operation. It seemed he knew that no one was ever to be brought to their home but he also knew that he and his mom were in desperate need of help.

We slipped and slid down the winding path for about a quarter of a mile until we came to a little bench on the hillside. The bench had been partly cleared of trees and there was a small garden plot beside a large pile of garbage. At one side of the clearing was a structure made of small logs, tree limbs, assorted boards, plywood, metal roofing, canvas and lots of cardboard. The structure more closely resembled a beaver lodge than a wood-frame building. Facing the cleared area was a hole under the edge of the structure. It was about two feet wide and nearly four feet high. The opening was mostly covered with a piece of very dirty canvas.

Ralph, now sobbing uncontrollably, pointed to the opening and indicated that we should go in there. One by one we duck-walked through the low opening and were met with the thick odour of urine and fecal matter. Once through the opening we came into an area about twelve feet in diameter, the ceiling/roof of which was from four to six feet from the dirt floor. Two other openings similar to the one through which we had entered indicated that there were further chambers beyond this one. A wood-burning kitchen stove was near one wall of the main chamber and a bare stovepipe went up from the stove through a piece of sheet metal in the material of the ceiling/roof.

Ralph's mom lay semi-conscious on the dirt floor near the middle of the room, victim of a massive stroke. It appeared she had been there for more than a week. We tried to find out from Ralph when this had happened but he had no concept of time. Ralph had been providing food as best he could but he had no understanding of the additional care she desperately needed. Her situation was truly awful. We carried her outside using a blanket as a body sling because the stretcher would not go through the opening into the structure. She seemed to be aware of our presence but she was unable to speak or move her body.

The muddy trail up to the road was a challenge but we managed to reach the road without losing our patient off the stretcher. Ralph was very reluctant to leave with the ambulance as we suggested he should. At times it appeared he was about to bolt into the bush back to his home. The local police corporal was finally able to convince Ralph that he should stay with his mother and go with her in the ambulance. Because of Ralph's obvious anxiety, the corporal led him to believe that we would all be coming to town right behind the ambulance. With that information, Ralph got into the ambulance willingly.

We were soon to find out why Ralph was so torn about leaving us there. We returned to the residence to search for any medical information or medications that the woman may have been using. After a long look around the outside of the hovel, we duck-walked in again with our flashlights providing the only light. Once inside the main chamber we were more than a little startled to hear some animal-like noises coming from one of the back chambers, accompanied by a metallic squeaking and clicking sound. We moved to the opening where the sound originated and our flashlights lit up a very strange vision: Ralph's brother.

Harold was on his hands and knees, hopping up and down on a rusted bedspring on the dirt floor. The spring was partially covered with the remains of a mattress and an assortment of dirty rags and clothing. Harold was obviously terrified by our presence. He cowered against the rough wall, his face contorted and his open mouth displaying several long brown teeth. His eyes were very wide and had the look of a wild animal caught in a leghold trap. Harold appeared about the same age as Ralph; they may have been twins, but we were never able to learn their history.

The sudden appearance of Harold presented another aspect to an already complicated situation. We wished that Ralph were there to comfort this man. We tried to talk to him but received no indication that he heard or understood. We tried to assure him that we were leaving and that his brother would be back later. We quickly made our way outside.

We were standing near the structure discussing what we had just seen when Harold hit the canvas flap from the inside and came out in full flight. The low doorway was no problem for Harold because he did most of his travelling on all fours. He came past us in a deep crouch at an amazing speed; he used the front of a closed fist to aid his propulsion and balance and in a brief moment he was out of sight in the forest. Harold wore bib overalls with only one shoulder strap fastened. The legs of his overalls were cut or torn open below both knees. He had a lumberjack shirt or jacket on his upper body, and this too was cut or torn up both sleeves past the elbow on both arms. The flapping loose material added significantly to the vision of Harold heading for the bush.

On our return to the village, we learned that Mom was in critical condition and had been taken to better-equipped medical facilities about two hours away. The local doctor was not optimistic about her chances of survival.

Ralph had been placed with a local family by the social services worker. He was struggling with the loss of his mother and with not knowing what had become of Harold. He was easily distracted from his grief, but as soon as his mind was not occupied with conversation or food he would revert to pacing and fretting about his family.

Everyone we talked to was amazed to hear of Harold. No one in the community had any idea that he existed. Even the social assistance people were unaware of Harold. Had they been told about him by Ralph or his mother it would have resulted in some additional funds for the three to survive on.

During the evening of the day we discovered Harold, the local police corporal returned to the residence with Ralph. Between the corporal and Ralph, they managed to talk Harold into the police car and bring him to the village. The two brothers then stayed with the family where Ralph had been placed earlier that day.

Ralph and Harold's mother died within a few days of this

incident. She remained semi-conscious until her death and was unable to provide any information about her family history. The social assistance people were able to find a facility in another part of the province where Ralph and Harold have most likely spent the rest of their lives.

Matters of
Life and Death

I grew up on an Alberta farm that was only a few miles from a large Native reserve. My early experience with the Native people was limited to occasional contact when we visited the local post office and the grocery store or when some of them came to our farm to work at land clearing or to help with harvest work. The Natives would come to our farm and set up a tent camp while they worked. The Native camps were most often made up of a complete family and everyone took part in the assigned tasks.

The store and post office facilities were together at the edge of the reserve and on the main line of the Canadian National Railway. My father knew many of the local Natives, having hired them over the years as he had cleared and broken the land of our home farm. Dad always enjoyed a visit with any of the Natives he encountered during our occasional excursions to the store and post office.

My family and most of our community were hard-working individuals who were driven to improve our lot in life by working to make the land more productive. We felt pity for the Native people, but we were unable to understand their laid-back, apparently apathetic attitude. Their conduct became the subject of many jokes and stories among us.

During my high school years I lived with my grandmother in the little community with the post office and store by the reserve. This change of residence was necessary for me to have access to a school bus and a twenty-five mile ride each way to a high school. I got to see a great deal more of the local Native people during those three years and I grew more perplexed about their way of life.

I was unable to see any outward difference between myself and the young Natives, and yet our approach to life couldn't have been less similar. My friends and I sought job opportunities despite a complete lack of experience but were hired and in most instances were contributing after a minimal training period. We worked hard and enjoyed the job satisfaction and income. With very few exceptions the young Natives made no effort to find gainful or meaningful employment, but just stayed on the reserve and existed from one day to the next. My friends and I couldn't wait to get out and seize life in our hands. Our Native counterparts seemed more inclined to lay down and die.

This background left me with a feeling of futility and frustration when I came into contact with the Natives of the British Columbia interior.

My first posting in British Columbia was to one of the few areas where there are very few if any Native people. I listened with interest to the stories told by the other guys who had worked in communities where the majority of the population was Native. I felt a little shortchanged. There would certainly have been a great deal more action at some of the locations described by my friends. In later years I had fond memories of the quiet and peaceful times at my first posting. We never miss the water until the well goes dry.

My next transfer in the Mounted Police took me to a town where a large part of the population was Native. I now found myself in direct contact with these people on a daily basis and the experience was not a positive one. With very few exceptions, they followed the same tragic course as those from my home district.

My new detachment commander, a tough old sergeant, took me aside on my first day at his unit. He welcomed me, and explained a few of the expectations of my job there. The main point of his orientation talk was about the unique nature of policing in a Native environment. The hard exterior of the old sergeant had a few small openings that revealed a soft and caring interior. He too had difficulty in understanding the conduct of most of the Native people but he had respect for them and for their right to live their life as they saw fit. I often saw him visiting with a variety of Native people whom he encountered on the streets of town. I thought of my father and how he enjoyed visiting with the local Natives.

Later, as my first summer at the new detachment wore on into fall and early winter I often heard the old sergeant lecturing on a variety of matters. One of the topics that stood out in my mind was his emphasis on the arrest of drunks during winter weather. He emphasized his lectures on this topic by saying, "It is a hell of a lot easier to arrest a drunk than to deal with a frozen corpse in the morning." I carried that lesson with me through the years of my service and when I became the supervisor of various groups of police, I often repeated his lecture. "When the weather is cold, throw them in the slammer at the first indication of intoxication." I liked to think that appearing tough had less to do with it than the simple fact that it is easier to book a drunk than to deal with a frozen corpse.

The press would be unlikely to be interested in a story about hundreds of intoxicated people being dragged, pushed or carried into police custody across the vast interior of British Columbia on an evening when the temperature had suddenly dropped to ten degrees below zero. The news stories the next day would be about other topics, unless the police had missed an intoxicated person somewhere and a frozen corpse was found in the first rays of daylight. This would make the news. One of the first questions raised by the news reporters would be rightfully directed to the police: "How could you have overlooked this person's desperate situation?" Answering such questions was difficult; we had tried to look after everyone, but we had failed. Transfers took me to several locations in my career, some where the Native population was the majority, while in others it was almost non-existent. We did not need a detailed statistical analysis to know that the number of arrests for Drunkenness in a Public Place was in direct proportion to the Native population in any community. Much is said and written about the police picking on the Natives and grabbing them at the first sign of intoxication; to this I say, "bullshit." In the winter we did this out of necessity. At other times we gladly let them move along unless they were about to come into conflict with traffic or other dangers.

At one Cariboo town, I met a Native man who had lived there all his life. Henry had worked and raised a family there and had enjoyed the respect of both the Native and non-Native communities. However, the years had taken their toll on him, his wife had died, and he had become a permanent fixture on the streets of the town. Henry was most often drunk and in that condition he became a nuisance. He would say very insulting things to women and children as they passed by. His bad behaviour was tolerated by most of the townspeople because of his past reputation. However, he was the subject of frequent complaints to the police and he often became a guest of the Queen in our establishment.

He was unable to make full use of a bank because he did not understand their hours and would not deal with the administrative requirements to open an account. When the welfare cheque was issued he would cash it at a bank and then he would seek out his trusted friend who operated a service station. He would give this man a wad of cash and then he would draw from it on a daily basis until it was gone. There was no record-keeping or counting of the money; the service station guy put it in a hiding place in the office and he was the only one who dealt with Henry.

The man at the service station was a great asset to Henry: the money was doled out sparingly to try and make it last until the next cheque was due. We all knew that Henry often got a few dollars out of the friend's pocket when he ran a little short. When Henry showed up drunk and wanted money his friend would not give him any and at times had to call us to take his angry friend to jail. Henry's first stop after getting out of our accommodations would be at the service station to apologize to his friend.

It was just before Christmas in a colder than average winter when the man from the service station called us to say that he had not seen Henry for several days. We canvassed all our members and none could recall seeing him for a while. He had not been in our cells for a considerable time. We made inquiries with all in the community who dealt with Henry, but no one had seen him. There was about three feet of snow on the ground so our search efforts were limited to the roads and a few trails around the town. Nothing came to light about Henry's whereabouts.

At the end of the school break, some elementary school

students were breaking their shortcut trail to school through the snow that had fallen over the holiday. The trail took them across an open field. As they tramped over the white blanket of snow they came to an area that had been heavily trampled by dogs. The centre of the dog-trampled area was where Henry had fallen in the snow and died. His frozen corpse had been badly chewed by dogs.

Our subsequent investigation found a very high blood-alcohol level in Henry's body. We were never able to determine how he happened to be in that location, which was not one that he had frequented to our knowledge.

A few days later I directed traffic as a long funeral procession took Henry to his grave at the edge of town.

Another posting took me to a village where the Native population was by far the majority. Here a good number of the Native residents had responsible positions in the community while many others chose to remain in the non-participation group. A Native man had been appointed a lay magistrate, and he was an asset to us and the community as a whole. If we had a prisoner to be taken before a magistrate, we could always count on this man to attend. When called, he would go to his home, get out of his work clothes and attend at our office in a suit and tie. His court decisions were always well thought out and carefully explained to the accused.

In spite of such efforts by some of the Native people, during my three years at this location I saw more violent and unnecessary deaths than during the entire remainder of my service.

One such incident occurred as Christmas was again upon us. The north wind began and the temperature dropped to the twenty-below range. On Christmas Eve, the local hotel beer parlor was full to capacity as the Native community celebrated the event. The weather had been the topic of discussion at our detachment and the word was out to throw the drunks in at the first sign of intoxication. When closing time came at about midnight, we were somewhat overwhelmed. The local taxi company had both their cars out to take the celebrants home, gratis for the holiday. This was a great help to us because at least eighty percent of the patrons were staggering when they left the bar. The police cars also made many trips to the residences on the reserve to get the partiers home safely. However, many Natives could not get a ride home because there was no vehicle access to their neighbourhood.

The town lay on one side of the river and a large part of the Native community was on the other side. The Canadian National Railway tracks crossed the river just below the town and a footbridge had been attached to the side of the rail bridge. The only other access to this part of the community was by a river ferry about two miles up from town. The river was now full of ice chunks and the ferry had been pulled out to prevent the ice from destroying it.

The day after Boxing Day, some Natives from across the river came to our office to report that a family member, a twenty-year-old man, had not been seen since the Christmas Eve party at the local bar. They had been in contact with everyone who they thought may have had knowledge of his whereabouts, but to no avail.

Several of the people who had partied in the bar on Christmas Eve were interviewed. Their recollection of the evening was quite clouded by alcohol but most recalled the young man being among them during the night. Some partiers recalled the young man having two thirteen ounce bottles of whiskey hidden on his person and that he was spiking his beer from these bottles. Most of the Native people were aware of the extreme danger of this practice. When they heard that the young man had been doing this, they were quite sure that he had come to a tragic end.

We searched the snow-covered ground and streets between the beer parlour and the railway bridge without any trace of the missing man. We crossed the river on the footbridge and started up the steep trail to the Native community about half a mile upstream. Near the crest of the trail we could see some faint marks on the wind-hardened snow below the trail. The marks were semi-circular scratches on the snow surface, as though someone had fallen and was sliding down toward the river. We made our way down the snow-covered bank to the first small crest where we were able to see a body curled around the base of a pine tree. The body was frozen solid and caught tightly to the tree.

We called the coroner and received his permission to remove the body to the local morgue. The problem at that moment was that we could not get the body to come free of the tree, which was ten inches in diameter and forty or fifty feet tall. We sent a runner back to town to get a chain saw and on his return the tree was felled and the body was then lifted off the stump. The unusual configuration of this body presented a problem in fitting it to the stretcher, but we were eventually able to carefully convey the remains back across the river on the footbridge to a vehicle that took it the remaining distance to the morgue.

Tragedies of this kind were not exclusive to the Native people, but the majority did involve them. Their attitude and conduct increased the odds very much in favour of such happenings. This behaviour no doubt has its roots in a complex and tragic history that still works inside them where nobody can see it but themselves, and perhaps in the final analysis nobody can really do anything about it but themselves.

Cultural Differences

The call was received around one in the morning on a mid-summer Friday night. The town was still very much awake and we were busy with all the usual problems brought on by week-end celebrations. We all had a backlog of paperwork that we hoped to get to once the town had quieted down. That was not to happen on this night. The call came from a lady at a remote ranch who was relaying a horrible story told to her by a terrified ten-year-old Native girl.

The little girl had run two miles across the open grasslands from her reserve community to the nearest ranch where a telephone was available. The only telephone at the reserve, installed as a goodwill gesture by the telephone company but regularly damaged beyond use, had been smashed by vandals.

The little girl told the lady that her two brothers, four and six years old, were playing with matches and she could not get them to stop. She had gone to try and get someone to help but she could not find anyone sober enough to care. When she looked back toward her home, it was on fire. She ran back to the house but could not get inside because it was full of fire; she could not find her little brothers by the house and she believed they were still inside.

The lady who had called us from the ranch told us that she could see a glow on the sky in the direction of the reserve.

The reserve was about thirty-five miles from town on a winding dirt and gravel road. If we had left immediately and driven the road as fast as possible it would have been almost an hour until we arrived there. There was little or no point in rushing to this matter, however, without having some firefighting equipment with us.

The reserve had only very basic firefighting equipment, consisting of buckets and barrels to bring water from a nearby creek. The already minimal potential of this equipment was lessened by the situation on the reserve that night.

The late spring and early summer had been extremely dry. Forest fires were spreading in several locations in our Forest Service district. The Forest Service people had been hiring anyone they could get to fight fire, and in many cases they used their authority to force any available people onto the fire lines. All of the able-bodied men from that reserve had been on the fire lines for about two weeks. That day, they had been paid and temporarily relieved from the fire lines. We knew that the influx of cash from the fires would result in a huge drinking binge.

After several attempts, we were able to find two men from the local Forest Service; they were near exhaustion from too many twelve and sixteen-hour days fighting fires. We explained our situation and asked if they had any portable firefighting equipment available. They found two trailer units that appeared to have been repaired and were ready to go back to the fire lines at their equipment facility. The equipment consisted of a water tank mounted on a trailer, at the rear of which was a small gasoline engine driving a high-pressure pump. Hose lines could be run from the unit to reach into places a short distance from the trailer. The little trailer units had stopped many small fires, but they were very limited by their small water capacity.

Thirty minutes later the two exhausted Forest Rangers were at our office ready to help. They had hooked the trailers to their four-wheel drive trucks, filled them with water and checked the pumps to ensure they were in working order.

The police car left for the reserve, followed by the two Forest Service trucks and trailers. We travelled as fast as the road conditions allowed, knowing that there was little if any chance of changing what had happened ahead of us. My partner was more experienced than I, and as I drove he recalled other incidents where he had attended house fires and recovered human remains. He had some experiences where there was nothing recovered, but all evidence indicated that there had been someone in the house. As usual, in such circumstances, some black humour was exchanged as we drove along. My partner complained about the smell from his neighbour's barbecue and how he often wondered what was cooking over there. The gross humour was a way of raising our awareness of what was to come without actually talking about the anticipated sights and sounds; the smell and feel of burned flesh, and the agony of the surviving family. We had not talked about it or even given it much thought, but the game plan was to see if either of us could make the other puke before we got to our destination.

The reserve village was laid out like nearly every other one in the central interior of British Columbia. There was a short roadway through the middle of the village with a row of houses on each side. In the centre, at the end of this little street, stood the Mission Church.

When we reached the reserve, we could see the glow of fire on the right side of the roadway near the church. My partner observed that the fire was nearly burned out and he speculated that there may not be anything left of the small bodies. He added a comment about how thin all the Native children were. We both felt that if there was nothing left our job would be much easier, but we would have to do a very close examination to be sure. I suggested that it would not be good public relations to have the reserve dogs running around fighting over some remains that we had missed.

The first house on the right side was the location of a loud and lusty drinking party. As we passed by, the few participants who noticed our presence screamed obscenities and then went back to their drinking. The reaction of these people was new to both of us. We knew they would be drinking. The verbal abuse was normal. But we were not prepared to find the party still in full swing considering what had happened only a few hundred feet away. Anger replaced our earlier fear and reluctance; we were now about ready to deal with whatever lay ahead. My partner commented that the two dead children may be fortunate to not have to grow up in the environment we had just observed.

We parked the police car where we would be able to see it as we examined the fire scene. Unguarded police cars on a reserve would be vandalized immediately.

We could see no indication that anyone had tried to fight the fire or remove any possessions from the stricken house. There was, however, a very old Native woman walking slowly around the burning building; she circled just close enough that the glow from the remaining fire made her partially visible. As she walked, she wailed an eerie high-pitched and mournful song. Tears streamed down her weathered face as she walked and wailed. I approached the old woman to try and find out if she knew where the home occupants were and if she was sure someone had died in the fire. She continued to wail and walk, so I walked with her for a couple turns around the fire; she refused to be interrupted, acting as though I wasn't there. It soon became obvious that I was wasting my time, unless I could or would sing with her. I later learned from a Native friend that this was the Death Wail; a tribal ritual that was intended to guide and soothe the spirits of the dead.

Shortly after we arrived at the reserve, a Native man approached to offer his assistance. He was obviously intoxicated, but he wanted to do something. The man appeared to be ashamed of his condition and that of the group at the party. He shrugged his shoulders and said that once the drinking got going, the only thing that would stop it was when the liquor ran out. We cautioned him to stay back from the fire and asked him to help get the water line to the creek; he did his best to help in spite of his condition. The old woman and the drunken man were the only adults from the whole community who seemed to be aware of the tragedy.

The fire had nearly finished its work on the little house; nothing remained standing except the concrete block chimney and a low concrete foundation. Inside the foundation was a layer of glowing ash and embers. The floor plan of the house could be identified from metal remnants of a cook stove, a wood-burning space heater, and bed frames with springs and wire strung over them.

One of the bed frames stood in a corner of the foundation; the steel angle-iron side rails had sagged almost to the ground from the heat of the fire and from the burning building falling on it. The fire had died down enough by this time to allow us a close look into the ashes. The remaining heat, however, quickly forced us away. We bent down to avoid the heat that radiated over the low foundation and searched for any clues to the location of a body.

We forced ourselves back to the searing heat again and again because the Forest Service men were preparing their water lines and we knew that the ashes and embers would be rapidly transformed once the water hit them. On one of these glimpses, as the wailing old woman passed by behind me, I saw what appeared to be burned rib bones protruding above the hot ashes under a bed frame. Closer examination substantiated this, and the appearance of a parallel row from the other side of a small chest confirmed it. I called my partner and pointed out what I had found; we took several deep breaths away from the direct heat before we concentrated our observations on that area and saw another set of slightly smaller rib bones under the same bed frame, but I tried not to dwell on the size and similarities between these little bodies and our own children. All unnecessary emotions had to be pushed aside and concealed, partially through the use of ugly humour and gross remarks. From our experience with our own children we surmised that the little guys had been playing with matches and their sister had been trying to put a stop to it; when the fire started they knew they were in trouble so they hid under the bed.

We had to cool the area and attempt to recover enough of the bodies to confirm the deaths and possibly to identify the victims. The Forest Service men had now laid a water line to the nearby creek, so we then had more than enough water to do what had to be done. The water pumps were started and a fine mist was allowed to fall over the corner where the bodies had been seen. The burned bones disappeared into the ashes as soon as the water touched them. The only sober Native adult in the community continued to circle the fire scene, singing the Death Wail.

During all this, a few hundred feet away, the party raged on, a radio played at maximum volume, voices could be heard screaming and laughing, each trying to be louder than the one nearest them. The party house was, like most of the reserve homes, a single floor with four or five small rooms. The window openings had no glass but it was quite likely that the glass had been gone before the current party began. A large part of the party was happening around the outside of the house. Many of the participants were lying where they had fallen in a drunken stupor. Some had become amorous from their excessive drinking and several bare asses were visible near the house.

Water was sprayed over the fire until the area was cool enough to allow us to walk in and move the bed frame from over the remains. Two small clumps of charred flesh were all that remained; bones that appeared to be parts of the femurs and spine were protruding from both. We wrapped the remains in emergency blankets and placed them in the trunk of the police car to be taken to the morgue.

Early summer daylight arrived before we were finished at the fire. With the first streaks of light came a gathering of Native children. We watched as their numbers grew. The children were coming out of the collection of derelict vehicles around the reserve. I asked some of them if they always slept there. They replied that it was better to sleep in the old cars when there was a drinking party.

The sun was rising as we finished our grim task. The fire equipment had been gathered and stowed for the return to town. The parents of the dead children were nowhere to be found, nor was the little girl who had been trying to look after them. Interviews and interrogations of these people would be best done at a later date.

The old woman was still walking and wailing as we got into the car to leave. I don't know how long she continued to do that. As we drove past the party house on our way out of the reserve, a young man staggered out into our path. He waved his uncoordinated arms for us to stop. I stopped and he approached my window to complain that someone at the party had stolen his last bottle of wine; he wanted mc to find it immediately and give it back to him. I suggested to him that obviously someone else needed the wine more than he did and that he should immediately get away from my car or something bad would happen to him. It must have been the expression on my face as I talked to him, because he did move away immediately in spite of his alcohol-induced stupor.

Modern police training now includes much emphasis on the understanding of Native and other cultures. In my time we learned about such things in the field; seeing and experiencing situations like this left us shaking our heads and wondering why. Culture was not a frequently used word. Our understanding of culture and the loss of it did not include an excuse or justification for what we had just experienced. There were no answers then and I doubt very much if we are any closer to an answer today.

The Shit House Shoot-up

Billy-Jack was well known to all of us at the detachment. He grew up in an isolated non-Native community an hour from anywhere, a place where everybody in town seemed to be related, some more closely than is recommended. If they had been located in the American south a lot of these people, including Billy's, would probably have been called "po' whites." We all knew that Billy had been dealt a hand with which he couldn't hope to win, but that didn't make it any easier to tolerate the verbal and occasional physical abuse that he used whenever he came into contact with the police. He had been trained to be completely anti-social and to be a dedicated police-hater. His elders provided this training—one of them no doubt his father, although none admitted to that possibility. On occasions when we were confronted by a drunken Billy-Jack at country boozing parties, these elders would gather around to egg him on and to add to the threatening atmosphere. The great pride they felt in their prodigy was evident in their faces.

Some or all of these elders were no doubt involved in teaching young Billy-Jack to drive and by the time he was fourteen complaints of him terrorizing the neighbours with his driving were a matter of routine. The elders would point out the damaged vehicles scattered around their shacks and brag about how "that boy" had crashed or rolled them. It seemed they were most impressed by him crashing end over end, and by his having learned the important point, much stressed by his trainers, that you hit the ground running and don't stop until you are sure the police are not around.

Billy-Jack had had his driver's licence for only a few months when the vehicle he was using at the time was found in a gravel pit a few miles from his home. Billy-Jack had reported the car stolen only minutes before someone who was walking by the gravel pit found it. Billy-Jack was nervous and agitated when interviewed about the car theft but stood firmly by his story that he had walked into the bush to relieve himself and someone had stolen the car.

The vehicle had been rolled several times. Tire marks in the area showed that the car had been going fast and was in a tight turn under full power when it started to roll. Under the car was the body of a fourteen-year-old girl, who had, like Billy-Jack, lived a few miles from the death scene. She had suffocated from being pinned between the car and the earth; had someone been available to assist her, she may very well have survived with minor bruises.

The girl had told her parents she was going to walk to the store about a mile up the highway from her home. She knew Billy-Jack from school but her parents had forbidden her from having anything to do with him. The dead girl was not a driver and had no interest in driving; her father had attempted to teach her to use a small farm tractor but she had been afraid of it.

Billy-Jack was a juvenile in the eyes of the law; therefore any interviews had to be done in the presence of his parent or guardian. His mother and any other guardians from his home environment were expert at repeating one of Billy-Jack's primary lessons: "Never say nothing to the cops; it ain't none of their business." We suspected Billy-Jack had picked the girl up, rolled the car and left her to die, but we had no hard evidence and the case was never solved.

Billy-Jack appeared in Family Court on traffic offences unrelated to the fatal crash and finally lost his driver's licence. Nevertheless, he continued to drive and was scheduled for more Family Court appearances as time went on. Nothing the court or anyone else did seemed to matter to him. Had the court known the full story of his home life, I believe they would have sentenced him to some form of detention. No penal institutional environment could have been a worse influence than his everyday home life.

The routine continued over the following year, with Billy-Jack continuing to drive an assortment of vehicles and the neighbours continuing to complain. Fear kept all the neighbours from going so far as to provide positive identification of the driver. Billy-Jack became more bold and aggressive each time we attended to interview him. He knew that until he was caught in the act by one of us, nothing would happen, and that even then he would enjoy the attention and the protection of the law. The others of his family were totally indifferent; they knew all of us by name and would insist that we stay for tea or coffee whenever we arrived to deal with the ongoing antics of Billy-Jack. They engaged in any conversation that did not deal with Billy-Jack and his behaviour.

One day I lost the contest at the detachment (the short straw or the last one back from coffee) and had to look into the current Billy-Jack event. I cannot recall the nature of the file but the usual coffee invitation was made and it seemed almost un-avoidable. Inside the residence I was immediately shown the new bathroom. A small corner of the living room had been walled off to become the place for the indoor plumbing. The bathroom had a toilet, a bathtub, and a sink. The sink was attached to the uncovered two-by-four wall studs in a position that prevented the door from opening fully. The pride at this new addition was evident in the faces of the elders. I had seen that look before. The new addition had at last made the outhouse obsolete.

Over the following months, Billy-Jack continued to refine his anti-social skills. He branched out into new activities: the immediate vicinity of his home was plagued with residential break and enter offences, as were business locations in the same area. Billy-Jack had reached the age where he lost his juvenile status in the courts, so it was now only a matter of time before he would get his first jail sentence. Billy-Jack, however, was confident that he was too quick and too smart to be caught by the slow-witted police. Fate has a way of fuddling the very best of criminal plans and Billy-Jack seldom worked from a plan. He needed some time behind bars to learn that and a lot of other things he had not thought of up to that time.

That summer two young cousins and their mother had come for a visit from the far end of the interior. The two boys were fourteen and seventeen years old and I am sure they learned a lot of things from Billy-Jack, who was close to nineteen by that time. On a late summer Sunday several other groups of relatives had driven up for a family gathering. The two young cousins had been learning to shoot a twenty-two rifle during their stay in the country and they had been wanting to do some shooting throughout most of the day. Finally their persistence paid off and they were allowed to take the rifle out on the back porch with a handful of twenty-two ammunition. The routine had been to go to the edge of the settlement and shoot at cans or bottles, but this time they decided to shoot at a knothole in the plywood wall of the now unused outhouse. The outhouse stood between the house and the wide open spaces to the east, beyond the building site; the doorway faced away from the house and thereby eliminated the need for a door. This arrangement also left the user to gaze into the distance during his or her stay there. Bullets could safely pass through the unused outhouse and spend their energy in the open land beyond. The two boys fired about ten shots at a selected knothole. Most hit into the second black layer of the plywood within the circle of the knot and a few were outside the mark by an inch or less. The rifle was then put away and everyone went back to their visiting.

It was late in the afternoon when the call came that there had been some mysterious incident at the Billy-Jack residence and a person was unconscious and urgently in need of medical assistance. We left immediately to drive through the wide-open countryside to the scene. We speculated as we travelled about what Billy-Jack had done to bring about this emergency, never thinking for a moment that there may be some other cause for the call. An ambulance left town with us and we were amazed to see this cumbersome unit nearly keeping pace with us in the powerful police car of that era. On a long, straight and level stretch of highway the ambulance was about a mile behind us. I was watching its progress, still surprised to see it so nearly pacing us, when it disappeared into a cloud of smoke. We braked and turned back immediately. On arrival at the ambulance unit we found that there had been a massive failure in the engine and transmission. There was no fire, and the crew was safe and had already called for a second unit to attend with us. The paramedic from the failed ambulance jumped in with us, and we resumed our rush to the scene.

As we arrived at the area of shacks and wrecked cars we were directed to the spot behind the place with the bathroom.

Everyone was outside and there was great concern and excitement in the air. One of the elders advised us, "Billy-Jack is unconscious in the shit house." The investigation revealed that with all the visiting folks around, no one had missed Billy-Jack until the evening meal was served and eaten. During the meal, questions had begun about his whereabouts and it was finally ascertained that no one had seen or spoken to him since around mid-afternoon. Billy-Jack's car was parked in the usual spot so they all knew that he had not gone far; an unorganized search of the building site began and soon ended with the discovery in the outhouse.

Billy-Jack was slumped into the corner of the one-holer, his head tight in the corner with his chin pressed to his collar bone, a copy of Playboy Magazine near his feet. At first glance it looked as though he could have fallen asleep during his mission there. The paramedic checked Billy-Jack immediately and determined that he was breathing and had a weak pulse but was in a deep coma. We had no knowledge of the shooting earlier in the day, so his condition was a complete mystery. Someone had covered him with a sleeping bag when they decided to leave him where they found him. We decided to move him out of the outhouse and place him in the three-quarters prone position on the ground. I placed a hand behind his head for support while moving him and became aware of a small amount of blood in that area. The source of the blood was a twenty-two calibre bullet hole just behind his right ear. The follow-up ambulance arrived shortly after we had removed him from the outhouse, and we immediately loaded him for the trip to the hospital.

Billy-Jack was attended by the medical staff, who advised that he was in critical condition and that they had very little hope for his recovery. He was placed on life support systems and immediately sent by air ambulance to a Vancouver hospital.

If there was any chance at all for Billy-Jack, the facilities at Vancouver could make the most of it.

Everyone at the residence at first denied knowledge of any shots being fired during the day. A search of all the buildings in the area located more than a dozen firearms, mostly shotguns and centre-fire hunting rifles, but only one twenty-two calibre rifle. This rifle was later identified by the crime laboratory as the one that had fired the critical bullet. The evidence was overwhelming and finally resulted in an admission from Billy-Jack's mother that the two visiting boys had been shooting the twenty-two rifle from the back porch of the house.

A conference among the residents of the house resulted in the fourteen-year-old boy coming out with his mother to say that he had done the shooting and that he was the only one to have fired the rifle that day. A few questions to the mother and the boy revealed this to be a lie. The family had decided that the fourteen-year-old would have a much better chance in Juvenile Court than anyone else. They believed that at seventeen, the other boy would be charged in adult court so the decision was made to cover for him.

The final story that had all the appearances of being the truth was that the seventeen-year-old had sat on the edge of the porch with one foot on the edge and the other hanging over. He had steadied the rifle on his raised knee and thigh and fired the first shot. The bullet had passed through the thin plywood sheathing of the outhouse and struck Billy-Jack behind the ear. Billy-Jack had slumped over into the position he was in when they found him, and all the subsequent shots had passed over his body into the open land beyond.

Early the following day we learned that all tests at the Vancouver hospital showed Billy-Jack was brain-dead; his mother and some of the elders were at the hospital when the decision was made to remove the life support systems. His respiratory system and heart stopped within minutes.

The seventeen-year-old boy was charged in Juvenile Court with dangerous use of a firearm. The charges were waived to his home district, where a guilty plea was entered with the assistance of a lawyer. He was placed on probation for six months and prohibited from using firearms for one year.

Horse Kill at Frenchman's Slough

The East Kootenay region of British Columbia has long been known as a good area for hunting big game animals. The improvements to the highway system in the early sixties brought hunters from all over the province, along with great numbers from the population centre in the Lower Mainland. The hotel and motel businesses enjoyed a small boom after the normal summer tourist season had ended.

The more dedicated and hardy species of hunters would rough it in tents and small trailers, but the greatest number preferred to have access to a hot shower or bath after a day in the woods. The hunting season ran well into December in those days and hunters could expect to encounter the worst that winter in the mountains had to offer.

This incident began with a telephone call about ten a.m. on a mid-November morning. The caller reported that someone had shot two of his old packhorses. The shooting happened in a popular hunting spot known as Frenchman's Slough. Frenchman's Slough was an area on both sides of the highway a few miles east of Cranbrook. The area was a crossing spot for elk, which came from feeding areas on both sides of the highway and often moved in small herds between the feeding grounds.

Hunters would go into the Frenchman's Slough area before dawn and wait at vantage points for daylight. The elk were so numerous in those days that this hunting method was very productive; the area echoed with rifle shots every morning as the first streaks of daylight emerged. Moose and deer were often caught in the open areas of the sloughs at dawn, along with the elk. The kills were always close to the highway. This took away much of the back-breaking labour required to get a large dead animal to the butcher shop.

We made a patrol to the horse-kill site, accompanied by the irate owner. The luckless horses lay dead in about a foot of crusty snow. They were about fifty yards from the base of a small hill and had been pawing the snow away to eat grass in one of the sloughs. The tracks of the hunters could be seen coming down from the small hill to where the horses lay. The tracks indicated the hunters had approached at a walking pace until they were near enough to see what they had done. They had paused for a moment, then turned and run back to where they had come from. The one set of tracks was much larger than the other; we thought it might have been a father and son outing which had gone terribly wrong.

The tracks in the snow led us to the top of the hill, where we found two tramped areas in the snow. This was the spot where the hunters had waited for daylight. Examination of the area showed that the smaller set of tracks in fact belonged to a woman. She and her partner had smoked several cigarettes while they waited. The cigarette butts discarded in the snow by the small boot tracks showed clear traces of bright red lipstick.

The hunters each had their favourite brand of smokes, clearly indicated by the printing on the paper near the cork tips. The hunter with the big boots had fired four shots from a .270 Winchester rifle, while the woman had fired three from a rifle chambered for the rather uncommon .250-3000 Savage cartridge.

We collected the cigarette butts and the fired rifle cartridges and took photographs of the boot prints. The tracks then led us to a trail off the highway where a small four-wheel drive vehicle had been turned around to head back out before being parked. The vehicle tracks showed how the vehicle had left the parking spot with all four wheels spinning in the snow. The tracks in the snow showed that the vehicle had a very short wheelbase. At that time about the only common vehicle built that way and with four-wheel drive was the army Jeep. The tracks in the snow also told us that this vehicle was equipped with four snow tires. Three of the tires were of the same snow-tire pattern, but the one on the right front had a different tread design.

The patrol returned to Cranbrook. We arrived in town knowing quite a bit about these suspects. As we reached the edge of town, we started checking the parking areas around the motels. At the second motel we saw a Jeep sitting by the door of one of the units. Without leaving our car, we could see the mismatched right front tire. We had our man and woman.

A knock on the door of the motel unit brought a man to the door to ask what was on our minds. He was told we were looking into an incident where some horses had been shot. He knew nothing about such a thing and volunteered that he had been hunting that morning west of Cranbrook, which was in the opposite direction of Frenchman's Slough.

A woman was present in the room but she remained in the background, choosing not to get into any conversation with us. She wore good quality winter outdoor clothing and bright red lipstick. A model 99 Savage rifle leaned against the wall just to one side of the door. Examination of the firearm showed that it was chambered for .250-3000 calibre. Another rifle in the corner of the room was a .270 Winchester. The room smelled as though the couple had been chain-smoking for several hours. The butts in the ashtrays were of the same brands as those at the shooting site.

The couple was advised that we would be seizing the firearms for laboratory examination to determine if our recovered cartridges were fired by either of the guns, and if bullets from the dead horses had been fired by those same rifles. They were also advised that we would have to seize the wheels and tires from the Jeep for comparison to the tracks in the snow at the site of the horse killing.

Both occupants of the room were extremely agitated. The guy, who was sweating like he had just played a period of overtime hockey, asked if he could speak to us outside. We stood alongside the police vehicle and heard a strange story. He immediately admitted that they had shot the horses. They had waited in the darkness until first light allowed them to make out the outline of some dark animals against the snow; they wanted very much for them to be elk and their imagination did the rest. On the count of three they both fired and then each fired several more shots. They walked down to the dying animals only to discover that they were horses, and then they turned and ran back to their vehicle.

The man went on to further explain their situation. He advised us that he and the woman in the motel were married but their spouses were not in attendance. They both lived in a community not nearly far enough away from Cranbrook. The possibility of being charged with a criminal or other offence and the media becoming aware would be devastating to them as well as to others.

We told him we would get back to him with our decision

at our first opportunity. We removed the rifles but left the vehicle and wheels with a stern warning not to remove or alter anything.

We met with the owner of the horses and told him we had found the shooters. He was very pleased with our work. He was not interested in seeing the shooters prosecuted, but he did want to be compensated for the loss of his horses.

Back at the office we learned that neither of the horse shooters had any police record. They were both long-time residents of their small town and had responsible positions there.

We returned to the motel and advised the nervous occupants that the matter could possibly be settled between them and the horse owner; we told them where they could meet the owner and they left with the tires spinning again.

Within a very short time we received a call from the horse owner. He said that he had agreed to sell the horses to the shooters and that he was satisfied with their offer and very grateful for our assistance. We did not find out what financial agreement was negotiated for the horses, but I suspect it was closer to race-horse value than to packhorse prices.

Our file was closed, the former horse owner was happy, and I suspect the two hunters were somewhat less than happy—but very relieved.

Hostile Homecoming

Much has been said and printed about the evils of the
Native residential schools. These institutions were operated in
Canada from about 1874 until the early 1980s. The schools were
funded largely by the federal government and operated by both
the Protestant and Catholic churches. The Federal Department
of Indian Affairs was created about the same time as the schools,
and their combined purpose was to facilitate the integration of
the Native people into the new dominant society. These institutions had many weaknesses and problems; however, they also
had some amazing successes. This story is about one of those
successes—almost.

The story begins in the early fifties with the birth of a baby
girl on a Native reserve in the south Cariboo region. This reserve was tragically similar to almost every reserve in the interior of British Columbia. The community existed without pride
or leadership from anyone. Alcohol was the only obvious moti-
vation and the abuse of liquor was astounding. Drunken parties

frequently resulted in deaths from gunshot and knife wounds, and each death was cause for another round of alcohol-fueled violence as the funeral potlatch raged on for days. The reserves lacked water and sewer facilities, as did most rural settlements in that part of the country during those times. The situation on the reserves was far worse because of the lack of anyone who cared enough to repair a water pump or dig an outhouse hole. This was the birthright of each child to be born into these communities.

This baby girl spent the first five years of her life in this hellhole and, like a child in any given circumstance, accepted it as home. As the law of that time required, at about the age of six she was taken to the residential school near Williams Lake to begin her education. The trauma of this move away from her parents must have been horrible for the little girl; however, children are very resilient and most of them adapt quickly to new surroundings. A clean bed, a regular bath and treatment for body lice and scabies must have been a treat for the new arrivals.

The school near Williams Lake was run by the Catholic church. The female students were taught and cared for by nuns, who were also resident at the school facility. There were no doubt exceptions to the rule but the great majority of the instructors and supervisors were very dedicated people who did their best to teach the Native children what they needed to know in order to cope with modern life.

The young subject of this story was obviously a bright and willing student who absorbed and retained the material presented to her. She gladly stayed with the school system that was available to her at the time and completed high school as an honour student. Through the influence and assistance of some of the nuns from the residential school, she made her way to a nursing school in eastern Canada and in a few years she qualified as a registered nurse. At that time she may have been the first and only Native girl to have accomplished such a feat.

The young woman stayed on at the nursing school after her training was completed and became a valued addition to the hospital staff. She shared accommodation with two other young nurses and she soon had a small amount of money in a bank account. One of her short-term goals was to save enough money to travel back to her home in the Cariboo for the Christmas holiday. She flew to Vancouver and took a bus for the long ride home, arriving there on Christmas Eve. She was dressed in clothing more suitable for the streets of a Canadian city than for the snow-covered trails of her home reserve.

Her mother had proudly told everyone on the reserve of her pending arrival, and the whole community turned out to see her. She and her mother had expected her arrival to be a happy occasion but the crowd stood around in stony silence and soon dispersed. Christmas was traditionally the excuse for a drinking binge on the reserve, and this one was no exception. The drinking on the evening of the young woman's arrival centred in a building on the reserve that was used for meetings and parties. In spite of the cool reception, the young nurse and her mother made their way to the gathering, where they were met with hostility born of jealousy and fuelled by alcohol.

As soon as they arrived at the meeting hall, some of the more drunken young men began to proposition the young nurse. According to evidence given at the coroner's inquest, several of them threatened her with rape, and some warned her that she would get fucked by all of them before morning. The young woman was terrified.

The reserve where this incident occurred was in an isolated location with only one access road in winter. This winter road led a few miles to a small community where the reserve residents did their shopping and got their mail. There was a summer-only road from the reserve over a low mountain pass to another small community about twenty-five miles away. This trail rose quickly away from the reserve and then passed through open, windswept alpine terrain until it dropped into a valley near the second community. If people were properly dressed for winter and in reasonable physical condition, they could survive the twenty-five mile hike to this community in spite of the snow and severe wind chill of the open country. A person dressed in clothing designed for city streets would have no chance of survival.

The young woman knew the road and trail to these places. She had walked and ridden along both routes on many occasions in her childhood. She probably knew that she would be followed and caught if she tried to go to the nearby community on the open road, but she must have thought she had a chance of getting over the twenty-five mile route to the other community. She left the gathering on her home reserve and ran for her life. I can only imagine the thoughts running through her mind as she fled from what she had thought would be a welcome home party.

On December twenty-seventh she was reported missing by her family. The police investigation began to reveal some of the happenings surrounding her arrival at the reserve. Some of us who attended were familiar with the area and soon realized that she might have tried to make her way over the twenty-five mile mountain pass.

There was minimal snow on the ground at the reserve, but the depth of the snow increased rapidly as we made our way along the trail toward the higher ground of the twenty-five mile trail. We travelled with a police four-wheel-drive vehicle, but we were only able to force the vehicle through the snow to a point near where the trail started into the open alpine country. We could see where a number of people had walked up the trail from the direction of the reserve to the point where we were stopped by the snow. All the tracks turned back except for one set of small prints left by pointed shoes with partially pointed heels. These tracks continued into the low alpine pass.

The snow at the point where our vehicle stopped and beyond had been hardened by the action of the wind and cold to the point that a person could walk on it and leave only faint tracks. Fortunately for us, there had been no additional snowfall since the disappearance of the young nurse. The little footprints were travelling fairly straight and taking about a twenty-four inch pace where we first found them. Two of us set out to follow the track; there was little doubt in our minds about what the track would take us to. A check of weather records on the night of Christmas Eve indicated that there had been a strong north wind and that the temperature was about fifteen degrees below zero.

After going less than one mile the little footprints were much closer together, the stride had shortened to about twelve inches and the track was weaving. Over the next half a mile the pace shortened until the footprints were almost heel to toe, and the meandering increased. In several places the tracks showed she had fallen down and staggered about after getting up again. Over the crest of the next little rise we found her frozen body where she had fallen for the last time and given up. She had fallen backwards, and she lay with her arms folded and her legs straight. This indicated to us that she had lost consciousness at the moment she fell. Had she been conscious, she would have curled into a fetal position to preserve warmth.

The coroner's inquiry was conducted. The cause of death was determined to be hypothermia and exposure. She was buried in the cemetery near the reserve where she was born. No charges were ever laid in connection with her death.

Terrorism in the West Kootenay

In March of 1962, I was posted to Nelson, British Columbia directly from the RCMP training facility in Ottawa. At the time the postings were announced, I received a lot of ribbing from my troop-mates about going to the area at the centre of what was then known as "The Doukhobor Problem." Even in Ottawa, the news broadcasts and papers were full of stories about a radical sect of the Doukhobor community who were known as the Sons of Freedom or Freedomites. The media made much of the occasional nude demonstration staged by these people and delighted in showing photographs of very obese middle-aged women parading in the buff. This caused a lot of the glee among the guys, but most of them were a little envious because my posting was to an area where we all knew something was happening. In contrast, some of the guys were so unfortunate as to be posted to the protective policing unit in Ottawa, where they knew they would spend the next year, at minimum, guarding the federal buildings on night shifts.

I drove across Canada on the way to my new posting. Every night I picked up the local paper and read everything I could find about the action in Nelson. During the trip I read of a dynamite explosion that had destroyed the major power transmission lines across a very large lake about twenty miles from Nelson. The transmission line was one of the longest cable spans in the world, and the damage was estimated in the millions. On my last day of travel, I boarded a lake ferry which crossed Kootenay Lake within a few miles of where the power line had been knocked down. Two uniformed RCMP members were observing cars and passengers at the ferry landings on both sides of the lake.

Tensions were very high in the mining community of Riondel on the east side of the lake near where the power line had been cut. The destruction of the power lines had shut the mine down and put most of the community off work. In addition, the working area of the mine was 3,000 feet below the level of the lake. Water from the lake and from other underground sources was constantly building up in the depths of the mine, and huge electric pumps were struggling to keep ahead of the seepage. When the line was cut by the dynamite blast, a full complement of miners from Riondel were in the pit. Auxiliary power was used to power the lifts and bring the miners to the surface, but the miners told of wading in knee-deep water before the lift was able to take them out. Only the lake lay between the irate miners and the Doukhobor villages of the West Kootenay region. The police responded to the threats of violence from the mining community with additional surveillance and twenty-four hour road checks. Fortunately, tough talk is more abundant than violent action: not a single person was hanged, let alone one from every bridge in the West Kootenay.

When I arrived in Nelson, there were one hundred and forty uniformed RCMP members working from the detachment. The normal body count for that unit was twelve or thirteen. Most of these uniformed policemen were working shifts at around-the-clock roadblocks, where every vehicle was checked and searched. The intent was that the road checks would deter the radical Doukhobors from moving their dynamite bombs. I cannot recall a single stick of dynamite ever being found at one of these checkpoints; the main effect of the road checks was to convey the impression that something was being done about all the bombs.

The main targets of the Freedomites were West Kootenay Power and Light and the Canadian Pacific Railway. These targets were selected because, in the minds of the radicals, these large corporations best represented free enterprise and the right to own property and possessions, both of which were considered evil by the Sons of Freedom.

The Sons of Freedom's favourite weapon was a timed dynamite bomb. Dynamite was not very well controlled in those days; almost anyone could buy it if they had some rocks to break or some land to clear. Every logging operation or road building contractor had a supply that was available for easy theft.

The Sons of Freedom bombs were crude, but effective. The dynamite was frequently placed in an inner tube, along with a battery and a pocket watch connected to an electric blasting cap. The watch was altered by removing the minute hand, and the hour hand was slightly bent upward to run close to the clear plastic face of the watch. An insulated wire was soldered to the back of the watch case and a tiny screw was threaded through a small hole drilled in the plastic face. The second wire was attached to the head of the screw. When the hour hand and the screw came in contact, the circuit was closed and the blasting cap would fire. The watch face could be positioned so the screw and hour hand would meet at the selected time for the blast, usually between one and four o'clock in the morning.

The inner tube method was a favourite for taking down wooden power line poles. The tube with the bomb was placed around the pole at ground level. The pole would be cut cleanly if the detonator fired and the dynamite was not too old to function. In many cases the dynamite had been hidden for years under less than ideal circumstances and it failed to ignite. These duds were of great concern when they were located; a perimeter guard had to be maintained until the military trained experts arrived to disarm them.

The railway was targeted in a slightly different way. The dynamite sticks were laid at a rail splice with the timing watch taped onto the bundle so that two sections of steel would be destroyed when it fired.

The probability of injury and death was always present, but the Sons of Freedom almost always placed their bombs in locations where the blast would be confined to property damage. One exception, years before, was a bomb placed in a passenger railcar which killed one of the Doukhobor leaders. Another tragic incident took place in Castlegar when a sixteen-year-old boy was setting the timing device on a bomb prior to placing it at the local post office. He was sitting in the middle of the back seat of a car with two friends sitting on either side of him and two more were in the front seat. The bomb ignited while he held it in his lap; he was identified by his mother, who recognized the colour and curl of some of his hair. The other four survived with shrapnel wounds and varying degrees of hearing loss.

The car was a strange sight. The passenger compartment was bulged outward in every possible way. The roof of the car had torn away at the windshield and the door posts, and it stood straight up from the back corners where it had remained attached to the car body. Glass particles were scattered over an area of several blocks, and shredded upholstery material hung from the wreckage and from nearby trees and buildings.

Some of the bombing exercises were just plain silly. One night, a huge blast echoed through the Castlegar area where the Kootenay and Columbia rivers meet. The blast was obviously much bigger than that which had become routine in the area, but it was also unusual in that it did not cause the lights to go out at the same moment. Following the blast, reports began to come to the police about rock fragments hitting buildings or lying on the roadways in the immediate area of the river junction. The investigation led to the site of the monument and tomb of the leader who had been killed in the train car blast years before.

The tomb was high on the mountainside overlooking the river junction and the benchlands where the Doukhobors had farmed for years. The bomb had caused heavy damage to the concrete monument and had torn a lot of rock away from the area surrounding the tomb. If the ghost of the dead leader was around the tomb that night, it must have suffered an awful fright.

There was no doubt that some individuals held much more influence than others, but the leadership of the radicals was not a clearly defined group or person. Various individuals surfaced from within or from outside the cult to become short-term leaders. One of the short-term leaders was a non-Doukhobor who showed up in the area and convinced the radicals that he had been sent by God to lead them to salvation. This gentleman displayed a flowing mane of rich red hair to near the middle of his back, and a matching beard to near the middle of his front. He was immediately accepted as their leader and was treated with great generosity. He was soon involved in their terrorist activities and fled to South America to avoid prosecution. It was widely believed that he was living there, in luxury, and that he continued to receive money from his impoverished loyal followers in British Columbia.

The number of jailed Sons of Freedom grew steadily as a result of the ongoing investigations done by the RCMP members who specialized in radical Doukhobor crimes. The special squad was made up mainly of RCMP members of Ukrainian and Polish decent who had some knowledge of the Russian language. The language skills were very important to the investigators because the sect members would frequently refuse to converse with the police even though they could all speak English.

A sudden breakthrough came when one of the influential sect members convinced his followers that each of them should confess to some bombing or burning that they had been involved in. This event came out of a promise to the sect members from the exiled bogus leader, who was then living in South America, that they would advance to a better life through the Canadian jails. Over the next days and weeks everyone was busy writing out confessions about incidents that, in many cases, went back to the early history of the sect. The courts were overloaded with the rush of Sons of Freedom who could hardly wait to get to jail. The crowd of prisoners was gradually moved through the courts and the temporary holding facility in Nelson to the new prison at Agassiz, where extra facilities had been constructed to accommodate the Doukhobor prisoners.

The Doukhobor people lived throughout the West Kootenay area between Nelson and Grand Forks. The majority of them were law-abiding, hard-working citizens who took an active part in their communities and their country. Many of these people were ashamed of the antics of the Sons of Freedom, and would assist where they could to try and put a stop to their destructive behavior. In some cases, families were split by some taking an active role with the Sons of Freedom and others being opposed to them. This had been carefully explained to me when I arrived in Nelson. I was then told that there was an easy way to determine the leanings of a

Doukhobor during an encounter: "The radical ones are light red, while the others are pink."

The radicals were scattered along with the law-abiding Doukhobors throughout the same region between Nelson and Grand Forks. There were small communities throughout the area that were almost entirely populated by Sons of Freedom radicals. The largest of these, known as Krestova, was between Nelson and Castlegar, near the junction of the Slocan and Kootenay rivers. Krestova was a collection of shacks made by the Sons of Freedom from salvaged scrap wood and whatever other material was cast aside by the affluent society they were so opposed to. At the edge of the shack town was a large sign that displayed five statements from the creed of the Sons of Freedom, in both English and Russian:

- The land cannot be bought or sold or taxes collected thereof.
- The land is the gift of God by the birthright inheritance of man.
- Down with private ownership.
- Down with boundaries.
- Let the world be a communal abode of all mankind for the kingdom of God is already with us on earth.

Over time, following the mass confessions, most of the population of Krestova had been jailed and moved to the prison at Agassiz. One morning in early summer, a mass burning was staged by the radicals. Throughout the area homes and shacks were burned, in most cases by their occupants. At Krestova, where nothing was left by noon, we were told that they were preparing for the better life they expected to come to them through our jails. Many of them were nude and were somewhat more than light red from being too near the fires that had consumed their shacks. Small children stood around with some of the women who were supervising them; they were wide-eyed with fright at what they had seen that morning.

A man of about eighty years, nude except for a pair of oxfords, was making an attempt to save his tiny greenhouse, which had been attached to the side of the shack that his wife had set afire. He had a garden hose that provided a trickle of water and he was scurrying around the tiny structure in a losing battle. There were tears in his eyes when he finally admitted defeat and stood aside to watch the flames finish their work. Each of the residents of the village had removed a small bundle of bedding and clothing before the shacks were torched; these were placed on the ground just out of reach of the fires. Many of these people spent the following nights in the open, or in vehicles around the ashes of Krestova.

The mass burning took on greater significance in other areas, where many of the original communal homes were burned by sect members even though they were also the homes of non-radicals. Many families had struggled to escape the cult thinking of the Sons of Freedom, but in some cases, Grandma, Grandpa, or a brother or sister were still caught up in it and torched the house to prove their loyalty and to be eligible for the better life they believed was about to begin for them. The day of the big burn was a great tragedy for many families in the Kootenays.

Several weeks after the big burn, we were all called out in the early morning. Something was stirring among the radicals, but no one was sure just what it was. I was sent out to the highway junction near Krestova to observe and report, and to be ready for whatever was about to happen. A group of us stood by near the Crescent Valley RCMP detachment and watched the goings-on. The detachment was on the bank of the Slocan River, just below the hillside leading up to the burned-out village of Krestova.

When we arrived, there was a group of Sons of Freedom standing around near the police building. Over the next few hours, more arrived on foot and in vehicles as the group grew to over one hundred. We were told by some of them that they were leaving the Kootenays to walk to the jail in Agassiz where they could be near their loved ones. Reports on our radio system advised that similar gatherings were forming in other locations throughout the West Kootenay. Agassiz was about three hundred miles away over mountain highways. By about noon the column started moving along the highway. The old, the weak and the crippled led the parade for the benefit of the press. By early evening, the parade had moved just a little more than a mile and the decision was made to camp for the night.

This went on for days until the group arrived in Castlegar, about eight miles from Krestova. When the parade left Castlegar and started into the mountain pass leading to Grand Forks, the pace suddenly changed. The walkers were picked up by vehicles, which made return trips for more pedestrians until, by the end of the day, the whole group had moved about seventy-five miles to Christina Lake, where they set up the next camp. From that day on, the group walked through the towns along the highway and then returned to their cars to travel the unpopulated areas of the route. Some camps lasted for several days before they moved again, while many were just overnight. By the fall of that year they were camped near the gates of Mountain Prison in Agassiz.

The conviction and jailing of many, and the decision to trek to the prison, seemed a turning point in the Sons of Freedom history. Over the years, the prisoners were paroled or released having served their sentences; they joined their families outside the gates and began to drift away. The frightened children from the morning of the Krestova burn will now have grandchildren. Obviously, they have made some great changes in their view of the world. Fires and bombs are now about as uncommon in the West Kootenay as in most other communities in Canada.

Canadian Beer

Many good stories have come out of a case of beer and some have come out of several cases. This one falls into the latter category; several cases, where even one may have done the job.

Four workers from a very large aircraft factory in the Seattle area decided they would drive to the Cariboo region of British Columbia for a few days of lake fishing. The day of departure came and the four met at the factory. They had everything with them for the trip and the plan was to pile into a brand new Chevrolet station wagon and leave right from work.

The fancy new station wagon was the pride and joy of its owner, and he had announced to the other three that he would be doing all the driving.

The four struck out to the north on Interstate Five and crossed the border into Canada on a beautiful summer afternoon. Their first stop in Canada was at a liquor store, where they laid in a supply of beer.

In those days, American beer was made with a very low

alcohol content—somewhere in the range of three to four percent—and these fellows were accustomed to their domestic product. Canadian beer, however, was a horse of a different colour. It had an alcohol content in the area of eight percent in the regular products, and there were a few brands that ran as high as twelve percent. The four pals were not unaccustomed to quaffing a few beer after work or on their frequent weekend get-togethers, but they were not prepared for the sledgehammer effect of our Canadian barley extract.

I did not learn whether it was by design or by accident that they chose one of the Canadian products with the full twelve percent alcohol rating, but choose it they did, and they repeated the same choice eight times before they left the liquor store. They packed their ninety-six bottles of beer into the station wagon and lovingly placed twelve of them on ice in their cooler. The cooler was positioned to allow quick and easy access in the event a thirst should seize them as they made their way to the legendary lakes of the Cariboo. Perhaps this story would have had a different ending if the four had done some simple mathematics and calculated that they were in possession of the equivalent of three hundred and eighty-four bottles of their own domestic belly wash.

The beer in the cooler had not melted much ice when the first four were uncapped and tossed back. It was a hot day and the warm beer was not very satisfying, so another round was definitely in order. The four may have wondered why they were experiencing a bit of a buzz from just one beer; if they did, they must have concluded it was a combination of the hot day and the warm beer. The next one would be colder by now and no doubt it would be much better.

The four fishermen carried on along the highway toward their objective with only brief stops to pee and replenish the cooler. They soon found themselves in the scenic Fraser Canyon, where the road twists and turns and occasionally goes underground in its historic struggle to take people to the interior of the province. There are many difficult trails through the mountains of British Columbia, and many of them are more challenging than the Fraser Canyon; however, this road is definitely one that requires the full attention of drivers. Our four friends were by now unable to focus their attention on anything for more than a fleeting moment.

The calls started to reach the police at both Hope and Boston Bar detachments. The callers told a variety of stories about a green Chevrolet station wagon with Washington State license plates and four male occupants. Most of the callers told of minor collisions with guard rails or other fixtures along the road, and many of them told us that the four men were drunk.

The first call to come directly to us at Lytton was from a truck driver who told us the car had crowded him to the extreme right edge of the road and then hit the trailer wheels of his unit. The station wagon lurched from the impact but returned to the right side of the road and carried on without a pause. The trucker got a good look into the car below him and he described the two men in the front as being "pukin'-through-the-nose drunk."

The incident with the truck had happened north of Boston Bar and the suspect vehicle was headed north. There were no police vehicles in that area so I drove south from Lytton to meet them. I soon began meeting drivers who flashed their lights and waved to get my attention, pointing and gesturing to make it clear to me that they had also observed the four fishermen. I carried on with my emergency lights activated. In a short time I met a northbound caravan of vehicles with a green Chevrolet station wagon in the lead. The station wagon was wandering over the full width of the highway and moving much slower than normal traffic. The traffic following the station wagon was not able to pass safely and therefore formed a line expecting to witness some sort of a crash.

I approached the vehicle with all emergency equipment in operation, yelling on the loud hailer. With the siren screaming, I drove the marked police car alongside; after several such approaches the driver turned his head toward me and tried to focus his vision. I could see that the other men in the car were trying to tell the driver that I was there, but they were not having any effect. The station wagon finally came to a stop in a cloud of dust, partly into the ditch on the right side of the highway. I approached the driver's window and was immediately hit by the smell of liquor; a quick look at the four occupants of the station wagon confirmed that they were all well beyond impairment and into the realm of intoxication. I reached into the car, shut the engine off, and removed the ignition keys. Now we could try to talk.

The extra-strength Canadian beer had truly done a number on these four lads. The three passengers were all big, well-filled-out men, all about six feet tall; the smallest of the three would weigh in the area of two hundred pounds. The driver was a small wiry man, about five foot six inches tall and in the area of one hundred and twenty-five pounds. I had little doubt that the smaller man had felt it necessary to match beer for beer with the others just to prove to them that he was their equal. The down side of a competition like this is the fact that alcohol distributes itself in the body in direct proportion to the water content and the total mass of the body. Assuming that the small man at the wheel drank an equal amount of beer as the others, his blood-alcohol content would be nearly double that of any of the other three.

The actions and conduct of the driver confirmed my theory. The three big passengers in the wagon were all drunk, but they were jovial happy drunks who laughed and told me that I sure had them "dead to rights." The driver, with his double load of beer, was a different animal. He was angry and abusive right from the get-go. I made a few notes and recorded the names and addresses of several witnesses who stopped to tell me how glad they were to see the station wagon off the road, and how willing they would be to give evidence if the court required it.

The three big jovial drunks were trying their best to calm their driver, but to little avail. The driver was into what we police referred to as the "excitement stage" of intoxication. I had asked the three jovial guys to try and keep their friend away from the traffic and to keep him confined to the shallow highway ditch on the right side of his car. The driver threatened to fight his friends because they were keeping him from fighting me. He was emotionally out of control, laughing one minute and crying the next—a clear signal to me that he was going to be trouble.

I approached the foursome, who were now beside their car and away from the highway traffic. The good humour of the three big guys was still evident, but the driver was becoming more wild as each moment passed. The three happy drunks were doing all they could in their diminished capacities to calm their friend and convince him that they would have to go with me until they sobered up a little. The driver would have no part of it. He had convinced himself that all he had to do was beat the crap out of me and then they could be on their way again. I tried as well to talk to the little man but he was unable to calm down enough to listen or absorb any conversation.

A few of the motorists who had stopped to offer assistance earlier had stayed with me because they did not like the odds of four to one. It was now time to try and load these fellows into my police car. I asked the biggest of the three happy drunks to keep the little driver away from the traffic while I escorted the other two to my car. Two or three willing motorists immediately agreed to see that he was able to do this. I showed the other two to the police car and they willingly got into the back seat behind the security screen.

The security screen was a recent addition to police cars at that time. The device consisted of a steel frame that was bolted into the floor of the car and ran up the centre door posts and across the roof of the car like a roll bar. There was a steel panel across the back of the front seat and a moveable Plexiglass panel that could cover the open area above the seat back and the headliner of the car. In this circumstance, I was very glad to have this addition in my patrol car.

I told the two big guys in the back of my car that their driver would be joining them very soon and that they must do everything they could to control him. They agreed to do whatever was necessary.

I turned to the group at the side of the road and asked the big drunk to hop into the passenger front seat of my car. He agreed to do so, but he pleaded with me not to hurt his friend. I assured him that I would only do what was absolutely necessary. The assisting motorists now moved near the police car to help me by watching my passengers. I moved close to the excited little driver and again asked him to come with me. He cursed and swung at me in slow motion with his fists. I ducked and dodged his efforts, and tried again to convince him to get into the back of the police car. It was now obvious that he would have to be forced; I was the only police member for about thirty miles or more, so I was on my own except for assistance from civilians. Thankfully, there were several people who had willingly come to help.

Early in my police experience I learned that it was folly to pre-judge anyone, male or female, when it comes to an all-out fight. Some of my most memorable fisticuff events were with small wiry men. What they may have lacked in brawn they made up for in experience proving themselves on the streets of life.

Fortunately for me, there would be no contest in this case. The driver was having balance problems and he was only able to focus his vision for fleeting moments.

I grabbed the little fellow and pinned him face down over the hood of his car. He struggled but was unable to escape my hold. I tried again to talk him into the police car, but he could not bring himself to give in. I stood him up and applied a sleeper hold with the crook of my arm under his chin. This was my first attempt at using this method to subdue anyone outside of training exercises, where pressure was never maintained until the subject lost consciousness.

The hold was in place for only a matter of seconds when I felt his body go limp. I immediately released the hold and lowered him to the ground, wondering if he was faking it. I did not wonder long, however, as he began to do "the chicken"—and in doing so, he sure scared the hell out of me.

The expression of "doing the chicken" comes from observing chickens that have had their heads chopped off. As a prairie farm boy I had seen the real "chicken" on several hundred occasions, but this was the first human enactment I had witnessed, and it was frightening. It seemed like an hour, but I suspect the whole thing was over in about a minute. The little man opened his eyes and blinked very slowly, looking around, clearly wondering where he was. I helped him to his feet and told him I would help him get into the car with his friends. He went along with it as though we were best buddies.

Two of my civilian helpers agreed to follow my car to Lytton and help me get my clients into the lock-up. There were no further difficulties whatsoever. The driver and his three friends talked about their current situation in quite a rational manner on the short trip to town. I booked the four into their accommodations and arranged for cell guards until the next morning, when the driver would face the local magistrate.

The next morning the driver entered a guilty plea to impaired driving, was fined two hundred and fifty dollars, and had his driver's license suspended for six months. The four men paid the fine immediately and I gave them a ride to the local garage where they got their first sober look at the remains of the brand new Chevrolet station wagon. They all stared in shocked silence as they slowly circled the vehicle and the full extent of their combined foolishness came home to them. The one bright spot in the whole event was that the car was still operable. The four had a brief discussion and decided to go straight home. The fishing trip was over, and so was their experiment with Canadian beer.

The Troopers of Williams Lake

In the late 1960s, Williams Lake was still very much a frontier town; a hard drinking, long-distance-driving sort of place. There were are a lot of truly great citizens in that part of British Columbia—and a lot of rather colourful characters too. Often the good citizen and the character were the same person.

Williams Lake was a place where people came and stayed because they liked it there and because there were opportunities to do business or to find work. This situation gave Williams Lake and its citizens a very positive spin. Policing was a challenge, as in most other communities, but the citizens were cheerful and appreciated what we had to do. Many other towns and cities in the northern and central part of the province were inhabited by people who went there because there was work; they stayed only to gather some money and then get out. In many cases these people found they had been in these places for half their lives and were still dreaming of leaving sometime soon.

It was midsummer when a ranch hand from the Chilcotin area came into Williams Lake for the day with his pickup truck and a list of tasks and supplies for the ranch where he was employed: stock salt, harness repairs, boots at the shoemaker, flour, wire, fence staples and more. The ranch was six hours of dirt road away and the trip was not taken lightly or frequently. The cowboy's last stop just before the six o'clock closing time was the liquor store, where he picked up a case of twelve twenty-five ounce bottles of rye whiskey. He set the sealed cardboard case in a safe front corner of the open pickup box and headed for home.

Williams Lake had another colourful group of citizens who were always around the centre of town. They referred to themselves as the "Troopers," and the police called them that too. The Troopers maintained constant surveillance on the liquor store through winter and summer. If any member of the Troopers was to come into enough cash for a liquor store purchase it was impossible for the transaction to be done without the knowledge of his compatriots. A furtive figure would dart out of the store and head into the nearest alley with his prize, only to be followed by the entire group. Once in the company of the eager followers, the hero would gladly share his prize among them. It seemed there were unwritten rules to this game; the carrier was not to run and the bottle was not to be tossed back in one shot to avoid sharing. Sharing was a traditional thing with this group, a tradition which had been part of their lives for generations before Williams Lake and the liquor store were there. The great modern benefit of this tradition was that the alcohol always went into a sufficient number of drinkers to eliminate the possibility of overdose. An "eighty-pounder" (the local name for a half-gallon of wine) would be enough to threaten the life of a single drinker, but shared among the Troopers it was hardly enough to slacken their collective thirst.

The cowboy with his supplies in the truck box was now heading toward the Chilcotin Road and the start of a six-hour drive to the ranch. He drove past the Maple Leaf Hotel, turned left at the Ranch Hotel, and went up the grade toward the Lakeview Hotel. The thought of a cold glass of beer before the long drive was too much for him to pass up, so he pulled over and walked across the street to the Lakeview bar for one quick beer.

One of the Troopers who was known and recognized by everyone in Williams Lake was Willyum Charleyboy. Willyum was a small wiry man with a good sense of humour. He loved to entertain people with his stories about life in the Chilcotin and life on the streets of Williams Lake, where he had spent most of his existence. He spent many nights as a guest of the Queen in our cells. He was always cheerful and bright in the morning when the overnighters formed a column for the march to the courthouse. Willyum was not alone in his morning attitude and outlook; most all of the Troopers would be cheerful and bantering with the police or among themselves. These people drank wine, hairspray, shoe polish and rubbing alcohol and yet they faced the next day with a smile and a chuckle. I, on the other hand, would drink good whiskey with water, and if I had had more than a couple I was not fit company for anyone the next morning—and I didn't get up to face a judge as the accused.

The court system at that time was very much aware of the circumstances in Williams Lake; the magistrate was a local businessman and the police lived in the community where they worked. The lawyers who occasionally appeared as defense or Crown counsel were also from the community and understood the difference between Williams Lake and Vancouver. The routine way of dealing with the Troopers was to jail them overnight and charge them the next morning under the Liquor Act for being drunk in a public place. The paperwork was prepared for each of them and they were paraded to the court where, following a guilty plea, they were sentenced to a fine of ten dollars or, in default, one day in jail. Since they had already been in jail for part of that day, the sentence had been served and they were free to go. In exceptional cases a charge was laid under the Criminal Code of Canada for causing a disturbance by being drunk. A criminal charge or several Liquor Act charges in a short time could result in jail time in the Regional Correctional Centre at Kamloops.

The magistrate and the police looked over the morning parade and watched for health problems. These observations occasionally resulted in a conference in the judge's chambers. The police prosecutor might say, "John Edgar is looking frail; I think he's lost weight and his cough kept some of the boys awake last night." A conference like that could, and frequently did, result in John Edgar being sentenced to thirty or sixty days in the Kamloops facilities where he would be "dried out," provided with three meals a day, and subjected to medical attention. After the sentence the Trooper would return to the ranks in town with a new lease on life, a new pair of jeans and a shirt. There was no doubt that these court-imposed interventions added to the lifespan of many of the Troopers.

Willyum was among those who benefitted from this untraditional court system. He often joked with us that he had more hours flying between Williams Lake and Kamloops than most of the young commercial pilots on that route. I recall a mid-June morning when Willyum was among the court parade. He had been a regular in the cells recently, and was not in good health. The conference before court led to the magistrate asking Willyum for a reason why he should not go to Kamloops. Willyum stepped forward and said, "Stampede is just a few days away, and I have never missed one."

The Williams Lake Stampede has been held on the July First

weekend for more than a hundred years. The event is a rodeo that is held in a natural amphitheatre formed by a semi-circle of hills near the lake at the edge of town. It is the region's greatest celebration of life in the Cariboo. Ranchers, loggers, mill workers and Natives all celebrate together, either as spectators or as contestants in the many events of stampede week.

The magistrate considered this submission, and adjourned sentencing to the week after Stampede. Bail was granted without surety but with the condition that should Willyum appear in court for any reason before sentence was passed, his bail would be revoked. Willyum thanked the court and did not come to our attention again until the evening of the last day of the stampede, when he really tied one on and stayed the night with us before flying off to Kamloops.

Closing time at the Lakeview came at two o'clock in the morning. The cowboy lurched across the street to his pickup and checked his load. A short time later he arrived at the police office to report the theft of a case of whiskey. The whiskey was gone, but all the other assorted goods in the truck were untouched. There was not much sympathy among the police. The cowboy knew that he would never see a single drop of the whiskey again, but he had felt it must be reported because the purchase had been made with the ranch owner's money. News of the theft was immediately broadcast on the police radio. The police around town watched for any unusual action among the Troopers, but the only clue was that none of them were visible in any of their regular haunts. The usual drinking places were checked, but there was still no sign of the Troopers. The experienced policemen on duty were quite sure where the whiskey had gone, but they were unable to locate any of the suspects during the remainder of the night. The body count in the cells that night was unusually low.

Daylight came and a few sweeps were made around town

between the typing of the required reports for the day shift. The whiskey theft was the highlight of the night and got extra attention because no one could believe that anyone would be foolish enough to leave a case of whiskey in an open truck box. This one would make the front page of the *Tribune*.

The missing Troopers were also obvious to the day shift. Most mornings a few would be hanging around the courthouse waiting for the overnight guests to be set free, but not this day.

It was near noon when a worker from the Pacific Great Eastern Railroad came to the office to report that he had found a corpse lying on a pile of railroad ties in the area known as the jungle. The jungle was along the edge of town, adjacent to where the cowboy had parked his truck on MacKenzie Avenue. MacKenzie Avenue, the creek, and the railway track all lay approximately parallel to each other along that side of town. Situated between the railway and the creek, the jungle was used as a storage area for railroad junk. It was a mass of thick willow growth with some trails cut through to allow access for railroad vehicles. Being away from the public view, the willow patches were great places for the Troopers to have wine parties, as they were seldom bothered there. Over the years they had carved away some of the brush to make openings inside the thick willows. These spaces had only small and difficult-to-find passages to the road. After a wine (or whatever) party, most of them would stay right there to sleep it off. This lessened the number of guests at our establishment and eliminated the paperwork required for arrests.

The railway worker led us into the jungle, where we found Willyum draped over a pile of railway ties. The medical examiner estimated he had been dead for about fifteen hours. A search of the entire area revealed no trace of the missing whiskey. By this time some of the Troopers were showing up around town, but none of them had any information about Willyum or the missing whiskey. According to them, they had spent the night in a great variety of places around town but not a single one of them had been in or even near the jungle. The blood alcohol level in Willyum's corpse was two hundred and seventy milligrams of alcohol in one hundred milliliters of blood. This level would indicate that he had drunk less than one of the twenty-five ounce bottles, considering that he weighed only about one hundred and twenty pounds. The autopsy revealed no specific cause of death. The coroner concluded the death was the result of alcohol poisoning. We were left to try and piece the story together mainly from observations and knowledge of their habits. It appeared that Willyum was alone when he spotted the prize in the truck box. He knew it could take flight at any moment so he must have grabbed it and tottered off into the jungle. In the traditional way of the Troopers, he should have called for the others to share his good fortune but he likely decided to have a few sips before doing so and the hard liquor took him out before he could complete his traditional duty. The fact the other Troopers went missing that night left no doubt that one or more of them had found Willyum and then the word had spread quickly. Some of them must have taken the liberated whisky to a place where they all gathered and held one hell of a wake for Willyum. They obviously figured the less we knew about it the better and we really couldn't argue with them on that.

The Gunpowder Cure

On an early spring afternoon, my partner and I were attending a call near the interior town where we were posted. It was that special time of year when everything was in the process of a new beginning; the ice was recently gone from the lakes and rivers, the evergreens were breaking new buds and the leaves of the poplar and willow still had their fresh colour and texture. The call was another of the little mysteries that people like to provide to the police. The caller had asked that we attend at his neighbour's place because he thought something was wrong. When pressed for details, the caller would only say that something was wrong and it was a police matter.

The call originated just outside the town boundary in a collection of small shacks, known locally as the "Camp."

The shacks had been built around a sawmill operation that had closed around the end of the Second World War. The little shells of buildings had served as living quarters for the mill hands and in some cases, their families. The mill and all the equipment were long gone, but the collection of shacks still served as home to a variety of people who could be described as "a little down on their luck." After the mill closed, someone had taken over the property and moved the shacks into rows, forming a little village. The rent was very low. However, if one was to look carefully at what these people received for their rental payments they were actually being gouged.

The residents of the Camp were all longtime residents of the region. Younger people who were unemployed or chose not to work would find their lodging in other places. The Native people who lived in the community or those who drifted into town to spend a few months would seek similar accommodation, but they preferred to gather in small groups in rundown motels closer to the downtown core.

The buildings of the Camp were all the same; each was about twelve feet wide and sixteen feet long. They were built on skids (logs laid flat on the ground that extended a little more than the sixteen foot length of the building). The skids under the buildings extended at the front and boards were nailed across them to form a little deck. Doors were slightly off-centre in the front end and there was a little peaked roof nailed over the door. Every roof in the Camp was covered with rolled roofing, which was a thick paper product saturated with tar and sand. Rolled roofing was quite durable, but its greatest appeal was minimal cost. Residents of the Camp were free to cover the bare wood frame on the inside of their home and to insulate the walls if they wished, as long as they paid their rent like everyone else and used their own resources for whatever costs they incurred. This arrangement resulted in some unique interior design; many walls were covered with salvaged cardboard boxes, some with the printed labels displayed and some with only plain brown cardboard. One resident of the Camp had covered his walls with beer cases. Each cardboard case was carefully flattened and stapled to the studs so the brand names and colourful labels were presented square and upright.

The heating for each shack came from a small, light metal stove with a stovepipe which passed through a sheet metal thimble in the roofing. When the outside temperature reached twenty below zero, the little stoves were kept glowing hot and the residents moved their chairs to be near the heat. Fires were not uncommon but up to that time had not resulted in any fatalities; the residents escaped with the clothes they were wearing and the shack was gone in about half an hour. Other Camp dwellers always made room for those who had had a fire. Life went on. Within a short time another shack would be moved into the empty spot and the original occupants would be back to their normal routine.

On this day, as we entered the Camp, everything appeared normal. Some of the residents who were visible stopped whatever they were doing and gave us a blank look, while others quickly moved inside their shacks. We stopped to talk to the "mayor" of the Camp. He was the resident with the telephone who made the decisions whether to call for outside help or to deal with problems right there. The mayor directed us to Maynard's place, and told us he was dead.

Maynard was well known to any of us who had been in town for more than two weeks. Some of the local folks would say that "Maynard had an air about him." He was a very strong-smelling fellow at any time, but after drinking a bottle of cheap wine his odour became outstanding. He was a regular guest in our establishment because of his insatiable thirst. We knew when he was in residence as soon as we opened the office door. If we approached the police office from the back, the parking lot was filled with the essence of Maynard. A small fan mounted through the wall struggled with the heavy task of pushing air out of the cellblock and into the parking area.

When Maynard was there the fan seemed to turn slower than on other days.

We moved the car to the end of the row that contained Maynard's place. Looking down the full length of the double row of shacks, the most obvious thing was the absence of any people. Normally on a beautiful spring day such as this, there would be someone on at least half of the little front porches; today there was no one.

Maynard's place was the third on the right. On the front porch we could see a crumpled body in a face down position. A straight-backed wooden chair lay on its side just off the edge of the porch. We walked the few steps to Maynard's porch. He lay with his head in a large pool of congealed blood. Between his body and the open door was a Lee Enfield army rifle. The stature of the body, the location, the familiar clothing and the smell left no doubt that this was Maynard. There was no sign of life. We called our office to have them contact the coroner and we began recording the details of the scene.

On closer examination we could see a jagged wound that began near the mouth or chin and extended into the left side of his face, involving both his eye and ear. It was a hideous sight. We wondered why Maynard had chosen such a way to end his life. I walked back to the police car to get a camera. When I returned, my partner had stepped onto the edge of the little porch beside the body; he was leaning over it with one hand on the wall beside the open door.

As police officers, we were often faced with situations like this. As a coping method we often used gross humour to carry us through. It was always very difficult to get the job done if one or both of us were vomiting. A crude remark or gesture could sometimes break the impact of the moment and allow us to get on with the task at hand.

Just as I reached the edge of the porch, my partner stepped

over the body toward the door of the shack. As he was astride the body he said, "At least the asshole came out here and didn't make a mess inside." At these words, Maynard lifted his head and upper body onto one elbow and turned to glare up at my partner with his remaining eye. He did not speak or try to. We were both frozen where we stood for a moment. We called for an ambulance. Maynard got to his feet but it was obvious he would not stay upright for very long. We assisted him into his shack and got him onto the bed; he was in severe pain but he remained conscious. The ten minutes until the ambulance arrived seemed like hours. Maynard was a sight that would remain with us for a long time.

He later told me how he had decided to end his life. He loaded the rifle and sat on a chair just outside the door. He placed the rifle butt on the floor near his feet and put his mouth over the muzzle. He then reached for the trigger with his right hand. In reaching for the trigger, he turned his head away from the centre line of the rifle bore. The bullet and the muzzle blast from the rifle tore into the left side of his head but somehow missed the vital areas. He was conscious when we arrived and he had been listening to our conversation. He was sure he was about to die, and he had been wondering why it was taking so long. When my partner made the crude comment, Maynard got so angry that he wanted to fight and he forgot about his intention to die. When he got to his feet he knew he was not up to a fight so he accepted our assistance and our assurance that we would get him to the hospital.

About two months later, Maynard came to our office to get his rifle and other effects we had taken for safekeeping. He was living at the Camp again but he assured me that he was never going to drink again. The medical reconstruction of his head had begun. Bone had been grafted to reconstruct his eye socket and he claimed to have fairly good vision from the eye that had been

dangling loose on the optic nerve and other tissues on the day
we insulted him. Over the next year many more medical miracles were done for Maynard. He was given a workable lower
jaw and fitted with dentures. Except for the huge scar area, he
was almost back to his original self. He never attempted suicide
again. Whatever had been bothering him had apparently been
shaken loose by the blast.

The Glue Sniffer
of Golden

Golden was a rather isolated community until the Trans-Canada Highway was opened after the completion of the Rogers Pass route in 1966. The people of the town had worked in the forest industry, either in the woods or in the mills that processed logs into lumber and plywood. A few more had found a living with the Canadian Pacific Railway, and a few others in the small businesses of the town. The opening of the highway changed all that almost overnight. Suddenly a flood of new people arrived to take advantage of the business opportunities brought there by the travelling public. In a few short years the town population had more than doubled to fill the needs of the service industry from the highway.

Along with the new people came a variety of drifters who would hang around town for a few days and then disappear as quietly as they had arrived. One of these was a young fellow in his late teens who was noted sleeping in the parks during nice weather and using whatever he could find in the rain. He carried a small club bag stuffed with dirty laundry and he had a very strong odour about him owing to his lack of personal hygiene. He soon became known to all the business people in town because of his frequent and poorly executed shoplifting. He also became well-known to us at the police office.

In addition to his sticky fingers this fellow had a habit of sniffing glue. His preference was for the type of solvent used in contact cement and model airplane glue. He seemed to lack the ability to interact with people. Even without the influence of liquor or glue he was one of the most obnoxious and abusive people I can recall in my police experience. We received calls every day about his anti-social behaviour, ranging from urinating in public places to causing disturbances at the elementary schools by cursing and verbally abusing teachers and students.

We had arrested him for intoxication on many occasions, and had attempted to have him committed under the Mental Health Act by using the many examples of his extreme behaviour as evidence. The process at that time was to take him before the local magistrate and give evidence about his anti-social conduct. The magistrate could also question him and observe his responses. When this was done the young man yelled and cursed at us and at the magistrate while in the courtroom. The magistrate quickly agreed that he had potential for danger to himself or others and sent him with us for the next step of the process.

The next step was to have him interviewed by two doctors, preferably from different medical clinics. We were unable to follow this at Golden because there was only one medical clinic in town. As it unfolded there was no need for a second medical opinion. The first doctor came to the office to interview him in the cells. Our prisoner answered every question in a sane and normal manner, and was not abusive in any way. He soon proved to the satisfaction of the doctor that he was not suffering from any mental condition that would require detention. As the first doctor had not been able to find any grounds to recommend psychiatric help, the prisoner was released.

The complaints continued and his behaviour showed no improvement. On the evening of the second day after his court appearance we were advised that a person with a serious facial injury was wandering around in the business area of the little town. Our young friend was found near the post office with his lower lip vertically split to the middle of his chin; there was blood everywhere. He had been walking around smearing the blood with his hands and wiping it onto windows and vehicles. He seemed to enjoy flicking his blood-covered hands to spatter others as they passed by. When we arrived to assist he went into a frenzy of splattering blood and we became his prime target. In a very short time we had his hands cuffed behind his back, but we were bloody from head to foot.

Our prisoner was absolutely wild; he thrashed around and cursed and screamed at us as best he could. We considered ourselves fortunate that he was unable to spit because of his injury. He was still able to splash blood around through his vigorous thrashing about.

The local hospital had no facilities to deal with this type of problem so we hog-tied him and took him to the police office. From the office I contacted the doctor on call and explained what we had. The doctor on call was a very experienced man who had dealt with severe trauma from a great variety of causes for many years. He had attended highway and industrial accidents where his job had to be done in extremely difficult conditions.

The doctor could hear our prisoner cursing and screaming in the background as we talked. He did not wish to deal with this person at the small local hospital where his abuses would be audible from one end of the building to the other. He asked me to bring the patient across the street to the clinic after he had enough time to get there and unlock the side door to the building.

We saw the doctor arrive at the clinic and three of us escorted the prisoner across the street and into the building. There were only the five of us in the building, so the wild behaviour of our client was not causing public concern. The doctor asked to speak with the young man alone. We backed cautiously out of the room, leaving the two of them alone, but we remained in the hallway ready to pounce should the prisoner assault the doctor or try to crash out the window.

The doctor tried every method he could think of to calm the prisoner and get him into a conversation about the injury and the urgent need to repair the damage to his face. The prisoner would have no part of it. He was not as abusive toward the doctor as he was to us, but he insisted that he be released to go about whatever he chose to do. The doctor was able to talk him down to the point that he stopped screaming and splattering blood, but not enough to get his permission to suture the gaping hole in his face.

The doctor came out of the room and one of the constables took over as the guard. The prisoner started to go wild again but was talked down by the constable, who assured him that we just needed some time to decide what to do with him. We held a little conference in the hall. The doctor was very concerned that the injury would leave a hideous scar if it was not treated as soon as possible. Our only course of action was to lock him in our cells until he came out of whatever was causing his wild behaviour. The doctor was concerned that the healing process would begin and that infection was almost a sure thing. After a lot of consideration the doctor stated that if we would hold him down he would suture the lip.

The young man was set upon quickly and held to the examining table with restraint straps and the three of us. The doctor did the best he could to freeze the lower lip and he then went about his work as quickly as possible. The fellow fought and struggled right up until the last stitch was in place. At that point we were able to converse with him in a limited way. It seemed the pain of the suturing and what we applied in holding him down had gotten through to him. He was placed in our cells and told that he could leave in the morning without charges provided he did not go out and cause another disturbance. He remained asleep in our facility until well into the next morning when he was given a breakfast and released. He disappeared from Golden that day and to our knowledge he did not return.

Small Town Justice

In my years of police work, between 1961 and 1989, I was continuously involved in the day-to-day workings of our system of justice. I came away from that chapter of my life with few regrets. I miss the companionship of the police organization with its huge dedication to a common task. I have, however, few fond memories of the courts and all the men and women who took the stage and played their role. Each had a part to play and they were guided and prompted through their performance by the grand director who sat in a leather chair on the raised section of flooring at the front of the room. Just before the final curtain the grand director would review the performance of each actor and award the prize (commonly known as a verdict) to whichever side had been judged to have made their presentation most compellingly.

Many people came to the court seeking justice, but all they received was an application of law tainted and distorted by the efforts of lawyers. The effort of the prosecutor was predictable, but the defense effort was in direct proportion to the financial ability of the accused. The final judgment was frequently hampered because the rules of evidence and the lawyers' interpretation of these rules would not permit the full story to be told.

I recall an occasion in the early part of my police service when I stopped a truck that was carrying a very large crawler tractor along a public highway. The tractor alone was too heavy for the truck, without taking into account the bulldozer blade and the rock ripper that were still attached to the machine as it sat on the truck. The load was more than double what the truck was licensed to carry, and far exceeded the absolute maximum allowed with special permits.

The truck and its load were owned by a local man who was well-known and well-respected in the community. I issued a traffic ticket for the overloading offence. He entered a "not guilty" plea and the matter was set over for trial in a few weeks.

At that time the police acted as both witness and prosecutor in traffic cases. I was quite concerned because this would be my first experience with this type of prosecution. I talked about the case with an experienced and very knowledgeable senior constable, and we laid out a detailed outline of everything that would be required for a successful prosecution. The trial day arrived, my witnesses were all present, and the senior constable was there to watch the trial. The judge, the accused, and his counsel were there and ready to proceed.

The senior constable and I had reviewed every aspect of the evidence that I had to present to establish my case. He had assured me that everything was in order; however, he also said that the man would not be convicted. I assumed he was trying to make me more nervous than I already was. I gave evidence and called experts to prove the weight of the machines, the weight the truck was licensed to carry, and all other requirements.

The defense lawyer asked only a few questions and called

no evidence. He summed up by rambling on for a short time about the fine reputation of the accused. The judge, without offering any reason or clarification, said he felt there was doubt and dismissed the charge. I immediately sought the senior constable and asked how he had known the result before the trial. He laughed and said that it was because of a secret organization. Later, over coffee, I learned that the judge, the defense counsel, and the accused were "Lodge Brothers." They all wore the same symbols on rings and lapel pins and therefore they looked after each other, notwithstanding the law and unquestioned sworn testimony.

The Prince George Security Shell Switch

This story took place in the RCMP Municipal Detachment in Prince George. By RCMP standards this was a very large police unit, with one hundred and forty uniformed personnel and a large number of civilian employees who filled support positions.

Prince George City Detachment was run by a large complement of senior non-commissioned officers and two commissioned officers. The office space occupied the entire second floor of a fairly large office building. The central part of the office was made up of open space with desks and low cubical walls; the area against the outside walls had small office spaces that were utilized by various units of the detachment. The back wall, the farthest from the public counter, had four larger private offices that were occupied by the officer commanding, his personal secretary, the administrative staff sergeant, and the officer second in command. This area could be said to be the nerve centre of the large unit; this is where the weighty decisions of everyday police work were made.

This story would not have occurred if not for the fact that the senior staff sergeant and the inspector, second in command, could not stand each other. Neither of these two could bring themselves to bid the other good morning even if they were caught in the only elevator taking them up to their neighbouring offices. They made no attempt to conceal their contempt for each other and the feud soon became the subject of office jokes.

Information important to our work was received by a variety of communication methods, and frequently one of the office combatants would make the rounds to be sure everyone was aware of information that had come in. A short time later the second of this illustrious pair would come around with the same questions and information. I do not recall any incidents where they really screwed something up but there was certainly potential for this to happen every day. I do recall the laughs we all got watching these two nimrods blustering their way along without speaking to each other.

One day a moving company was hired to relocate one of our subsections out of the main office. The move was not completed on the first day and the movers left some of their equipment in a corner of the office. Among this equipment was a two-wheeled furniture dolly; a simple machine that enabled a lone man to pick up and move very heavy articles.

A standard piece of office furniture in those days was a heavy steel cabinet with an iron door and combination lock, similar to a business vault or safe. This unit was large enough to hold a standard four-drawer steel filing cabinet, and was used to store personnel files and any other sensitive documents. Each of the back offices in the nerve centre had one of these units. They were called security shells and each was exactly like the other except that each had its own combination.

Sometime during the long hours of the very early morning, when the night shift was on and the nerve centre was not occupied, the furniture dolly was engaged in the moving of two security shells. The two shells involved were those of the staff sergeant and the inspector who did not speak to each other. It was not a long-distance move between the adjoining offices, and great care was taken to place the exchanged shells into the exact spot on the carpet where the other had come from. The entire deed was completed in a few minutes and the perpetrators returned to their duties with visions dancing in their minds of the impending results of their handiwork.

The next office day began like any other. Everyone was busy with the documentation of the events of the night before and with preparation for the day at hand. There was, however, a rumour around the office that something was about to happen between the two warring clowns in the nerve centre. Everyone was watching discreetly, but no one was letting any cats out of the bag. There was an obvious increase in the pedestrian traffic to the photocopy machine in the back corner of the office.

The first indication of mischief was when the old staff sergeant was observed in his office with his chair pulled up close to the front of his security shell. He had both hands on the dial of the lock and was in very deep concentration. On the floor between his feet lay his notebook with the pages splayed open to reveal some numbers scrawled across the page. A passing glance into the office next door revealed a remarkably similar position being executed by the inspector. The two combatants struggled with their individual problems until well into the afternoon; both being careful not to let the other know because they knew that the problems of one would bring joy to the other.

In those days the RCMP in British Columbia had a special section with the responsibility of servicing and procuring security equipment. This section was located at headquarters in

Vancouver. The first break in this mystery came when two employees of the Vancouver security equipment section went for coffee. One mentioned that he had to fly to Prince George to repair a faulty security shell. His coffee partner was planning the same trip! Their conversation over the next two minutes solved the problem.

After their coffee break the security experts called the unspeaking pair in Prince George and suggested that they go to the other's office and try their own combination there. They were none too willing but—wonder of wonders—the respective doors swung open.

The ensuing rage was unrestrained; the two combatants were in full agreement for the first time in years, but there was nothing spiritual or uplifting about this huge breakthrough in human communications.

They both demanded a full investigation of this deplorable act. Fortunately, the officer commanding was a diplomatic fellow who was well aware of the childish behaviour of these two. He pointed out to them that the entire thing would not have happened without their juvenile conduct, and his best advice to them was to shut up and try to learn something from the experience.

A Grizzly Ending

This incident took place on the east slope of the Rogers Pass. Here, the Trans-Canada Highway and the Canadian Pacific Railway follow the Beaver River valley out of the mountains of Glacier National Park, one on each side of the river. The railway had built and maintained a footbridge that crossed the river to allow train crews and other railway workers to have access from the highway. This bridge was a cable suspension structure that hung quite low over the river. That year the spring flood of the river had destroyed the bridge.

The river was still high, but it was below flood stage when a work-crew began to replace the bridge. They put a small aluminum boat into the river and rigged a rope harness to the stern and bow. The harness of the boat was then secured by a long line to an anchor point upstream. Changing the angle of the harness caused the boat to be pushed from one side of the river to the other by the current. Several crossings had been successfully made by this method when a sudden surge of water twisted the boat and filled it with glacier-cold water in an instant. The man in the boat was fully clothed in working gear, with heavy leather boots laced well above his ankles. He surfaced and was seen struggling to swim toward a small island a few hundred yards downstream in the racing water. The current and his efforts to swim almost took him to the island. Witnesses told us how it appeared he would make it to the island but a change in the current caught him when he was just short of it. He was last seen struggling in the water near the island he had hoped to reach.

The riverbanks were rocky and thickly forested; this prevented other workmen from running along the shore to help. Neither the railway nor the highway was close enough to the river to allow a view of the water below the accident scene. The others could only watch from where they were and hope he could save himself. The island where the man had last been seen was the first of several below the bridge site.

The islands were covered with impenetrable willow brush, tangled by years of spring flood water. At the time of the accident, the river water was still well into the willow brush on the islands. The rising and falling water, over the years, had cut some paths through the willows and the gravel-based soil of the islands. A person could pass through these openings in a deep knee bend or on hands and knees.

Within hours of the accident, a helicopter had searched over the river to the point where the Beaver River joins the Columbia. No sign of the man or any of his gear was found. Police and the remaining workers walked the river wherever the terrain allowed, but also failed to locate any trace of the man.

It was well into the summer when railway workers found the first clue. They were working near the downstream end of the rail siding when they found a pair of muddy and torn work pants that still had a leather belt buckled on them. They called our office in Golden and two of us drove to the siding location.

The replacement bridge had been completed and we were able to cross the river to meet the railway workers.

The smell of the clothing left no doubt that the pants had recently been on a decomposing body. The trousers had been found near the railway tracks in an area where animals frequently cross the river. As this area is on the border of Glacier National Park and is home to grizzly bears, it was with more than a little concern that my partner and I entered the river channel to search for more evidence of the dead man.

The river was now low enough that the islands were accessible on foot. We worked our way into the tangled brush on the first island and began searching. The only accessible areas were the shorelines of the island and the paths cut by the river. It was in one of these passages that we found the tracks of a grizzly in the muddy ground. We left tracks less than an inch deep, but the bear had sunk much deeper into the same mud. My size eleven boots would fit inside the bear tracks with room to spare; an observation that caused the hair on the back of my neck to stand on end. I assured my partner that by the time we were able to see the bear in that bush, it would be so close that I couldn't miss it with the rifle I carried.

At the upstream end of one of the paths through the island, we found a heavy leather work boot. The boot was laced, with the leg bones still inside, bitten off even with the boot tops. A depression in the mud near the boot was likely where the body had been washed up by the river on the day of the drowning. The depression was at the beginning of drag marks, caused when the bear pulled the body deeper into the brush. The drag marks led a short distance to where the bear had obviously tramped around for some time, mauling and eating the body. A second boot lay in the midst of the tramped area. Like the first, the bones had been snapped off evenly with the top of the boots. Nothing other than the boots remained there.

The trousers may have been dropped near the railway tracks by the bear, or by other animals, possibly coyotes or wolverines. A complete search of all the islands and the surrounding area revealed nothing more of the man or his gear. The bear had either carried away some of the body or completely consumed it. The trampled area indicated to me that it had been eaten right there. The femur bones of a man are large and tough, but a grizzly can chew them into pieces small enough to swallow.

The boots and trousers were all we had to establish that the remains were those of the workman from the bridge. The recovered items were tentatively identified by family members, and were taken by them for disposal at their discretion.

This was another situation where basic safety measures had not been followed. Had the lost worker been wearing a personal flotation device, he would most likely have suffered some degree of hypothermia and a little embarrassment. There have been huge gains made in the use of safety equipment by workers today. At that time, however, the workers themselves would make fun of someone who chose to use basic safety gear on the job. Progress in these areas comes slowly, and at a tragic price.

Bear in the Air

The use of aircraft to detect speeding drivers and any number of other violations was a common practice on British Columbia highways during the 1980s. It was a very effective method in the wide open spaces of the Cariboo. The system was simple: wide white stripes were painted across the highway at five hundred meter intervals for two and a half kilometres; then an intercept area of at least one kilometre was left open, followed by another two and a half kilometres marked again with the measured white stripes. Only the intercept area needed to be straight and level, for safety purposes. Two or three of us would take part in the measuring and painting of the marks so that any one of us could give evidence as to the accuracy of the marks and how they were measured and placed. The police officer in the airplane was trained for timing, recording notes and keeping the suspect vehicle in constant observation until it was assigned a number and turned over to the member on the highway in the intercept area.

We decided to run an aircraft operation one Friday afternoon on Highway 97 south of Quesnel. One member headed
south in a marked patrol car to work routine patrol checks
while waiting for the aircraft and police observer to get in position. About the time he reached the marked air patrol zone, he
overheard urgent radio calls from Williams Lake detachment,
which is about seventy-five miles south of Quesnel on Highway
97. The patrol cars and members from Williams Lake were in
pursuit of a stolen car and were headed north toward Quesnel.
The Quesnel member drove south to assist the Williams Lake
patrol cars.

Meanwhile, I was clearing up some routine matters in
Quesnel in preparation to work in the intercept area with the
first patrol member, who was now involved in the stolen car incident. Soon the aircraft was airborne and had established radio
contact with the Quesnel office and with me in my unmarked
patrol car. In a few moments the aircraft was over the operation
zone, but I was still in town.

The officer who had responded to the stolen car call was
now about thirty miles farther south of the intercept area where
the car thief had left the highway and was trying to become
invisible in the forest on a network of secondary roads. We decided to assist with the aircraft. It took only minutes for the
airplane to reach the area where the stolen car had left the highway. The thief had chosen an area with a network of roads, but
he was so obvious from the aircraft that there was no contest
at all. He finally abandoned the car and ran into the bush in a
desperate attempt to get away. The trees in that area were small
and thin, enabling the aircraft spotter to keep close tabs on his
progress. With some skilful flying and signalling, the aircrew actually herded the suspect out onto a road where a police car was
waiting.

While all the excitement was going on with the car thief,

I had finished my errands in Quesnel and made my way to the aircraft zone. I was waiting for the airplane to get back from the area where the luckless car thief was now in custody. I set up my radar and was measuring traffic speeds in the aircraft zone. It was not long until I was ticketing a driver for a radar-detected violation, and before I had finished writing the ticket, the aircraft returned.

Within a minute of his arrival, the aircraft spotter was calling me and counting down cars to identify speeders he had timed. In no time at all, I had four drivers waiting for their tickets and the plane was slowly circling at a discreet distance overhead. In all the rush, I had forgotten to turn off my radar set. I was a little snowed under so I called the aircraft and asked that they hold off unless they spotted a really hot one.

The aircraft made a wider circle and cruised a little north of the marked zone to give me a chance to get caught up. I was writing at maximum speed and hoping the second car would soon return from the car-thief chase. About the time I had cleared one of our backlogged customers, the radio crackled and the aircraft observer called to advise they were watching a hot one and were waiting for him to get to the first timing mark. The spotter in the aircraft estimated the speed at one hundred and forty kilometres per hour.

I tried to write faster.

The aircraft observer called again to confirm the vehicle was timed in the first zone at one hundred and forty-five kilometres and was closing fast on my location. The airborne observer told me that the speeding car held that speed until it was less than one kilometre from me, where it braked sharply and continued at a speed of about sixty kilometres per hour. The aircraft called to inform me of the colour of the car and finally to confirm that the next one coming to me was the violator.

I still had two vehicles waiting. I stepped out to signal the now slowly moving car to stop. The lone male driver moved to the right but continued past me about fifty yards to where he finally stopped on the right shoulder. I jogged over to the car and advised him that he was being stopped for speeding, that I would require his papers, and that I would get to him as soon as I was clear of the other waiting cars. I returned to the other violators.

What I did not know at the time was that this guy had a radar detector. The detector had warned him of my radar set and he had not seen the aircraft overhead. He sat for a moment, assuming that I was a one-person radar operation, and thought about his situation and mine. I was busy with the other violators and would not likely be able to give chase; he had a very fast car and could probably outrun me if I did chase him. I heard the roar of the engine and the howl of the tires as he sped away. The unfortunate fellow was heading toward the second police car, which was now returning from assisting with the car thief. I called the airplane and saw it make an immediate sharp turn to pursue the luckless runaway. The airplane was in position and timed him out of the marked zone at speeds up to one hundred and ninety kilometres per hour.

The airborne policeman was now in radio contact with the other police car, which was preparing to stop the runaway a few kilometres down the road. Imagine the cold sweat when his radar detector told him there was another police car nearby! What should he do now? He wisely pulled over and faced the music.

Given a choice of three Motor Vehicle Act offences—two speeding tickets and one for failing to comply with police directions—or one Criminal Code offence for dangerous driving, the driver chose the three traffic tickets.

Both the pilot and the policeman in the airplane agreed that that afternoon had been the most fun and exciting few hours they had enjoyed in a long time. As for the high-speed driver, he got his driver's license back after a few months, gave his radar detector away, and became a much more prudent driver.

Policing the Fringe

The isolated interior community of part-time loggers, miners and welfare recipients in this story was typical of many small towns to be found in the dark corners of British Columbia in the 1970s. Many of its citizens would fit the popular definition of rednecks that says if their porch fell down it would kill more than four dogs, they think "harass" is two words, and so on. It was forty miles from the detachment where I was stationed but it was in our policing area.

The little village had a community hall, a building from a bygone era that had been built by a sawmill company in the fifties and early sixties. The hall was the local citizens' gathering place for weddings, birthday parties, funerals and other such celebrations. The hall was also used for community dances from late spring until fall. These dances frequently ended in all-out brawls where many received injuries from drunken bare knuckled fighting and the occasional use of weapons.

At that time communities like this harboured a strong spirit of independence and wanted to be left alone to do whatever they would tolerate among themselves. The police were not welcome unless one or more of the locals had suffered severe injuries in a fight or accident. Even when the police were required to sort out one of their frequent problems, there was a serious lack of cooperation, so we made sure we had a good reason before we got involved. The violence increased with each event and local grudges grew as the dance season wore on.

The regular combatants began to arm themselves with a variety of tools that could serve as brass knuckles, and a few chose to carry knives. The situation was exacerbated by young people from our community and those from another place beyond the trouble spot who flocked in to see the action and to enjoy the wide open liquor and pot-smoking scene. In spite of our limited police resources, it became obvious that some intervention was necessary.

Four of us and two cars were dispatched to try and cool the next expected debacle. During the forty-mile drive to the scene we learned by radio that there had been a vehicle incident of some kind at the dance hall, and a young woman was injured. An ambulance was en route somewhere behind us. Our somewhat reluctant pace up to that time suddenly became an emergency requiring lights and sirens. We arrived at the front of the hall and were met with a barrage of liquor bottles thrown from among the crowd around the door. It seemed that the accident report had been false, or that the majority of the celebrants were not aware of it. Either way, it was not a healthy environment to be in.

A person approached our cars from the back and advised that the accident was on a lot adjacent to the hall, where overflow vehicles were parked. We moved our cars to the accident scene where we found that a young woman had been squatting behind a vehicle to urinate when the car had suddenly backed up. She had found herself tipped over and partly under the rear end of the car. Her screams had alerted the reversing driver and he had stopped, leaving her with minor injuries and a bare ass for all to see as they tried to assist. We organized a group of the less intoxicated partiers to lift the rear of the vehicle, and the girl was freed from her predicament. The ambulance arrived as she was removed from under the car and they took her away to the hospital. She was discharged upon arrival there.

We then turned our attention back to the hall. The arrival and departure of the ambulance right next door had to have come to the attention of most of the crowd, but it seemed to have no effect on their conduct. The crowd surged around us as we approached the door of the hall. They continued to drink beer and the air hung heavy with pot smoke. They yelled obscenities and threatened us.

This was the first time I had observed a phenomenon that was to become more common in later years: several of the women in the crowd exposed their breasts by grabbing the front of their clothing and lifting it up over their faces. I still do not understand the purpose of such flashing, but it was certainly the topic of conversation among us on our way home. We made our way to the front of the hall where we found the source of the music: a drummer, a guitarist and a violin. We informed the band that the party was over and that one of them should tell the crowd and then leave. One of the band people thanked us heartily and followed our instructions immediately.

We absorbed a great deal of abuse over the next hour as we seized and destroyed liquor and marijuana. We gradually forced the crowd out of the hall and secured the place, and then began to confiscate liquor and pot as fast as we could deal with it until the crowd faded away. We were fortunate that even here on the very edge of the thin veneer of civilization where there was no respect for authority, there was still fear. We needed to and did provide justification for that fear. We came away with some pains and bruises, but many of the crowd fared much worse. Another night on the fringe was over.

This little village was also notable for being home to one of the very few out-of-the-closet homosexuals that any of us knew of at that time. This man was part of the community because he had forced himself on them; he was aggressive and a very capable fighter. Some of the local establishment had tried to run him out of town; however, he had refused their suggestions and sent them away with a variety of injuries that only a very skilful and fit fighter could inflict. Once he had overcome the initial resistance of the villagers, things went smoothly for the most part. He was gradually accepted by the majority and would tell any of us that he liked living there and hoped to live out his life there. At that time, most of us were only beginning to understand the situation of the homosexual in society; we were, however, truly amazed that this fellow could live and survive in that environment.

During the first year of his being a part of the community he began a close relationship with a young man who had lived there all his life. The two were always together. They both found work in a nearby town and they commuted together. The local tongues wagged but no one took any issue with them. Later when we talked with people of the village, we learned that the young man had been very uncomfortable with the relationship. He avoided all his former friends and if he became caught up in any conversation with his peers he would, out of necessity, firmly deny that there was anything beyond friendship between him and the newcomer. I believe that had this young man confessed to his local friends that there was a homosexual relationship going on they would have beaten him severely or killed him.

Months went by and then the young man suddenly packed his belongings and moved to our community. He found work at the local lumber mill and rented a bachelor place for himself. In a very short time he had met and married a local girl. They lived in a rented trailer at the edge of town and were accepted as the "newlyweds" by the residents of the trailer park, who threw a grand baby shower shortly after the birth of their first baby. All appeared to be normal and good with the new young couple and their baby.

Just after midnight on a late fall Saturday night we received a panic call from the little village forty miles away. The police were required immediately. A few questions to the caller revealed that someone had tried to blow his head off with a shotgun. The caller was the former friend of our new resident and father. He denied knowing who had shot at him but said that he would talk to some of his neighbours and that he thought he would know the identity by the time we arrived. We later learned that he did know the shooter and that he had talked with him briefly after the shot was fired.

On our arrival at the scene of the shooting we spoke to the victim. He was very shaken up and was having great difficulty hearing us. He told us there had been a knock at his door. When he got up and opened the door he was confronted by a man with a shotgun. The shotgun muzzle was pointed at his head and a shot was fired at the same instant he opened the door. We could plainly see where the blast from a twelve gauge shotgun had gone into the ceiling just inside the front door of the little cabin. The path of the shot charge was visible through his hairline and in line with scratches on his forehead; his frontal scalp, eyelashes and eyebrows were lightly singed. His eyes were bloodshot and very tender from the hot gas of the gun blast, and he said that his ears were ringing like they had never done before.

In the first part of the interview, the victim advised that the shooter was the young man whom he had considered his friend and who had moved to our town. He emphatically denied any knowledge of a motive for the obvious attempt on his life. He refused our suggestion of medical attention and after we recorded a detailed statement, we left him at his residence. Prior to leaving the man, we learned that the perpetrator had driven back to his new hometown and turned himself in at our office. He had confessed to the shooting attempt and was prepared to plead guilty to whatever charges resulted from it.

The young man gave a very detailed statement of the events leading up to the attempted murder of his former lover. He stated that he had experienced homosexual thoughts and fantasies since his early stages of puberty. He had willingly entered into the relationship at the first opportunity after the man showed up in his village. What he was not able to deal with was the attitude of his former friends and neighbours. The relationship became more and more stressful; he was no longer accepted by his peers and his lover became very dominating and violent. He decided to "cut and run." His greatest regret at that moment was that he had not run far enough. He rambled on about how he should have gone to eastern Canada or the United States.

Shortly after he moved to our town he met his wife, and in a very short time she was pregnant with his child. For a few months his life was quite pleasant; he was still torn by thoughts of his former lover and his home village, but he had decided to present an image of what he considered to be normal. He and his young wife were excited about becoming parents and they were well accepted in their little neighbourhood.

Within a few weeks of his arrival in our community, he began to be visited by his ex-lover from the village. On some occasions the visits were quite pleasant but it became obvious that his ex-lover wanted him to move back and live with him. Whenever this topic arose during their visits things became very unpleasant. The young man insisted that he was going to make a life with his wife and expected child, but the older man was not prepared to accept this. Their visits often ended in both verbal and physical violence, with the young man always getting the worst of it.

The trauma of the visits intensified. Shortly after the birth of his child, the new father was confronted with an ultimatum: either he would return to his old love, or their relationship would be explained in detail to his wife. The stress was almost unbearable. He considered suicide. On the night of the shooting, he snuck the shotgun out of their trailer and put it under the seat of his car. He told his wife he was going to do some errands and would be home soon. He drank a large amount of liquor, hoping that would make it easier to end his life. While struggling with this state of mind he dwelt on his intense hatred for his former lover, and he found himself driving to his home. He knocked on the door and was prepared to kill him. As soon as the door was opened and he was sure of his target he fired at his head. The outcome would have been very different if the young man had been more familiar with firearms or less intoxicated. He simply misjudged the upward angle at which he was holding the shotgun.

His intended victim immediately grabbed the shotgun and took it away from him. The young man ran back to his car and drove away. No doubt we met him on our way to the incident. He had planned that he would kill the man, whom he saw as the source of his problems, and then end his own life. He was not sure if he would have been able to commit suicide. The loss of the shotgun took care of the need for that decision. As he drove toward home he decided to go to the police and lay it all out before them.

The young man was sentenced to two years less a day. His marriage ended, and his ex-friend chose to pursue other interests.

Bush Madness

In the fall of 1970, two young men set out from the Vancouver area to hunt deer. They were directed into the Lytton area by experienced hunter friends who had taken a good number of mule deer from the Fraser Canyon. They had been told about an unused logging road that left the road between Lytton and Lillooet to climb the canyon wall to the rim. Here, the steep wall gave way to rolling hills where past logging activity had left large open areas. The new growth in these clear-cut areas was a favourite browsing ground for deer and moose.

The two young men had been childhood friends; they worked and played together and had been on hunting adventures before. This trip to Lytton was their first hunt with just the two of them. Their plan was to spend two days on the east side of the Fraser River in the area about fourteen miles north of Lytton. They would take a room at Lytton and spend their daylight hours in the search for deer.

They left home early and reached the foot of the old logging road at about ten o'clock. The road was rough and rocky, but they were able to drive up with no difficulty until they reached the elevation where the early snow had not melted. They installed their tire chains and continued up the hill, the snow on the ground becoming deeper as they continued their climb. They were about to give up driving any further when they realized that the road grade had suddenly flattened out: they had reached the rim of the canyon.

It was about noon when they found a place to get their truck off the roadway. They shared a lunch as they prepared for the hunt. There was about a foot of snow on the ground, a few inches of which had fallen the day before. Everything was coming together for them. The new snow would show them the fresh tracks of deer and it would quieten their footsteps.

The sky was overcast with a high cloud layer that was thick enough to prevent any determination of direction from the sunlight. The two friends made a hasty plan; one chose to walk along the road beyond the truck while the other would climb a ridge to the right of the roadway. They were to meet at the truck after about two hours.

The hunter on the road walked about a mile beyond the parked truck. He told us that along the way he saw several sets of deer tracks and took the time to follow some of them a short distance from the road. His tracks were observed the following day and it became quite obvious that this fellow had a great respect, or fear, for the unknown woods. On the first occasion that he encountered a deer track, he paced around on the road but did not step over the edge to follow the tracks. He repeated this action at the next two sets of tracks. On the fourth encounter, the deer tracks crossed an open area and could be clearly seen for several hundred feet from where they crossed the road. The hunter followed these tracks to a point just past the middle of the open area before returning to the road in his own tracks.

That little jaunt was the greatest distance he had been off the road in his entire walk of about one mile and back. He was about one mile from the truck when he heard a rifle shot from the direction his friend had gone. He heard a second shot within a few minutes of the first.

The road hunter returned to the truck after hearing the shots and waited there rather than following his friend's tracks into the woods. It was about eight p.m. when he came to the police office in Lytton to report that his friend had not come out of the bush. The missing man was dressed for the conditions and had some experience as a hunter and camper; we concluded that there was no immediate need to attempt a rescue in the darkness. The man took a room in town and arrived at the police office early the next morning. We suggested that he return to their parking spot as he would likely find his friend waiting there. A helicopter had been requested and we planned to search from the aircraft as soon as it was available.

The helicopter arrived in Lytton about nine a.m. and within a few minutes we were over the area where the hunter had last been seen. The truck was parked again where it had been the day before, and the hunter who had contacted us was nearby. It appeared that his fear of the woods was greater than his concern for his friend who had been out all night.

The missing hunter's track from the truck was clearly visible from the helicopter. He had climbed about half a mile to the top of a ridge and then walked along the ridge, which slowly angled away from the road. At a point where the ridge top was about three quarters of a mile from the road, he had shot a deer. We landed the helicopter nearby and examined the kill site. He had properly field-dressed the deer and cooled the body cavity with snow. After tying a short piece of rope to the antlers of the small buck he had started to drag it straight down the side of the ridge, knowing that the road ran parallel below him. Under the overcast sky and with the excitement of the successful hunt, he had lost his bearings and gone down the wrong side of the ridge.

We returned to the helicopter and started to follow his tracks down the hill. We had flown about half a mile when we saw the missing man lying face up in the snow where he had dropped and died from exhaustion and hypothermia.

We landed again and confirmed that he was dead. Examination of the tracks took us to a point nearly two miles from the kill site where the young man must have realized that he was lost. He left the deer and started to walk back in his tracks but after a short distance, panic overtook him and he began to run. He fell several times over the next few hundred yards but scrambled to his feet again and continued running. At a point about a mile from the deer carcass he threw his overcoat into the snow and continued on; after another short way he left his rifle and staggered on. He fell and got up several times in the short distance from where he left his rifle to where he died.

Although the coroner's inquiry ruled that the man died of exposure and hypothermia, the real killer of the young man was a condition that experienced backcountry people call "bush madness." He had been well equipped to spend the night in the woods if necessary; he had dry matches and adequate clothing, and he could have eaten from the deer to keep up his body heat and energy.

There is a great fear and embarrassment in men to admit that they are lost. This fear leads to irrational behaviour and needless tragedy. I have been told of search parties observing a lost man actually hiding from his rescuers when they arrived to guide him out of his trouble.

Had the confused hunter stopped long enough to gather his thoughts, he would have realized that all he had to do was backtrack himself to the road. Had his partner gathered his courage and tracked his hunting companion after hearing the shots, the two of them would have found strength from each other and made it out with venison and a good hunting story.

Deadman Floater

Word had reached us at Lytton Detachment that a woman had fallen into the flooding waters of Deadman Creek. Rescue efforts and a search of the creek had not been successful, and she was presumed dead. Deadman Creek flows into the Thompson River from the north near the west end of Kamloops Lake.

The incident had happened about four miles from where Deadman Creek flows into the Thompson River. The Thompson then tumbles down its canyon for nearly seventy miles through Ashcroft and Spences Bridge to where it joins the Fraser River at Lytton. We had been informed of the incident because we were in the downstream water system and the body might pass through or become lodged in our area.

There had been nearly three weeks of beautiful warm spring weather since the woman had gone missing. A couple driving up the highway decided to take a break at Goldpan Campsite, about fifteen miles up the Thompson River from Lytton. They parked their car and went for a walk along the edge of the river.

Their walk was interrupted by the sighting of the partially nude and grotesquely swollen body of a woman floating in a small eddy. The man rushed back to his vehicle and returned with a few feet of light rope. As the body came around in the eddy he was able to toss a noose over one foot and tie the body to a small tree on the shore. His wife drove to the nearest business place and called us. She then returned to the campsite and remained there with her husband until my partner and I arrived from Lytton.

We recorded the information that the couple provided and they gladly left the area. It was obvious that identification of the body by appearance would not be possible, so there was no point in having one of her family members attend there. It was also quite evident that the body could not be pulled from the water in one piece without some special equipment.

We called the RCMP detachment at Ashcroft, where the original incident had been reported, and advised them we had most likely located the body of their missing person. The detachment commander at Ashcroft was very grateful for our assistance. He requested that we recover the body and turn it over to the regional coroner at Kamloops. This would necessitate my taking the body to Lytton for storage while I did the paperwork to get authorization to move the body to Kamloops. I responded that although we were always glad to be of assistance, I had no intention of taking this body back to Lytton. The body would have to be taken to Kamloops for autopsy and identification, so there was no point in starting out by taking it farther away from there.

Just as the radio conversation began between me and the detachment commander, the last of the uniformed police members at Ashcroft left the office on the run. Overhearing our conversation had somehow caused them each to suddenly recall a very urgent investigation that required their immediate attention.

The Ashcroft commander then tried another flanking operation. He called the regional coroner's office at Kamloops and was able to convince them to send someone from one of the funeral establishments to recover the body.

My partner and I waited out the two hours while keeping the floater under constant observation and being ever aware of the fickle air currents near the river. We watched the river and observed how floating objects would enter the little eddy on their way downstream. Each bit of debris that came floating down the river would enter the pool and circle slowly in a counter-clockwise direction. On the fourth rotation it would again enter the river and continue downstream. The quick action of the passing motorist had prevented our guest from continuing her journey to the sea. His action brought closure to the grieving family and, without question, was a commendable act. We both wished he had done his good deed somewhere else.

The man from the funeral home was experienced and capable. He came equipped with hip waders and a very large body bag. He waded into the water and easily slipped the open bag under and around the floating body. He was then able to partly close the bag. With our assistance, the body was easily pulled out of the river. Once on shore, most of the river water escaped from the bag, allowing it to be completely closed and placed in the funeral home vehicle for the trip to Kamloops.

The coroner was able to identify the body as that of the missing woman from Deadman Creek. The autopsy established that she died by drowning.

Poached Venison

The deer of Vancouver Island are small but they make up for their size in numbers. During the time we lived in Comox the deer were at the top of their population cycle and were a nuisance in many ways. We tried to grow a garden but found that without a very high and expensive fence, the deer would take their share first and leave us to make do with whatever they left. They would eat anything that had been planted in a garden plot, but they had their favourites; green beans were at the top of their preference list, followed closely by carrots, lettuce, corn and peas. If any rose bushes were available they would take a break from the garden to eat all the new shoots from the roses.

One beautiful fall evening at about eleven p.m., a couple were sitting in their living room when they saw movement below a street light a few doors from their home. Closer observation revealed that there were several deer wandering along the street; the people turned off their lights to get a better look.

There were four or five does in the herd and a proud little four-point buck. The little buck was keeping a close watch on his does, but he did allow them to romp around under the light for a few minutes.

Suddenly a shot was heard. The deer ran in every direction, but the little buck lay dying under the street light. The observers were very upset and immediately phoned the police. While they were talking to the dispatcher, they reported that a pickup truck had just pulled up beside the deer, and that two men had grabbed the dying animal and thrown it into the truck box.

The police arrived shortly, but by then there was nothing at the scene except a pool of blood. The witnesses had not been able to see the men well enough to identify them, but they did notice an unusual paint-job on the truck. This information was broadcast on the police radio from the scene and another police member recognized the suspect truck from having had dealings with the driver a few days prior. He passed the information to the car at the scene and gave them an address.

The address was checked and found to be in total darkness. Further checks at the rear of the property located the suspect truck parked near a small shed. Small streaks of light could be seen coming through cracks in the little shed. Tiptoe approach to the shed revealed that the truck engine was hot, there was blood in the truck box and three men were inside the shed drinking beer and dressing a buck deer.

The patrol retreated to the street so as not to be detected. A decision was made to let the poachers finish the messy job before announcing the police presence. About fifteen minutes later the door of the shed opened and one of the men came out and got a garden hose from the back of the house. The three were allowed to finish washing the venison before they were given the bad news.

The truck, the rifle and the deer were seized. One of the three plead guilty to a charge of dangerous use of a firearm, and all three plead guilty to poaching charges. The venison was given to the Native community.

Orphans

On a beautiful cloudless day in early June, a young couple were driving along a northern highway with their two sons. The parents were in the front of the compact car and their three and one-year-old sons were buckled into seats in the back. They were almost home from a short holiday trip to visit grandparents in another part of the province.

The young mother was driving their car when a full-sized pickup truck came toward them, travelling in the opposite direction. The highway was straight and level with shallow ditches on both sides. Another driver following the small car told us that the approaching truck slowly crossed the centre line and the small car began to move to the right to get away from it. At the last moment, the small car braked sharply and drove into the shallow ditch on the right side of the road. The oncoming truck continued across the highway and into the ditch where it slammed head-on into the now almost-stopped car.

The larger, heavier and higher truck rode up over the front

of the small car until its bumper was near the headrests on the front seats of the car. The two little boys in the back seat were not physically injured because their parents had taken all precautions for their safety; they were in properly fitted child restraints, properly fastened to the vehicle. But in that instant, the little passengers became orphans.

The driver of the truck was not seriously injured, but he was obviously drunk. He consented to a blood test, not because he was required to but because the cop who attended knew how to manipulate a drunk. The mess on the highway was cleaned up; the orphans were picked up by the devastated grandparents they had just visited, and the drunk was released on bail without deposit.

At the time of this incident, the Motor Vehicle Act of British Columbia provided for the immediate seizure of the driver's license of any person who caused the death of another person by a criminal act. A short time before this incident, however, the newly proclaimed Charter of Rights had made major changes to Canadian law, requiring that all statutes that allowed any form of sanction against an accused person before conviction be amended.

The bureaucrats in every provincial capital in Canada must have been on unlimited overtime to get this done. However, although they had done their utmost to amend every relevant statute, this provision of the Motor Vehicle Act of British Columbia had been overlooked. When they reprinted and distributed the revised copies of the statute, this offensive portion was still included.

I seized the killer's driver's license pursuant to the overlooked section, because that offensive clause was still part of printed law. The drunken driver was no stranger to the court; he had been convicted of impaired driving less than a year before he killed the young couple. He called his lawyer from my office. His lawyer, the same one who had defended him in the previous case, immediately called me and informed me that the existence of that law was an oversight and that I must return the license without delay. I suggested that I did not believe him and that I had no intention of returning the license.

This sequence of events caused a great stir in the legal system: lawyers called on judges, judges called their superiors, and the storm rapidly spread to the Attorney General's office. The reaction, and the speed of it, was amazing. One would think that the drunken killer's life had been threatened, rather than his right to drive a motor vehicle. In less than forty-eight hours I was called to the office of the Regional Crown Counsel, where I received a lesson about the new Canadian Charter of Rights. I was again asked to return the driver's license.

I suggested that the law I had applied was still valid because no amendment had been passed to alter it. I also indicated that I would turn the seized license over to the Crown Counsel and that he could return it to the killer if he felt that that was the proper thing to do. At that point, the Crown Counsel did not wish to have anything more to do with me, or the license. The following day, the driver's license was returned to the killer by one of the more senior and compliant police officers at the detachment.

The amendment to the Motor Vehicle Act, removing that offensive section, was drafted and passed within sixty days. The killer was eventually convicted of impaired driving, although it took more than six months, during which time he was free to drive all he wanted. He was fined a few hundred dollars and his license was suspended for one year.

The orphans and their devastated grandparents were heard from no further—at least by the court.

Incident at Tank Hill

Tank Hill is one of the many landmarks along the canyon highway between Hope and Ashcroft. In good weather it is hardly noticed by motorists, but when snow or ice covers the surface it can become a very memorable challenge. Tank Hill is in the Thompson River canyon about nine miles east of Lytton. In the years that I worked at Lytton I do not recall hearing any history about this location and I have no idea how or why it got that name. The only significant thing I know about it is that it is the highest point on the highway between Lytton and Spences Bridge.

Three teenaged men from the Vancouver area had been on a brief holiday in the interior of the province. Their holiday was possible because they had borrowed a very old travel trailer and one of them owned a Rambler station wagon. The old Rambler was not the type of car that was popular with young people but it was fairly reliable and it was all they had. The old car had pulled the trailer and carried them and all their gear as far as Prince George and into a lot of side trips along the route.

The three were now heading home with a lot of good times behind them and no money. They had enough money to cover their gasoline and they were looking forward to getting home for something to eat. Their lack of funds was the main reason that they were still travelling at about one o'clock in the morning.

The three travellers with their Rambler and their funny old trailer were winding their way down the Thompson River canyon toward Lytton. They weaved along the river's edge and then up the steep grade known as Tank Hill. As they came around the long left curve over the top of the hill, they saw the lights of an oncoming vehicle.

The young man driving the station wagon realized at the last minute that the oncoming vehicle was well to the left of the centre line. He braked and moved to the right; there was a wide shoulder at that spot and he moved over completely onto the shoulder. The oncoming vehicle continued toward him in spite of his evasive move. The car and trailer could go no farther away from the path of the oncoming vehicle, which hit the old station wagon about on the hinges of the driver's door. Fortunately, the oncoming vehicle was travelling quite slowly and the old station wagon was very nearly stopped at the moment of impact.

The offending vehicle was an International Travelall. It was bigger and heavier than the old Rambler; it scrubbed along the side of the station wagon and shoved it sideways as it went. The International then disengaged from the station wagon, but the old trailer had swung over and was directly in front of it. The International hit the trailer squarely and totally destroyed it in an instant.

The three young men could hardly believe what had just happened to them. The driver tried to get out but his door was jammed; the front passenger jumped out and the driver slid across and got out behind him. The third young man was in the back seat and he got out on the right side from the back door. The three then ran around the front end of their car and along the damaged side. There was just enough moonlight for the three to have some limited visibility once their eyes became accustomed to the partial darkness.

The left side windows and the back window were all broken out of the station wagon. The trailer was gone except for the floor and the axle. The three then noticed that the vehicle that had hit them was nowhere to be seen. The first thing that came to their minds was that the Travelall had carried on around the curve behind them and left the scene. The three boys stood bewildered by their fate for a moment until they heard the echo of something crashing down in the canyon far below them.

It was about a thousand feet down from the edge of the highway to the Canadian Pacific Railway tracks. The three young men followed the trail of debris from their trailer across the gravel-surfaced area to the edge of the cliff, where it was obvious that the other vehicle had gone over. They had heard the last echoes of the crashing of the Travelall as it plunged down toward the railway tracks.

The Travelall carried three people in their middle twenties: two men and a woman. They had come to Lytton from Merritt to visit some friends, and had spent the late afternoon and all evening in the bar at Lytton. After the bar closed at midnight, they visited outside the bar for a short time and then set out to drive back to Merritt. They were all intoxicated. Whichever one was at the wheel probably passed out or fell asleep.

The report of a very serious accident reached us at Lytton and we attended immediately, along with the local ambulance. The information that there may be a vehicle and people on their tracks was immediately passed to the Canadian Pacific Railway. We were unable to see any sign of the vehicle or people from the highway. Our knowledge of the terrain told us that it was very unlikely that any of the bodies or parts of the vehicle had stopped before reaching the railway. We drove back toward Lytton about half a mile to a point where it was possible to walk from the highway down to the railway tracks. We made our way to the tracks with flashlights and then walked back to the area where we expected the wreckage to be.

The bodies and the wreckage were all in close proximity. The three bodies were laid out head to foot in a shallow ditch on the uphill side of the railway tracks. There was no sign of life and nothing to indicate that any of them had been alive when they fell there. The main part of the crushed Travelall lay just beyond the bodies in the same ditch. The ambulance crew confirmed that there were no signs of life and that the vehicle was clear of the tracks. The emergency was over. Now we had to recover the bodies and gather all the available evidence for the coroner.

There was no place where we could get a vehicle near the railway tracks between the accident scene and Lytton, and the same situation existed for ten miles or more in the other direction. We contacted the local railway track service crew and asked if they could assist us with a track patrol car and something to carry the bodies. The crew responded with their motorized track patrol car and a little flat car that they towed along. We met them at the scene and loaded the three bodies. I rode with the two railway men and the bodies for the nine miles to Lytton, where we transferred the bodies to the ambulance at a level crossing.

The following day the wreckage of the Travelall was picked up by a railway mounted crane and hauled to Lytton. Our investigation showed that the vehicle belonged to one of the dead people. It was not licensed or insured. The young owner of the old Rambler had only the most basic of insurance, so they were unable to recover anything of their property. They were fortunate to have escaped injury, and their financial loss was small.

The Curse of
Jackass Mountain

A young Prince George man had spent several months working for a local manufacturer of machinery for the logging and sawmill industries.

So far he had been working around the company yard, which he did not like, but there was a good chance he could move to a driving job if he stuck it out until one became available. He had recently obtained his upgraded driver's license and the necessary air brake certification to drive highway transport trucks.

The company had a shipment of steel plate and logging equipment to go to a location in the Lower Mainland. The trucks normally used for such hauls were all away on other deliveries. There was an old and tired unit available; it was kept on the job to take care of local deliveries and work inside the company yard. The customer needed the shipment immediately so a decision was made to send the old unit. This bad decision was compounded by a shortage of experienced drivers and the young man volunteering to make the delivery.

The inexperienced driver left Prince George late in the afternoon, intending to get to his Fraser Valley destination early the next morning. He had either overlooked the requirement to do a thorough brake examination or had been unable to convince the owners that the truck and trailer were in crucial need of repairs.

The old truck lumbered along the highway until near midnight, when it reached a popular truck stop at Kanaka Bar in the Fraser Canyon. A steady rain had been falling for an hour or more. The young man guided the truck into the parking lot and set the trailer brakes before walking across the highway to the coffee shop.

While parked, the trailer brakes on this old rig were held by compressed air. The air pressure turned a cam mechanism, which spread the brake shoes and forced them against the brake drums. The brake linings on this old trailer were almost completely worn away, and the drums were worn until there was only a small portion of their original thickness remaining. These two factors caused the brake cam to turn beyond centre on one of the trailer wheels so that it jammed.

After enjoying a piece of pie and coffee and a visit with some old-time drivers, the new driver returned to his truck. He released the trailer brakes in preparation to drive away. The jammed brake on the over-centred wheel remained applied, but there was no indication to the driver at that point. He pulled out of the parking area and onto the highway. As he pulled up the first grade toward the top of Jackass Mountain, he realized that the truck engine was working much harder than it had on similar grades. Through his mirrors he was able to see the reason: the trailer wheel with the jammed brake was locked up and skidding. The truck was now in a narrow and winding part of the highway where there was no place to stop safely. The driver decided to drag the crippled trailer to a place just past the summit of the mountain where he could pull onto a wide shoulder.

The parking spot chosen by the young driver was a good safe place to pull over to be clear of other traffic, but it was at the top of the long and steep downgrade known as Jackass Mountain. This placed the truck and trailer on a downward slope with only the parking brakes holding it from careening away down the grade. The roadway was cut into the side of the mountain. At the right edge of the spot where the truck was parked was a drop-off of about a thousand feet toward the Fraser River.

A quick examination of the trailer brakes, with the aid of a flashlight, showed the driver why that wheel had been skidding. The correct thing to do would be to park the truck until the worn parts could be replaced, but the young driver understood just enough about air brakes to know there was a haywire way he could free up the jammed brake and continue with the rush delivery. In order to work on the one brake that was jammed, however, he had first to release all the trailer brakes.

To prevent the truck from rolling forward and taking off down the hill, he decided to block one wheel with a boulder. He found a wedge-shaped rock about twelve inches around and four inches thick. He placed this rock in front of one of the truck's drive wheels and released the parking brakes. He then went to the rear end of the trailer with his flashlight and a hammer. He crawled under the bed of the trailer in the darkness as mud and water dripped down on him. He got himself into a position near the back of the rear axle where he could get at the air brake assembly. One good whack on the stuck brake caused it to let go. The truck lurched forward and nearly stopped when the drive wheel came against the rock he had placed there to block it. It nearly stopped again when the next set of wheels came against the rock.

The driver was now fully aware that he had either underestimated the size of the rock required to hold the truck or that he had not placed it tightly enough against the wheel. The trailer had now moved away from above him. He sprang to his feet and raced toward the cab of the accelerating unit. He caught up to the cab in time to get his foot on the step in the side-mounted fuel tank and his hand on the door handle. At that instant the truck tractor tipped as the right wheels went over the edge of the roadway. The driver threw himself backward, away from the doomed machine.

The young man landed in a heap at the edge of the thousand-foot drop. For a moment he thought the truck had hung up on the edge of the roadway in the darkness, but he then realized he could no longer hear the idling engine. He then heard the first major impact far below, like an explosion that echoed around the canyon walls and was followed by several lesser crashes as the machine and its load disintegrated and came to rest.

In daylight the next morning, the scene was quite amazing. The largest remaining piece of the unit was the deck of the trailer. It lay among the debris of the truck and load, with a half twist in its length and the wheels no longer attached. The frame and drive wheels of the truck tractor were next in size. The engine and transmission had torn away from the frame and were somewhere among the debris. Neither the cab of the truck nor any pieces of it were identifiable from the point where it had gone over.

The naming of Jackass Mountain had nothing to do with this story. According to Fraser Canyon lore, a heavily loaded jackass, nearing the summit during the gold rush of 1860, suddenly reared and threw itself over the side of the mountain. The legend was that the animal had chosen death rather than continue the life it was experiencing. It is not known if the young man, upon realizing what he had done, entertained thoughts of following the jackass's example. After considering all the circumstances we chose not to prosecute the driver in connection with this incident. He seemed to fully understand how close he had come to certain death and how the condition of the old truck had contributed to his near encounter with the Grim Reaper. I do not know if the young man chose to remain in the trucking industry; but as he stood with me at the edge of the highway that day he swore he would never again drive a vehicle of any kind unless it was in perfect mechanical condition.

The Dog Who Wouldn't Flee

The winters in the North Columbia area of British Columbia are known for their abundant fall of snow. The highway through Rogers Pass crosses the northern end of the Selkirk Mountains and was constructed to eliminate the old road known as the Big Bend. The Big Bend followed the Columbia River valley around the end of the same mountain range and it was well-known as a tough trip in the summer and something to be avoided in winter. The Rogers Pass highway shortened the trip from Golden to Revelstoke by nearly a hundred miles and four hours.

The main problem with the Rogers Pass route is the extreme snow conditions encountered there. The summit of the highway receives about five hundred inches of snowfall every winter. This heavy snow area extends throughout that region from the Arrow Lakes, south of Revelstoke, all the way up the Columbia River to its source at Columbia Lake.

This story happened in the Invermere area one winter when the snowfall was a little more abundant than average. Keeping the roads open that winter had been a constant challenge. A man who lived near Invermere was employed in the struggle to keep an access road open to a logging area. He had parked his truck and was walking along a freshly snowplowed road. His purpose was to mark where the side of the road ended and the plowed snow began; without marks on the totally white expanse, the logging truck drivers could not tell exactly where they were in relation to the road.

The man worked along the side of the mountain probing the snow with a metal rod and marking where he found solid ground. The markings were made by placing small evergreen tree limbs into the snow. As he worked along the steep slope, the thick layer of fresh snow gave away from the slope above the road and it sloughed down over him and the freshly cleared road. The man was knocked down and buried in a great mass of powdery snow.

Fortunately, the snow had not come from a great distance up the mountain. It was more than he could free himself from, but it was not as heavy as major avalanche snow.

There were other workers in the immediate area and they noticed the slide almost right away. The man's truck was nearby but he was nowhere to be seen, so it was obvious that he had been buried by the slide.

The local avalanche rescue group was called and they attended with their snow probing equipment. They used a systematic search method. A line of people would start from a marked location and work their way across the area where the missing person was thought to be. Each person had a thin probe stick that was long enough to reach to the frozen earth or rock under the accumulated snow. They would each sink their probe into the snow until it struck bottom, then lift their probe out, step forward one pace in unison with the other searchers in the line, and probe again. This system worked because if a body was lying somewhere in the snow, the probe would be stopped short of the normal ground level. A body would also produce a noticeably different feel through the probe to the hands of the searcher.

In this situation, the rescue people assumed that the man had been swept up by the sloughing snow and carried down the mountainside to where the bulk of the snow had stopped, about a hundred yards from the road. The roadway where he had been working was completely filled in with snow.

The snow had fallen throughout the previous night and about eighteen inches of fluffy dry snow had accumulated. When morning came the storm had moved out of the area, leaving a beautiful clear sunny day. There was no wind and the sunshine was so intense that most of the searchers were working in their shirtsleeves. The probe work had gone on for several hours with no positive result. Hope was fading of finding the man alive.

A friend remembered that the missing man had a mongrel dog at his home near Invermere. The dog was not obviously intelligent, but he was very fond of his owner. The friend drove to the man's farm and brought the dog to the snow slide. He had rigged a leash on the dog, and as soon as he arrived he took him out of the truck and led him down to where the searchers were working. The dog appeared very uninterested. He walked around on the leash, sniffed at the snow, and peed on the piles of snow here and there. He gently tugged on the leash, wanting to go back up to the road.

The friend, discouraged by the dog's inability to help, took the leash off, thinking that the animal would find its way home. But the dog did not return home. Instead, it trotted up to the area where the road lay buried under the avalanche and sat down on the snow, watching the searchers working below. The friend again put the leash on the dog and brought him down to the search area. The dog repeated his actions, and as soon as the leash was off, went back to the snow-covered road and sat down in the same spot as before.

The short winter day was coming to an end. The searchers were tired, but they speeded up their efforts, knowing that there was no chance of the man surviving if they did not find him before dark.

The road led to an active logging area high in the mountains. A crew and several logging trucks had gone into the area to work that morning, and they were now caught above the snow slide. The decision was made to use a large front-end loader to scoop up the snow from the roadway and carry it to a safe place to dump it so as not to interfere with the search activity. The loader started its work. It scooped up big bites of snow and carried them to a point just down the road, where it dumped them over the edge. The work was slow, but it would be completed by dark so the people above the slide could drive home.

While this was going on, the dog remained rooted at his chosen spot near the middle of the snow-covered section of roadway. As the machine worked its way toward the place where the dog was sitting he seemed to become a little agitated, but he would not move away. The removal of the next scoop of snow would obviously tumble the dog down to the freshly cleared roadway, but still he remained there. Suddenly, as the machine backed away with a load of snow, the dog jumped over the edge and stood by the waving hand of his master.

The man was quickly freed from the snow. He was very weak, tired and cold but otherwise unhurt. His dog was very excited and obviously glad that the workers had finally got around to digging his person out.

The man told us that he had been knocked to the ground suddenly and buried right where he had been standing. The snow was soft enough that he was able to clear a small area in front of his face and chest but he could not move any farther than that. He was about ten feet under when the slide stopped. He could see the shadows of people walking around above him in the bright sunshine. He yelled as loud as he could, but no sound reached the surface.

Obviously, the dog had known where the man was all along but no one at the scene could read the signals it provided. The little mongrel enjoyed a much-improved reputation around Invermere during the following weeks.

Bear Lovers Beware

This story comes out of the summit of the Rogers Pass on the Trans-Canada Highway where the Illecillewaet Glacier stands guard over the beautiful valley crossing the top of the Selkirk Mountains. The highway was new in 1966, as were all the facilities in the summit valley. The most impressive of the new structures was a full-service hotel that catered to the highway traffic and to those who went there to hike and experience the alpine wilderness.

This valley had been the original route of the Canadian Pacific Railway when it first crossed the nation in 1885. The mountain environment fought the railway with everything it had. Over five hundred inches of snow were dumped on the area every winter, and the resulting avalanches were truly awesome. In one incident, an avalanche crashed to the valley bottom and came so close to hitting a steam locomotive that the wind from the avalanche actually knocked the engine off the tracks. The railway company fought back by building snowsheds and by cutting trenches deep and wide enough for a train to pass through and then building timber roofs over the trenches. The sheds and the roofs of the trenches were often smashed by avalanches and the trenches were filled with concrete-like snow. The snow conditions were so fierce that in a single winter the railway lost nearly their entire track crews from both Revelstoke and Golden. An avalanche struck near the summit and killed the Revelstoke crew of forty men. The crew of about thirty-five men from Golden rushed into the valley in a rescue attempt, only to be struck and wiped out by another avalanche from the opposite side of the valley. Following that winter the railway company made the decision to construct a five mile tunnel to get the railway line out of the path of many of the deadly avalanches. The Connaught Tunnel was completed in about 1915, and the summit valley was again left to nature until the Trans-Canada Highway followed the original route of the railway five decades later.

The highway and the new hotel brought civilization to the wilderness with a bang. The valley hosted more people for the highway opening than had been there in the previous fifty years. Many people got jobs with the highway maintenance crews or as hotel staff and so became part-time residents of the valley. This new population in the wilderness would have an impact.

The route of the highway and the railway traverse both Glacier and Revelstoke National Parks. The summit area of the Rogers Pass lies near the centre of Glacier National Park. The National Park Service established an office at the summit to observe the human activity and to enforce their regulations.

During the early summer of the first year of the new highway, the Park Services people became aware of a grizzly sow with two cubs. The bears had established themselves in the valley of Cougar Creek, which rises away from the main valley a few miles west of the highway summit. Cougar Creek had lush forest in its natural unspoiled state, and had no doubt been home to a bear and her cubs every summer forever.

The National Parks people knew that the valley of Cougar Creek was too near the new population centre for the bears to be left entirely alone. The parks people observed the bear family for a few days until it was obvious that they were not transient; they considered the valley their home.

The park wardens made the decision to advise the new human population of the bear family and to request that everyone stay away from that area until the bears had moved along. Printed notices were placed in every location frequented by both tourists and the resident workers.

The staff at the new hotel included a young couple who were avid outdoors enthusiasts and amateur photographers. These two were very interested in the reported bear family; they could hardly wait for their next day off so they could get some great close-up photographs of these cute and cuddly little cubs. Their day off came and they were already walking along well into the valley of Cougar Creek when the sun came up. They had crossed some avalanche debris from the previous winter and had found signs of the bears feeding in the new vegetation along the edges of the slide path. Their excitement grew as they made their way along the side of the valley within earshot of the rapid creek below. They were now quite sure they were in the right area to meet the bears; the forest was more open, there was less undergrowth and the larger trees were more separated. There were open patches with new spring growth of alpine plants.

Without a warning sound the woman was suddenly knocked to the rocky ground and run over by the grizzly sow. In the terror of the sudden impact she became aware of a searing pain as the bear grabbed her upper arm in its jaws. For some reason the bear released the arm rather than shaking her like a rag doll. The woman's arm was punctured to the bone by the bite, and her shoulder was dislocated.

The woman was most likely spared by the presence of her friend and the need for the sow to deal with two threats to her young. After dropping the woman, the bear immediately knocked the man to the ground and began to chew at his head. He tried to get away but lost consciousness in a very short time.

The attack had come from behind at a time when the man was leading their way up the valley. The man and the bear were a few steps farther into the valley from where the woman lay on the ground. The woman sprang to her feet and ran for her life. She ran like she had never run before and hoped never to run again. The terrible pain in her arm and shoulder was completely out of her mind as she tore through the forest toward the highway.

When she reached the highway she was not a sight that tourists wanted to see, with blood flowing from her upper arm and shoulder, but she flagged down the first vehicle to come along and was taken to the first aid station at the highway summit. Her horror story spread rapidly around the little community. Luckily, there happened to be a helicopter doing some work in the area and the machine was commandeered by the local rescue group to determine the fate of the man in Cougar Creek.

The helicopter crew soon located the man and to everyone's surprise, he was alive. He had suffered horrible damage to his head and neck but no major arteries had been broken and he lived to be rescued in spite of massive blood loss and shock. One of the rescue crew said that there was more skull bone showing than there was remaining face and scalp. The man was rushed to medical facilities in Calgary where he underwent the first of what would be years of skin grafting and reconstructive surgery.

The man had very little recall of the attack. He was aware that the bear had hit his girlfriend and knocked her to the ground and that it had then attacked him. He figured that the bear had bitten at his head two or possibly three times and then left. The bear may have been distracted from the second attack by the first victim running away or it may have considered the job done and just walked away to care for its cubs. The bear was being guided by instinct, which demands that she provide protection for her young. She did not have any intention of eating the intruders, or she would have been more deadly in her efforts and she would have killed and buried both of them. Grizzlies seldom eat much of a fresh kill, preferring to cover the kill with whatever material is at hand to let it age, perhaps improving the flavour.

When the crisis of the rescue was over, the national park wardens held a conference to determine the fate of the grizzly sow and her cubs. The cubs were too young to survive without their mother even if they were captured and cared for at the best available facilities. By ignoring the warnings and provoking the attack, the nature-loving intruders had sealed the fate of all three bears. The day after the attack, another helicopter flew into the pristine valley of Cougar Creek. The sow and her two cubs were easily located in the alpine meadows and all three were shot dead.

Roadblock at Ten-Mile Bridge

Car chases are and always have been a very controversial issue among the police.

In my time there was little or no firm policy in British Columbia; the responsibility was left up to the individual involved at the outset of the incidents. Detachment commanders were expected to deal with the problem at their level and to accept the consequences of whatever took place on the roads within their jurisdictions. This non-policy had value in that the officer was allowed to make his or her own mistakes and to make a judgement call on all the facts that played a part at that moment. The capable detachment commanders would pass the discretion on to their officers and depend on their good judgement. Some commanders who feared responsibility would go so far as to put out a firm policy that no one was to enter into a car chase under any circumstances. The word would soon spread far and wide that the police at certain detachments would not pursue a vehicle and that the only thing to do in those areas was to run for it.

Hand in hand with the pursuit question was that of blocking the roadway to stop a vehicle that refused to pull over for the usual police signals. There seemed to be some consensus on the idea that an established case law prohibited the absolute blocking of a roadway. In spite of this, there were situations when a cop found himself faced with the decision of "stop this thing or some innocent person will almost certainly die."

This incident was one of those. A man who lived in Calgary had let his life get into such a state that he felt there was no hope or help available and that nothing could turn things around for him.

One evening his wife advised him that she could no longer remain in their relationship. This announcement was made, like most such proclamations, just as he came home from having a few too many drinks and a line or two of coke. This was just too much for him. His job was in jeopardy, he had huge debts, an insatiable thirst, a great liking for nose candy, and now his inconsiderate wife was leaving. He thought about the whole thing for a few seconds and then did the only thing that came to his fuddled mind: he beat her senseless.

Now believing that he had committed murder, he went to a small locker in the bottom of the hall closet and got his .44 Magnum revolver and a box of fifty rounds of ammunition for the big weapon. He then left the house without checking the condition of his wife, who was still lying on the living room floor in a pool of blood. He walked to the garage where he had parked his van, backed it out and left in a cloud of smoke from the spinning tires. The noise of the van was very unusual and got the attention of all the neighbours.

The van was equipped with a huge engine block and every possible accessory to get the absolute maximum power out of the big motor. All this had contributed to the man's financial problems, but the van could almost fly, and he was very proud of it. Notwithstanding his infatuation with the van, he was not known in his neighbourhood as a bad driver. His high-speed driving was always done on the open highway. Whenever he was around town he drove carefully and with respect for others, except for the sound of that great big engine. This very obvious change in his routine was the reason that his noisy and smoky departure got the attention of his neighbours. One of them walked over to his house, found the woman, and got emergency aid for her.

No one knew why he drove away from Calgary toward Banff, but he was clocked by a radar patrol as he headed west near Cochrane, Alberta. The van was running over one hundred and thirty miles per hour when it passed through the radar beam; the policeman in the patrol car thought he had a ghost reading until he saw the flash of the headlights and felt the shockwave as the van passed his police car, which was parked on the highway shoulder. The radar operator turned on his emergency equipment, called on the radio that he had a hot one going west, and started after the disappearing van. The highway patrol cars in those days were not short of power so after about three miles the police car was closing on the target van.

The van suddenly slowed, turned on the right signal and pulled over onto the shoulder of the highway. The patrolman pulled in behind the van, radioed that he had the speeder stopped and walked up to the driver's window. The driver was laughing and he said, "I guess you got me good." He produced a driver's license and the registration documents for the van. He was apologetic about his speed and said he was just blowing the carbon out of it. The policeman smelled liquor and was suspicious about the driver's behaviour. He told him he would get back to him shortly and returned to the police car to run the data on the police system. We now had the suspect sitting in his powerful van and the cop in his car immediately behind; this situation lasted only long enough for the name and address to be transmitted by radio.

The policeman in the patrol car was startled by the throaty bellow from the exhaust of the van as it rocketed forward and moved into the travelled lane of the highway. The chase was on. The radio operator in Calgary put high priority on the data just received from the pursuing police unit and requested that all radio channels in the Calgary-Banff area be left clear. Banff detachment was requested to assist and they were provided with frequent updates on the rapidly changing location of the racing vehicles. The van and the pursuing police car shot through the east gates to Banff National Park at a frightening speed and were now very close to the next effort to stop the pursuit. There was little time to prepare anything. A marked police car was positioned at the side of the highway with all the emergency lights in operation and flares were set out on both sides of the westbound lanes. Two officers stood near the police car waving flashlights to signal the vehicle to stop. The runaway van slowed to about a hundred miles per hour when the emergency lights were first visible, but it was accelerating hard when it shot past the checkpoint.

The van driver's name had been run through the RCMP system and no record of any kind had been found. The name was passed to the Calgary Police and an alert operator overheard the request and advised that their units were presently on the scene of a domestic dispute involving people of the same or very similar name. Calgary Police were able to advise that a woman had been severely beaten and that the likely suspect, her husband, had left the scene in a high-powered van. The name was passed to the officers on the scene of the beating and they confirmed the match.

It was now near midnight. Only one of the two police officers at Lake Louise was available. He had less than fifteen minutes to make preparations. His effort was very similar to the one at Banff, and the van driver gave it about equal consideration. The van was now leading a high-speed parade. The radar unit had been joined by two additional police units from Banff, and once the Lake Louise policeman had regained his composure he decided to bring up the rear. The van stayed on Highway One and headed toward the BC Alberta border. He may have thought that the border would end the efforts of the police from Alberta, but he was wrong.

The parade was now onto real mountain highway. The road was narrow and winding with steep grades, and it would get worse as the vehicles got closer to Golden. The Golden detachment members had been advised of the chase when it first began. They knew that the chase had run through two checkpoints. They were also aware that the driver of the van was a strong suspect in a possible homicide at Calgary. No one was aware, at that time, that the runaway driver was armed with a .44 Magnum revolver.

There were three constables on duty at Golden, two of whom were experienced policemen. They discussed the circumstances and decided that the best place to force the vehicle to stop was on the highway bridge over the Kicking Horse River, ten miles east of Golden. They called me at my home and advised me of the circumstances and of their plan to go to the Ten Mile Bridge with our tired old Ford police car, which was about to be replaced due to high mileage. Their plan was to put the old car crossways on the bridge deck, leaving insufficient room at either end to get around it. I advised them to do what they felt was adequate to stop the pursuit—go for it—but to be extremely cautious for their own safety.

The chase had now encountered a few sharp corners and

some grades that had apparently scared the hell out of everyone involved, including the driver of the van. Their speed had come down to seventy to eighty miles per hour. The van was using the whole of the highway in entering and getting around corners. The pursuing police advised that the van driver had lost control at the top of the Spiral Tunnel Hill near Field, BC, but had managed to catch it again just before the edge of the mountain. A few feet more and the chase would have become a certain fatality.

Three marked police cars raced up the canyon from Golden to the selected bridge at Ten Mile. The drivers of the cars were aware that the chase had slowed somewhat but they still had very little time to set up. Their plan was to send the first car about half a mile east of the bridge location to stop all traffic coming from the direction of the chase. Eastbound traffic would be stopped short of the bridge deck by one of the other two members. This would prevent any other traffic from being on the bridge deck if a collision occurred.

The Ten Mile Bridge was well-known to everyone who used the Trans-Canada Highway in that area. Westbound vehicles approached the bridge on a very steep downgrade. At the bottom of the grade, the road turned nearly ninety degrees left, onto the bridge deck. At the other end of the bridge, the road turned very sharply to the right and continued down the narrow canyon. The bridge deck was about three hundred feet long, nearly level and had a slight "S" bend. Traffic coming west to the bridge would see a mass of black and yellow reflective warning arrows pointing to the left and a large checkerboard pattern, also in black and yellow, directly in front just as they turned onto the bridge. There were also flashing amber lights to emphasize the severity of the corner onto the bridge. The bridge deck was only wide enough to allow a minimal single lane in each direction.

The first police car from Golden crossed the bridge and reached the top of the hill, where he stopped a transport truck and directed him to the extreme right side of the road. He placed the police car with emergency lights flashing to provide maximum visibility to westbound traffic and asked the trucker to remain in his unit with his emergency flashers on. He then called to his two partners at the bridge to advise that he had the traffic stopped, and that he would warn them at first sight of the target vehicle. The end was near.

The two policemen at the bridge set up at the west end of the bridge deck. The old police car was positioned squarely across the two lanes of the bridge, and the other car was parked a short distance beyond the end of the bridge. In a short time, a few units of traffic had stopped by that police car, and the drivers were asked to stay in their cars and leave their emergency flashers on. A transport truck was among this traffic. The driver was asked to assist by telling any new arrivals to remain in their vehicles with emergency lights on. The truck driver was glad to assist when he heard a brief account of what was coming toward them. The two policemen then took up positions behind the massive concrete pillars at each side of the end of the bridge. This location left them close enough to the doomed police car to take immediate action if the driver attempted a turn or tried to run.

The wait was very short once the vehicles were in place. Within a few minutes of the police taking up their positions behind the bridge abutments, the call came from the car at the top of the hill: "Here they come!" Again, the van took no notice of the signals to stop. The pursuing police were asked to move up as close as possible to the van as they came down the steep grade to the bridge, and to use their cars to shut off the entrance to the bridge in case the van turned and came back at them.

The two policemen and the other traffic on the west end of the bridge watched the little parade streak down the steep grade on the other side of the river. The speed of their decent made it appear that none of them would be able to slow down enough to get onto the bridge. The screeching of locked brakes echoed across the canyon as the speeding vehicles came into the final sharp left turn onto the bridge.

The police drivers and the man in the van were able to see the emergency lights of the old police car and the second police unit at the west end of the bridge as they came down the hill. There were also lights visible from the other traffic that had been stopped just short of the blocked end of the bridge. It was fairly obvious that this was not another courtesy checkpoint where the driver was invited to stop if he chose to do so.

The van came into the bridge approach with its wheels locked. It slowed just enough to get onto the bridge deck, and then slowed more as the old police car came into view. The pursuing police cars entered the bridge and two were placed side by side to prevent the van from getting off again if it turned around.

The van continued toward the blocking car at a much reduced speed. However, it was still a long way from a safe speed in those circumstances. At a distance of about a hundred feet from the old police car, the bellow of the big engine was heard again as the driver pushed it to maximum acceleration. In an instant the van was in collision with the left rear side of the car. The sound was explosive. The old car lurched away from the impact and swung to one side of the bridge deck, leaving enough room for the van to get around it. The impact also took a heavy toll on the van, crushing the front end back enough to disable the steering. It continued forward and hit the old police car again, this time more toward the centre of the body. The two explosive impacts were followed by silence. The two policemen behind the bridge abutments had grabbed fire extinguishers and were running toward the wreckage when they heard a muffled blast from the van. They both recognized the sound as a gunshot. Without hesitation, they found themselves once again behind the abutments.

The next sound they heard was running footsteps on the bridge deck. They could not tell if this was from someone running toward the van from the other side of the bridge or if the suspect was now running away. In another moment they identified the runner as one of the policemen from the Alberta cars. They both yelled out to take cover because they had heard a gunshot. However, the running policeman was now right at the rear door of the van. He was in a very vulnerable position. One of the two behind the abutments then moved up using the wrecked police car for cover. The fire extinguishers had now been set aside and replaced with revolvers. The two police nearest the van were able talk to each other. Neither had seen the driver, and they were unable to detect any movement in or near the van. After some time, a flashlight beam was used to light the windshield and driver's window of the van. The light showed that this area of the inside of the van was heavily covered in blood and gore.

The driver of the van had placed the muzzle of his big handgun under his chin and discharged a bullet up through the area where his head had been at the moment he fired. He died instantly. The autopsy found no evidence of other life-threatening injuries. There was every indication he would have survived the crash without serious harm.

The dead man's wife survived the beating he had given her and collected on a fairly large life insurance policy. I can only hope that the remainder of her life was a better experience than she had with this fellow.

Bullies at the Bar

This story begins on a winter day at the summit of the Rogers Pass. Snow had been falling for several days and travel conditions were terrible. The highway crews had been working to their maximum ability but the continuous snow was getting ahead of them. The highway authorities were considering the possibility of closing the Trans-Canada Highway through Rogers Pass.

It was just after noon that a transport truck approached the summit of the pass heading west. The truck was driven by an experienced driver. For some reason the driver failed to observe the amber flashing light hanging over the middle of the highway intersection. He also failed to realize that he was overtaking a bright yellow snowplow grader with an amber flashing light on top of the cab, large bright-red lights on the rear, and all of its road lighting equipment in operation.

Several independent witnesses stated that although the snow was still falling at the time of the incident, visibility was adequate for them to see the grader from a distance of a quarter of a mile or more.

The grader operator had signalled a left turn and started his move to leave the highway into the service area to his left. The transport truck moved to his left at the same time and struck the slower-moving grader on its left side, toward the rear end of the machine. Fortunately neither the grader operator nor the driver of the truck was injured. The crash resulted in many thousands of dollars of damage to the two machines.

The highway intersection was divided into several lanes at that location. There were designated lanes for left and right turns from both directions; however, none of these traffic aids were visible because of the snow covering the roadway. The only available traffic control device, other than the caution lights on the grader, was the single amber flashing light that hung over the centre of the intersection on a cable.

The investigating police officer concluded that the truck driver had failed to react correctly to the situation, and issued him a traffic ticket for the offence of driving without due care and attention.

The matter came to trial in Golden the next summer. Witnesses were called from several locations in Alberta and British Columbia, and the operator of the snowplow grader was among this group. The Crown case was being laid out before the court in the routine way. Several witnesses had told their stories of how they were able to see the crash developing. The case for the prosecution seemed very strong.

The final witness for the prosecution was the grader operator. This man had worked in the Rogers Pass section of the Trans-Canada Highway for years. He was considered the most skilled machine operator of the entire crew on that part of the road. He was adept with every machine that the highway maintenance crew had at their disposal to deal with the most adverse winter conditions in the whole country. This man was an expert in his field.

We all have our strengths and weaknesses. This man was a very shy individual with a great fear of speaking in any sort of public venue. He also had a speech impediment. It took a long time for him to tell his story of that winter day in Rogers Pass, but with the understanding support of the Crown Counsel, he did get it done in a clear and concise way.

The company that owned the transport truck had hired a highly reputed lawyer to defend their driver. This action by the trucking company was no doubt motivated by the strong possibility that they would have to buy a replacement road grader if they were found responsible in this crash. This lawyer had not found much opportunity to ply his trade during the straightforward evidence presented by the witnesses prior to the grader operator. After hearing the grader operator's laboriously told tale, the lawyer began his cross-examination of the grader operator by shouting his first question as he jumped to his feet. The grader operator was visibly shaken by this sudden outburst. The lawyer saw the result of his first assault and immediately took full advantage of his victim. He led the man through a series of questions that were deliberately designed to confuse him. He had the man describe the numerous traffic lanes that were under the snow at the time of the crash and then tricked him into saying that all those lanes were there and available on the day of the crash.

I sat and watched this travesty unfold. I wondered why our system allowed for such deliberate and planned obstruction of a witness, especially one who has no prior experience in court. I was more distressed by the fact that both the Crown prosecutor and the judge were obviously highly amused as they watched their brother lawyer ply his trade. Their years of university education and experience in the field of law must have allowed them to see this tragedy in a different way than I viewed it. I am still angry and disappointed by this display of disrespect for what I consider to be the due process of law.

The judge dismissed the information. I have no concern with that action. My concern is with the deliberate and vicious attack on a witness by an officer of the court, which led to that witness's inability to respond correctly to the situation.

This must be justice as it was intended to be. I cannot believe that our law schools would teach such tactics, yet such things can be observed in any court on almost any day.

Would it not be wonderful if fate could put that lawyer into a snow removal machine in a mountain pass when avalanches are screaming as more snow falls—and then allow the skilled operator to just walk away?

The Wyoming Elk Call

The variety of the wildlife resource in British Columbia, consisting of 1,138 vertebrate species, is one of the richest in North America. If you live anywhere but in the major cities you will encounter wildlife almost every day. Even in the heart of Vancouver one will occasionally hear of a black bear or coyote. Sometime in the past few years a cougar was cornered by wildlife officers in the underground parking area of the Empress Hotel in downtown Victoria.

The town of Golden lies by the junction of the Kicking Horse and the Columbia rivers. This area has always been a winter haven for a variety of large game animals. Moose, elk, deer, and mountain sheep would wander the edges of town and occasionally came right in the business district to do a little shopping.

Yoho National Park lies only ten miles east of Golden, and Glacier National Park is only a little farther away to the west. All forms of native wildlife abound in the parks on a year-round basis.

Many of the residents of Golden enjoy a fall hunt for large game animals as well as ducks and geese in the abundant marshlands along the Columbia River.

During one of the years that I lived and worked in Golden, some friends of mine were planning a hunt for elk in the approaching fall season. One of them had driven to Calgary and visited his favourite sporting goods store to see what they had to ensure success during the upcoming hunt. He had found a variety of hunting and camping equipment that he could not do without, and he came away with several hundred dollars worth of new toys.

Among them was an instrument that looked like a miniature French horn. It was known as a Wyoming Elk Call, and it came with a tape recording of instructions for its proper use. My friend listened to the tape several times during the three-hour drive back to Golden from Calgary. When he reached Golden, he felt he knew all about the art of calling elk. His only regret was that he had come through the national parks after dark and had not been able to test his new knowledge on some of the pet-like animals there. He could hardly wait for an opportunity to return to the park and conduct some tests.

It was well into September and the elk breeding season was on. During the rut season the elk bulls are in a frenzy as they each try to gather a herd of cows and then fight off the other bulls who are constantly trying to woo some of the girls away. The competition is fierce and results in some truly bizarre behaviour. During this season, elk and moose bulls will charge machines and people they encounter in their travels. Many ranchers have stories about moose and elk bulls falling in love with their domestic cow herd and refusing to take no for an answer. These stories usually end with the rancher having a supply of wild meat for the coming winter.

The first evening that my friend was able to find some spare time, he was on the telephone to see if anyone could accompany him on a quick drive to Yoho Park. No one was able to get away so he set out alone. He was driving a very nice camper van that he used on hunting trips throughout the fall.

Just as the sun was setting over the mountains he arrived in the park along the Kicking Horse River. This area had a large population of elk and he was sure he would be able to test his new bugle under actual conditions.

He drove off the highway into an open area that was surrounded by forest. He parked his van and shut the engine off. He got out and stood quietly by the van for a few minutes to determine if he could hear or see any animals. None were evident. He then put the call to his lips and gave a blast that he felt sounded exactly like the demonstrations on the instruction tape. Just as he took the horn from his lips he heard what he thought was an echo; the shrill whistling scream came from the forest just at the edge of the clearing where he had parked his van. The echo-like sound was accompanied by some heavy crashing and clattering in the brush.

In the next moment a bull elk barged out of the forest into the clearing. The sight of this creature was frightening; its entire body was steaming in the cool evening air as the elk slashed away at imaginary enemies with its huge rack of antlers. My friend jumped into his van, not wanting to have anything to do with this fellow. The bull walked on stiff legs as it glared at the van. Vapors from his hot breath could be seen as he snorted and whistled a challenge to the van. This phase of the encounter went on for ten minutes or more until the elk seemed to feel that he had met the challenge and had frightened the intruder so badly that it would not cause any further threat.

The bull began to lose interest and moved gradually back to the forest from which he had appeared.

Just as the bull was about to disappear into the forest, my

friend leaned out the window of his van and gave another blast on the call.

He should not have done that.

Without hesitation, the bull turned and charged. He came with his head lowered and his huge antlers slashing from side to side, spraying urine as he galloped toward the van. He struck the side of the van with such force that the man inside thought it would roll over. The elk went to his knees for a moment as the van rocked back onto its wheels. A side window of the van had exploded into a million pieces. The bull sprang to his feet and circled the van as he jabbed and slashed at it with his antlers, each slash and jab resulting in several hundred dollars of damage. When the second window exploded, he stood back and glared his defiance for a few minutes before turning away to the forest. The second shattered window seemed to convince the bull that he had killed the intruder. This time my friend allowed the bull to leave without any further insults or challenges.

It had been an expensive lesson but my friend had no doubt whatsoever that the Wyoming Elk Call was very effective.

Hitchhiking Girls

The introduction of the Canadian Police Information Computer system, or CPIC, made profound changes on routine police functions and effectiveness. I was stationed at Golden, on the Trans-Canada Highway near the Alberta border, when we received our first computer unit during the early part of 1973.

The detachment commander of Golden at that time was the finest example of a member of the Royal Canadian Mounted Police I encountered in my entire twenty-seven years of service. He ran his detachment with basic principles and straightforward policies. The detachment members worked very well together because this man made the entire operation run that way. He motivated his people to do their job in a fair and just way and he taught them about the rewards for conducting themselves in that manner. The police at Golden were highly motivated and they found great satisfaction in their job, all because of the detachment commander and the way he conducted the day-to-day police work.

It was into this very positive environment that the new computer was received. The commander advised his people that we now had a piece of equipment that could and should change the policing picture across the world. Everyone was encouraged to make use of the computer at every opportunity. During the year 1973, Golden detachment apprehended more occupied stolen cars than all other police units on the Trans-Canada Highway in British Columbia. People who were the subject of outstanding warrants were apprehended daily, simply by entering their data on the system. Warrants for offences from ignored traffic tickets to homicide were executed.

Our detachment commander told us, "There is no need to ever feel idle or bored as long as that highway is over there; go out and check a few cars and you will have some excitement before you know it." As usual he was right on the money!

The story I have in mind begins on the Trans-Canada Highway in the Fraser Valley near Langley in the lower mainland of British Columbia. Two young women were hitchhiking across Canada on a camping holiday. They had reached the west coast and were starting on their return to eastern Canada. It was late morning on a beautiful summer day when they reached the highway with their packs and started thumbing. Young women have little difficulty finding a ride on our highways and before long a man had stopped to offer one.

The man was driving a very distinctive yellow, black and green car with a license plate from the United States. He was about twenty-five years old, six foot six inches tall, and two hundred and eighty pounds. The young women were reluctant about his offer of a ride, but he spent time with them and talked them into getting into his car. He told them he was on his way to a new job in New York and that he had chosen to drive across Canada because he had travelled the United States route many times. He stated that he would appreciate their company for as long as they chose to travel with him. The two held a little conference and decided to take a chance on him.

The remainder of the day was spent along the Trans-Canada Highway, getting from Langley into the Rogers Pass. The driver was a gentleman in every way and there was a good rapport among the three of them. When they stopped at the summit of the Rogers Pass the young women sought information about where they could camp for the night; they were directed to a campground a few miles east of the summit. The women expected that their driver would drop them off at the campground and then go on to find himself a room somewhere.

What the two women did not know was that their driver was a psychotic killer. During his recent travels he had raped and killed two women in a motel in Virginia and had taken another woman on a terrifying ride through several states. He had abused this prisoner in every way he could, but she had survived from day to day and at last escaped from him. The police were looking for this man from coast to coast in the United States.

The two women were glad to have made the decision to take a ride with this fellow. Their day had been perfect, they had enjoyed his company and they had travelled through some of Canada's most beautiful scenery in ideal weather conditions. They were now looking forward to getting their tent set up and having a good sleep.

They all watched closely for road signs as they descended the mountain away from the summit of Rogers Pass. At last the signs directed them to turn left from the highway to access the camping area they had been told about earlier. The driver pulled off the highway where the women suggested he could drop them off with the least inconvenience. At this point they were still of the opinion that he would drive on to find himself a room for the night. He insisted that he would drive them right into the campsite and help them get their gear ready before going on his way.

The two young women registered at the camp office and told the camp attendant that the man in the car would not be staying. They were assigned a tenting spot and their helpful driver took them right to the assigned location. At the campsite, he helped get their things out of the back of his car and he tried to help them make their camp. He was obviously not someone who had any experience in camping; he was clumsy and had no idea of what had to be done to set up a tent. In spite of his lack of skill in this area he insisted on having his great bulk in the midst of the activity. He watched with interest as one of the women used a claw hammer to drive small metal tent pegs. They carried this hammer in their tent bag just for this purpose.

The tent was set up in a short time and the two again tried to say thank you to their helper. It was now becoming obvious that he was reluctant to be on his way. The women were only mildly concerned about this development as he had shown only kindness and consideration for them during the day and they expected this to continue.

The three sat around the camp for some time and talked about their day's travels. Some time during this conversation the killer announced that he would sleep in his car by the campsite. He told the women how much he had enjoyed their company and that he would be very glad to continue their trip the next morning whenever they were ready to leave the camp.

The conversation by the camp went on for several hours until the driver said good night and settled his bulk into the car as though he intended to be there until morning. The two young women rolled out their sleeping bags in the tent and were asleep in a short time.

Some time shortly after midnight they were jolted awake as their tent crashed down on them. The huge bulk of their driver friend was on top of the tent and he was slashing at their heads with their claw hammer. The attack went on for what seemed an eternity to the two victims. They each received several blows to the head and shoulders from the claw hammer. They were not sure if either or both of them lost consciousness during the assault.

The rain of hammer blows finally ended. The women in the collapsed tent could hear their attacker trying to get his breath after the great exertion he had put into swinging the hammer. They were too frightened to move or say anything, which must have led their psychotic friend to think they were dead. This was a logical conclusion on his part because the medical people at Golden felt that their survival was a miracle.

As the two lay motionless in their tent they heard and felt their attacker return. He gathered the four corners of the tent together and dragged it to the edge of the slightly raised camping site. He then pushed and kicked the tent and its contents over the edge and down into the bush. Again both women somehow managed to remain silent through this phase of their ordeal.

They lay still, wondering what was next. No sound could be heard until the car started and moved away slowly.

The events after the car left became very foggy. One of the women lost consciousness and her friend thought she had died. The other woman struggled in the collapsed tent and the darkness until she was able to find the zipper and free herself. She could detect only total darkness yet she was sure there had been a sky full of stars and a bright moon when they had gone to bed. She then realized that both her eyes were completely swollen shut. She pushed the swollen tissue away from her eyes with her fingers and found that she could still see.

Forcing her eyes open, she saw a small light nearby. She knew that she had to get to that light immediately. The light source was a tiny nightlight on the side of a camp trailer. The woman struggled toward that light, stopping frequently to force another visual check on her objective. She had no idea how long it took her to crawl the fifty yards to the light but she was able to awaken the occupants and the rescue began.

The people from the neighbouring trailer took charge of the horrendous situation. They awakened everyone in the campground. An ambulance was called, the police were contacted and people were posted as guards to prevent the possible return of the attacker.

These two young women had amazing strength and a huge will to live. They were both drifting in and out of consciousness when the ambulance and police arrived but they were determined to do what they could to apprehend the animal who had done this to them. They wanted to tell their story to the police even before receiving attention from the ambulance crew. Between the two of them they gave the attending police officer a detailed description of the man and his car.

As the ambulance raced toward Golden with the victims, the police constable called his office in Golden by radio and relayed the details of the incident and the suspect's description. The person on duty at Golden immediately went to the CPIC and passed the story to every location in Alberta and British Columbia. This new computer technology provided a means of simultaneous broadcast to the street level of the entire police organization.

The first streaks of daylight were appearing across the open country near Cochrane, Alberta when a police constable heard the information relayed by the radio control centre at Calgary. The police constable was sitting in a marked police car at the side of the highway. He scratched a few notes on a clipboard as he thought to himself that the suspect could now be in his area. He thought that this one would not be difficult to spot, with the tri-coloured car and the huge man driving it. As the constable looked up again to the highway, a car passed by. It fit the description right to the great bulk of the driver.

The constable called his Calgary radio centre to say that he had visual contact with the suspect and that they were heading toward Calgary. The Calgary radio operator cautioned the constable to wait for another police unit before attempting to stop the suspect. The constable had now pulled onto the highway and was a short distance behind the suspect. Before he was able to acknowledge the caution from Calgary, the suspect car braked and pulled onto the shoulder of the highway. The constable passed this development to Calgary and jumped out of his car.

The suspect was arrested without any resistance. He was returned to Golden where he admitted to the offences against the women. A search of his car produced the twenty-two caliber pistol that had been the weapon in the double murder in Virginia. The man pled guilty to all charges in Canada and was sentenced to nine years. Within a few months of his being incarcerated here, a deal was arranged to have him returned to the United States to face their charges. He was eventually sentenced to several hundred years, only because the United States jurisdiction where he was tried no longer invoked the death penalty.

Only a few months before this incident, the vital information would have passed through many more hands and may not have reached Alberta until regular office hours the next morning. That would have been far too late. The CPIC system had again proven its great value and Golden detachment had demonstrated their skill and determination in using it to the maximum.

Safe Driving Week

Over the years in Canada, the first week of November has been designated as Safe Driving Week. Since its inception, this idea has been promoted by safety organizations and all levels of government across Canada. Many activities are undertaken during this time to educate the public about better ways to use our highways, streets and sidewalks.

The police play some important roles in the campaign, one being to submit statistical reports on the total number of vehicle crashes indicating which had resulted in death, injuries or property damage. Additional information was required about any activities we had undertaken to promote the Safe Driving Week theme.

In the fall of 1971, I was stationed at Lytton in the Fraser Canyon. The autumn had been warm and dry, as it was most years in that part of the province. Routine policing was being attended to and some minor preparations were made for the annual Safe Driving Week campaign, which was to run from 12:01

a.m. Monday until 11:59 p.m. of the following Sunday. The appointed time for the start of the campaign arrived along with a
very noticeable change in the weather: the temperature dropped
to just below the freezing point, the wind blew from the north,
and snow began to fall. The temperature warmed somewhat
when the snow began to fall heavily at about midnight. I went
to bed with a feeling that something bad was sure to come out
of this weather. Meanwhile, on the highway, the wet snow was
compressing into a solid sheet of ice as each wheel passed over
it. The steep grades and sharp curves that made up most of my
patrol district would combine with the ice to cause something
that would get me out of bed before the morning light.

It was just before four that morning when I was awakened
by someone pounding on my door. I opened the door to a very
excited man who told me of finding a transport truck all folded
up against itself about one mile south of Lytton. The truck was
the type known as a "B" train, meaning that it consisted of a
tractor and two trailers. The first trailer rode with the front end
on the truck tractor, while the second trailer was on a completely independent set of wheels and attached to the rear of
the first trailer by a heavy steel drawbar and hitch. The driver of
the truck had attempted a quick stop that resulted in the unit
folding until the three sections were all pressed together alongside each other. The truck driver had told my visitor that a car
had tried to pass him and that it had gone over the side. No one
had been down to the car before my caller left to get assistance,
but the truck driver was sure that no one could have survived
when the car hit the side of the mountain. I noted the name and
address of the man at my door, thanked him for assisting, and
prepared to get to the scene.

The reason the man had come to my house was that a marked
police car was parked on the street. Calls were so frequent that
one of us always took a car home to save the time needed to get

to the office before we could respond and establish radio contact. I dressed, started the car, swept off the four to five inches of snow that had accumulated on it, and began rocking it back and forth to get it away from the curb. Less snow was falling than at midnight. Visibility was much improved, but the road was extremely slippery and it was very difficult to get the car up the hill out of our little community and onto the highway.

Everything was covered with a fresh layer of clean snow. All the trees were bent over, and telephone and power wires were sagging between their poles under a load of wet snow. The canyon would be a great place for a photographer when daylight came that morning. The highway was completely covered in snow. There was nothing visible to show where the main travelled portion of the road lay, but I could discern the banks of the ditches, sign posts, guardrails, trees and rocks that bordered the edges of the highway. With these markers and the experience of having driven that road many times, I made my way toward the crash site.

The man who had been at my door had told me that the truck was located in a sharp curve in the roadway, one mile south of the Lytton Junction. I knew the exact location as soon as he gave me that description. The place was locally known as Cristie's Curve, and it was one of the most common locations for vehicle crashes in the Lytton section of the Trans-Canada Highway. The highway is built along the wall of the canyon; in many areas it follows the route of the original wagon road that was pushed through during the Cariboo Gold Rush of the 1860s. At Cristie's Curve, a deep ravine in the canyon wall had to be crossed. The construction engineers had to do the best they could with the available budget. This resulted in the highway entering a gradual curve into the ravine from both sides and then taking a sudden hook to the point where the least fill or bridge construction would be needed to span the gap. The curve was marked with warning signs from both sides, but even the best reflective signs are not visible when heavy snow is falling.

In the apex of Cristie's Curve I found the truck tractor and trailers folded as the man had described them. The truck driver had placed incendiary flares at both sides of the crash site, and he was standing on the road with a flashlight to assist passing motorists. A young man was sitting in the passenger seat of the transport truck cab. The driver told me he had been southbound, going slowly because of the slippery road and the falling snow that restricted his vision. A car had been following him for a few miles. The car had moved up close behind him several times, indicating that the driver intended to pass, but each time it had dropped back again. As the truck and car neared Cristie's Curve, the car again moved up close. The road was straight and level in the area just before the curve, and the car moved to the left and started to pass. The truck driver saw the warning signs that the roadway was starting into the left curve. He knew that the pass could not be completed safely, and he began to slow the truck as quickly as he could. The driver of the car may not have been able to see the warning signs because the truck was in his line of vision and was also stirring up additional snow. The truck driver knew the canyon route well, and he recalled the nature of the curve ahead. He knew that the car, now beside him, could not possibly negotiate the sharp curve, and he threw on a full application of brakes. The truck folded and slid to a stop facing toward the edge of the highway where the car had just gone over.

The trucker watched the car for the instant that it flew down and away from the highway to where it struck the solid rock of the mountainside. He had never seen such an impact. There was a fireball that lit the area like a lightning bolt when the car hit the snow-covered rock. He expected the car to continue burning. However, he was relieved to not see flames after the initial explosive impact.

The trucker concluded from what he had just seen that there could be no one left alive in the car. He immediately gathered his safety flares and lit one at each end of his truck. He then ran a short distance ahead and behind the truck where he put up additional flares. By this time, the falling snow was visibly lighter than it had been just minutes before, and by the time I arrived at the scene the snowfall had stopped. After placing the flares, the truck driver returned to the cab of his truck. He was standing on the highway trying to decide if he should stay on the road to direct traffic or go down to the wrecked car.

He was leaning toward staying on the highway, partly because of the belief that no one could have survived the crash and partly because of the additional danger created by his disabled truck. Another transport truck arrived and the driver parked nearby and offered assistance. Just as the second truck arrived, a twenty-year-old man scrambled onto the highway from the direction of the wrecked car. He told the drivers he had been in the passenger seat in the front of the car when it had crashed.

The young man said there were five of them in the car. In the total darkness, after the crash, he had called their names but got no reply. He suffered severe bruising and abrasions, but had no broken bones or internal injuries. To add to the miracle of his survival, he was released from the hospital after two days.

When I reached the scene, I spoke to the truck drivers and the young survivor. The ambulance was on the way. I then went over the bank to the wrecked car. I could see where the survivor had crawled out through the opening where the windshield had been. He went straight up the steep broken rock bank of the highway to the lights of the disabled transport truck. Inside the car, I found four bodies piled together like rag dolls: two males in the extreme left front, and a female and a male against the left rear door. There was no indication that any of them had moved after the impact, and there was no detectable pulse or breathing. There were jagged cuts that exposed bone on the upper leg of one and the upper arm of another but there was almost no bleeding from these wounds. The autopsy examinations found multiple injuries to each of the four that caused instant death.

The car was a 1969 Ford sedan. This vehicle was advertised by the manufacturer as "the car with the big living room" because of the design of the right front seat area. The dash panel on the passenger side dropped down from the bottom of the windshield, leaving a large open area in front of the passenger seat. I examined the wreck thoroughly to try to determine how the one man had survived, but there was nothing visible. The large open area may have contributed in some way, but the most probable contributing factor was that he was cushioned by the bodies of the other two people in the front seat. The greatest impact was to the left front, which threw everything and everyone to that side.

The car was from Calgary, Alberta. Three of the young people who died were friends from Calgary; the car belonged to the parents of one of them. The car was to be used that evening for getting around in Calgary, but the three friends decided, on the spur of the moment, to go to Vancouver. The three youths from Calgary had picked up the survivor and his friend where they were hitchhiking near Kamloops. These two were from Ontario.

The bodies were removed to the morgue with the permission of the local coroner, and before ten a.m. on Monday the wrecked car had been removed to secure storage. The transport truck received some minor repairs and carried on down the canyon. I contacted the RCMP detachment in Calgary and handed them the task of going to the door of each of the dead youths. The families would be frantic by this time; the attending policeman would only have to show up at the door in uniform and nod in the affirmative. The same task was handed to an RCMP detachment in Ontario. Safe Driving Week was off to a tragic start.

By the middle of the afternoon on Monday, the snow had turned to slush in the warm sunshine. The continuous flow of traffic and highway maintenance machines had thrown the slush onto the shoulders of the highway and the road was reported to be bare and wet. Tuesday was an uneventful day. Most of our efforts at the Lytton Detachment were directed toward the follow-up administrative work that results from a multiple fatality.

Tuesday evening brought another snowstorm. The temperature was just at the freezing point, the snow was falling in fluffy chunks, and visibility was almost nil. There was no need to consider closing the highway: after a couple hours of that sort of snowfall, the highway was blocked by vehicles that were unable to get up any of the grades in the canyon. The highway maintenance department had all their equipment rigged with tire chains and they were doing whatever they could to get traffic moving again. The snow continued until about three a.m. Wednesday. Once the snowfall quit, most of the traffic was able to get going again within an hour. The air stayed warm after that and the foot of snow rapidly turned into very heavy slush; the sky was clear and the morning sunshine was melting the slush quickly. The traffic soon cleared a set of tracks in each direction, leaving ridges of slush in the middle of each track and along the centre line of the highway. There had been more minor collisions than we cared to count, but no one else had been seriously hurt or killed.

It was almost ten o'clock Wednesday morning when we were called to Cristie's Curve again. This time, the crash was in the gradual bend leading into the sharp hook of the curve from the south. A heavily loaded transport truck had just come out of the sharp hook of the curve and was picking up speed when the driver saw a small car meeting him. The small car moved a little to the right, possibly in an attempt to give the truck more room, but it hit the slush ridges and went out of control. The driver steered left to correct, but succeeded only in putting the car into a counter-clockwise spin. The truck driver had only enough time to slam on his brakes as the little car completed a full spin and crashed, head-on, under the front of the truck.

The small car did not come into hard contact with the truck until the low front end hit the front axle of the truck tractor. This contact was simultaneous with the windshield meeting the front bumper. Three university students, on a short break from their studies, had been on their way into the interior to visit friends and family. The three died instantly.

This crash was unusual in that the two vehicles engaged from a head-on attitude and they remained together after the impact. The little car had gone under the truck tractor; this resulted in the front wheels of the truck leaving the road surface. The vehicles were in that position when we arrived. From the little we could see and feel through openings in the wreckage, it appeared there was nothing to be done for the three bodies in the crushed car. The truck driver was not physically injured, but he was emotionally out of control and showing symptoms of shock. The first people to arrive after the crash told us of the driver trying to pull the car out from under his truck with his bare hands. Fortunately, the ambulance crew had arrived with us and they were able to assist. The driver was removed from the immediate site into the protection of the ambulance unit. Two women and a man, all in their late teens, had been in the small car.

A heavy towing truck arrived about an hour after us, and the front of the truck was lifted to allow another tow truck to pull the car away from the transport tractor. Further examination of the little car and its grisly contents confirmed our earlier conclusion that nothing could have been done for the three young travellers. The scene was cleared as quickly as possible and we began, again, the passing of messages to the police at the home areas of the dead. Unlike the earlier deaths, these families would receive the information without the slightest forewarning.

The remainder of Wednesday and all of Thursday were spent in the administrative work and other follow-up from the two multiple fatalities. Thursday evening the temperature dropped again and snow began to fall. By eight p.m. the highway was covered with a thick layer of slippery, compressed snow. The snow had stopped falling and visibility was excellent but the highway surface was dangerous because of the extreme lack of traction and because drivers could not see where the road and shoulder met or where the centre line was.

At ten o'clock that night I was sitting at a typewriter in the police office. I could hear the sounds of the traffic passing above the village on the Trans-Canada Highway. Two loaded transport trucks were heading up the canyon toward the interior. They were directly above the village when I heard the unmistakable snort of engine brakes, followed immediately by an explosive crash. In the following moments, the sound was repeated by an echo from the far side of the canyon. Then there was silence.

I got up from the typewriter and put on my winter coat and boots. It took five minutes until the phone rang. A motorist had just seen a car go under the front end of a transport truck and then bounce back out. The person reporting to me had not stopped at the scene; other traffic was stopping and he felt it best to get the information to us as soon as possible. From having seen the impact and the damaged car, he had very little hope for anyone in the car.

I called for the ambulance and drove to the scene. When I arrived, I found a group of students from a nursing school attending to the driver of the car. Fortunately, the driver was the only person in the car. The students did what they could, but it was futile. Had the body been in the best equipped and best staffed operating room in the country, there would have been no chance of survival.

The crash site was on a straight and level section of roadway with a hill rising at both ends. Two trucks from the same transportation company had been travelling up the canyon together. As they reached the start of the straight section, the driver of the lead truck saw a car meeting them. The car appeared to be travelling at a reasonable speed for the road conditions, and visibility was good. As the vehicles came nearer, the car moved to the right and then suddenly crossed to the left and crashed squarely into the front of the truck. There was a tremendous impact as the car went under the truck and then twisted itself around and bounced out again, returning to the side of the road where it had come from.

The Fraser Canyon highway through my area was mainly two blacktop lanes with gravel shoulders. Some of the long grades had been widened to three lanes, allowing the uphill traffic to use the centre lane for passing. The gravel shoulders presented a problem of erosion in heavy rain. The normal traffic entering and leaving the paved portion would throw the gravel aside, leaving a groove along the edge of the paved surface. There was a typical groove, about six inches deep and one foot wide, along the edge of the pavement in the area of this last fatality. The driver of the car had moved to the right as he was about to meet the two trucks. The road was icy and the snow-covering made it difficult or impossible to see where the pavement met the gravel shoulders. The car suddenly dropped into the groove and went out of control. It came back onto the paved portion and continued to the left into the path of the oncoming truck.

The car and the truck came together squarely; a ten-inch

section of the front edge of the roof of the car was folded down at a ninety-degree angle. In the centre of this folded portion was the clear imprint of a cleat that was bolted to the centre of the front bumper of the truck tractor. The trailer of the truck unit was lying on its side on the highway. The driver of the truck was bruised, but not seriously injured. The second truck was driven by a friend of the lead driver; the second driver provided verbal support and warmth in the cab of his truck until the ambulance attendants arrived.

The remainder of Safe Driving Week went by with no more serious crashes. The bulk of the required reports were completed in the following week, in addition to the statistical return outlining our dismal record for the safety campaign.

Clinton 1, Bikers 0

Shortly after the end of the Second World War, motorcycle gangs began to fester in North America; they became a large-scale problem in the United States before they reached that stage in Canada. The malignancy progressed rapidly, however, and by the early sixties Canada too had a major infestation of these criminals.

It was during the summer of 1968, while I was working at Williams Lake, that I had my first experience with a motorcycle gang. The call came from the police detachment at Clinton advising that a gang of about fifty motorcyclists had stopped there and it appeared they were intending to camp overnight. There were many indications that this group would be the source of problems for the local citizens and for the police.

The gang had arrived in the little community about mid-afternoon. They rode around in the village for a few minutes, making all the residents aware or their presence. After their initial noise-making ride, they pulled to the side of the highway at the edge of town and began setting up camp.

Shortly after their arrival, a group of them rode up to the police building on the pretence of a friendly courtesy call to the local police. The first three arrived in the parking area and came to the front counter, where they were met by the detachment commander and his only constable. The three thugs announced that they were staying overnight in town and did not want any trouble. They made no promises or suggestions about their conduct but made it clear that they expected the police to leave them alone. During the visit at the police office, more motorcycles arrived outside, riding over the lawn and into the small flower beds around the building. It was obvious that they intended to do whatever they pleased during their visit to Clinton.

The detachment commander thanked them for coming to the office and advised them that while he most certainly did not want trouble, they were only welcome in Clinton as long as they conducted themselves as any other guest of the community should. Following a few more thinly veiled threats, the group left the office causing a great noise with the wide open exhaust systems on their machines. They rode a few circles around the village in a ragged bunch, making very loud noise and breaking traffic regulations at every opportunity. After a short time, they joined the others where they were making their camp at the edge of town.

One of the regular clients of the Clinton Hotel beer parlour was a retired cowboy who had worked his lifetime on British Columbia cattle ranches. He was a man of about seventy years who really enjoyed his beer and lived a very modest existence in Clinton. The old cowboy spent the early part of each morning around his little shack, and he would be standing nearby when the bar opened at eleven. The rest of the day was spent nursing a few glasses of beer and visiting with anyone who happened into the bar. He had friends throughout the Cariboo and Okanagan areas, having worked for some time at nearly every cattle ranch in those parts of the province. Tourists marvelled at their good fortune to have met a real cowboy, and often stayed for hours to hear his fascinating stories about cowboy life on the ranches. He frequently became the dinner guest of travellers who gladly bought him a meal to hear more about his vanishing way of life.

At that time, the provincial liquor laws required beer parlours to close each evening for one hour from five-thirty until six-thirty. This break in the flow of beer was intended to cause all the husbands and fathers to go home and enjoy the evening meal with their wives and children. When the required closed hour was near, unless he had a dinner invitation, the old cowboy would buy a few bottles of beer at the bar and find a quiet place nearby to drink the beer and wait out the hour. In this man's routine, he would drink more beer during that hour than during the rest of the entire day.

The motorcycles had no doubt been the subject of much conversation in the Clinton bar that afternoon, but the old cowboy saw no reason to change his routine. He bought four bottles of beer and left the bar at closing time with the beer in a brown paper bag. It was a beautiful sunny summer afternoon so the old boy was slowly making his way to a favourite spot not far from the bar. He regularly enjoyed his off-sale beer in a small park overlooking the valley below the village.

The old cowboy was crossing a gravel street just behind the hotel when a group of four of the visiting motorcyclists happened along. One of the bikers rode his big Harley Davidson across the man's intended path and forced him to stop walking. The other three immediately formed a rough circle with their motorcycles and began to make fun of the old man by asking pointless questions and poking at him with their hands. The old man was terrified. He offered them his beer, hoping to pacify them. The bikers took the beer, opened and drank it immediately, then threw the bottles on the street. They continued harassing the old man for a short time until it appeared they were about to move on. At that point, one of the bikers knocked the old man to the ground and kicked him as he curled into the fetal position to try and protect himself; some or all of the others kicked at the old man before they rode away. A passing citizen took the old cowboy to the local first aid station, where he was found to be badly bruised but to have no broken bones or internal injuries.

Word of the beating of the old man spread rapidly through the small community. It was less than an hour later that two young men from the village arrived at the biker camp armed with an old single-shot twelve-gauge shotgun and a baseball bat. The local men stayed on the edge of the highway, knowing better than to walk into the centre of the camp where there were fifty or more bikers. Words were exchanged and the bikers soon realized that these two would not likely fire the shotgun. The two vigilantes now found themselves partly surrounded by a mob of loud-mouthed bikers, and it was very obvious to them that they had made a big mistake. The two young men were beside their old car, and were wishing they were somewhere else. The bikers were becoming more bold, but were still somewhat concerned about the shotgun. The vigilante with the shotgun grasped the barrel of the firearm and swung it like a golf club toward the nearest biker. The biker was standing in a defiant posture, with his legs spread and his arms folded across his chest. The wooden stock of the shotgun broke when it came in contact with the biker's crotch. The biker screamed and dropped to the ground. The two vigilantes dove into their car and drove away with great haste.

The news of the bikers at Clinton spread rapidly through the police detachments in the central region of the province.

The administration headquarters at Kamloops sent a request for all available men and cars to get to Clinton immediately. Williams Lake detachment responded with six members and three cars. We left without taking time to go home for a change of socks or a toothbrush. Police units were very quickly on their way to Clinton from nearly every detachment within a hundred mile radius. The city of Kamloops had the largest pool of uniformed police members in the region; we heard by radio that they were chartering a small bus to move their contribution of members. In addition they were sending several cars with full complements of men.

The broken shotgun incident resulted in a bad situation becoming explosive; a group of bikers rode to the police detachment and demanded full and immediate police response to this assault. They made threats on the lives of the two Clinton policemen. They said they were prepared to exact revenge against the citizens of Clinton by every imaginable means.

The corporal at Clinton did some quick thinking and requested a brief meeting with two of the gang leaders. The meeting was held in a side office of the detachment. The corporal asked the leaders to restrain their members as best they could. He advised them that every home in Clinton had at least one firearm, and that the people of Clinton would not tolerate any attack against their community. The leaders left the police office believing that any vigilante action by them would be met with deadly force from the local residents. The group held a brief meeting outside the office and then went back to their camp. The biker who had been crotched with the shotgun butt was able to stop vomiting by this time and, while he did not look well, he decided to stay at the camp and lie down in one of the conventional vehicles that were part of their cavalcade. We heard very little more from that fellow during the remainder of the adventure.

307

The group of us from Williams Lake arrived in Clinton within a few minutes of the bikers going back to their camp. The two guys at Clinton were overjoyed to see us. In the next fifteen or twenty minutes we were joined by police units from Hundred Mile House, Ashcroft, Lillooet and Lytton. The largest group from Kamloops was now en route and would arrive soon.

The bikers had been bold and abusive to the police as long as there were only the two Clinton police on the scene. We decided to present a show of force. With two or more of us in each of the six police vehicles, we drove to the camp. We came up the highway in a close formation and pulled onto the shoulder as a unit. The moment the cars slid to a stop we burst out as though we intended to make arrests. All activity in the camp stopped except for that of one of the bikers, who ran away through the bush like a deer. Our spokesman, the corporal from Clinton, announced that we had heard that some of the local citizens were on their way to the camp and that we had come to provide protection for the bikers. He implored that the bikers stay away from the village because of the extreme anger about the beating of the old cowboy. He did not want any more assaults or worse incidents. At that time the additional police units and the bus from Kamloops arrived to join us on the side of the road by the camp.

About an hour after we arrived at the camp, the motorcyclist who had run into the bush came sneaking back into the camp. He tried to be inconspicuous but was razzed by his companions for his cowardly display. We called him out to the highway to identify him and determine if he was subject of a warrant. It turned out he was just a very nervous type and fear had gotten the best of him. He was extremely embarrassed.

By this time it was well into the summer evening and the sun was setting. We positioned the cars so we could light up the entire camp with the headlights and we remained there through the night.

The camp was on a flat area beside the highway; there were a few small pine trees in the camp area but not enough to obstruct a clear view from the highway shoulder where we were located. At the edge of the camp, away from the highway, the ground rose quickly into a small range of hills. The slope of the hill rising away from the back of the camp was covered with small evergreen trees and underbrush that left only small openings where a person could walk and be seen.

Most of the bikers lay on the ground beside their machines in the flat area near the highway. We were not aware that a few of them had moved into the bush on the hillside behind the camp and were sleeping there.

With each movement or sound from the camp, the headlights were turned on and we all jumped out of the cars. The bikers were learning quickly that it was not a good thing to have our close attention.

By midnight the bikers were all into their bedrolls and it was quiet. We were sitting in the police cars, with three or four of us in every car. We tried to get some sleep on a rotation basis, with only limited success. The news of the biker incident at Clinton had spread far and wide; almost every vehicle that passed by on the highway would give a blast on their horn.

Just after two o'clock in the morning a shot was heard. The sound appeared to have come from the brush-covered hillside rising away from the back edge of the camp. We all jumped out of the cars to try and find out what was happening. Our first thought was that someone from the camp had fired at one of the police cars. The shot sounded like the report of a hunting rifle or a shotgun. It was definitely not the sound of a twenty-two caliber rimfire round. We were about to start checking our vehicles for bullet holes when a biker came running from the camp, screaming hysterically and saying that he had been shot.

The screaming biker was grabbed and held by the first two police that he came near. He opened his shirt and showed us a bleeding wound in his abdomen just to one side of his navel. The wound appeared to be from a small caliber firearm, most likely a twenty-two caliber. It was definitely not a wound from a shotgun or hunting rifle. Further examination of the man showed that the bullet had gone through his body either from front to back or back to front. He told us that he had been lying on his back in his sleeping bag and that he was not sure if it was the sound of the shot or the bullet hitting him that had awakened him.

The wounded biker was one of a few who had chosen to sleep in the bush on the hillside behind the camp. A second biker had been sleeping quite near the one that was shot, but he could offer very little to assist us. He had been awakened by the shot and then heard his friend screaming. He had not heard anyone leaving the area where they had been sleeping.

We called for an ambulance and learned that the nearest one would have to come from Hundred Mile House, about an hour away. The wounded biker was made as comfortable as possible on sleeping bags from the camp and his wounds were covered with bandages. There was almost no bleeding from either wound. He remained awake and alert while waiting for the ambulance.

About the same time that the shot biker came running to us, another person was heard running away through the bush. The runner was crashing into things in the dark but was jumping up and running again. He hit a barbed-wire fence, causing the wire to screech through the staples in the fence posts, but he untangled himself and ran again.

Inquiries with the bikers in the main part of the camp

confirmed that the second runner was indeed the same one who had taken to his heels when we first arrived. Someone from our group suggested that this fellow should try out for the Olympic cross-country running team.

Some of the bikers in the main part of the camp had been awake at the time the shot was fired, and they told us that there was no sound prior to the one shot and that they had heard nothing immediately after. They all agreed that there had been only one shot. Some of the bikers were familiar with firearms, and they all agreed that the shot they heard was not from a twenty-two caliber rimfire firearm. All the bikers were rousted out of their bedrolls and the entire camp was searched because of the possibility that the shooting may have been an inside event. We did not use a great deal of care in taking bedrolls apart or in arranging their personal effects during the search. After the search had satisfied us that there were no firearms in the camp the bikers spent a long time finding their stuff and getting back to bed. Some of the blankets and ground sheets that were too high in the trees remained there for the rest of the night.

The ambulance arrived and took the shot biker to Hundred Mile House. About two hours later, we heard an ambulance coming from the direction of Hundred Mile House. It passed by our location with the lights and siren activated. We then learned that the doctor at Hundred Mile House had determined that the bullet had gone through the man's liver and surgery was required. The hospital there was not equipped to deal with that circumstance, so the man had to be taken to Kamloops immediately.

In spite of the long ambulance ride, the shot biker recovered and was released from the Kamloops hospital after a few days.

It was never determined who shot the biker. The people of Clinton were unable to assist the police investigators. No one in the community had any idea who may have done such a thing.

Most of the citizens of Clinton did not tell the investigators that they would not have said who it was even if they had known, but many of them did utter those or similar words.

The search of the area where the biker was shot revealed nothing. No fired cartridges were found and the bullet was not recovered. The bullet had passed through the body, but it stopped in the fabric of the sleeping bag. When the wounded biker got up to run out to the road, he took the sleeping bag with him. He dropped the bag partway to the highway and the bullet was lost somewhere along his route.

We suspected that two attackers might have come to the edge of the camp through the bush. One of them stood over the biker in the sleeping bag and fired a twenty-two rimfire rifle with the muzzle very near or touching the sleeping bag. In that circumstance the shot would be quite muffled. The second person fired a shot into the air with a shotgun or hunting rifle at the same moment. Another theory was that one person armed with a double barrel firearm had done the deed. The twenty-two shot was fired into the sleeping bag and the second barrel was fired into the air immediately after. The person or persons then quietly walked away in the direction they had come from.

As the first traces of daylight came onto the camp, one of us saw someone sneaking toward the camp from the direction our running biker friend had gone. We waited until he was very near the camp and then we all burst out of the cars and ran toward him yelling as loudly as we could. He displayed an amazing burst of speed but the unlucky fellow hit the same wire fence again and became tangled in it. He was struggling bravely to free himself when he looked up and found himself surrounded by a bunch of laughing policemen.

The excitement of the running biker got the whole camp up and on their feet. By the time that excitement had died down, daylight was there and the bikers were no longer trying to get some sleep. They held a brief meeting and decided they wanted to get back to the Vancouver area where people were more tolerant of their ilk.

By six o'clock most of the bikers had their machines running and they started away toward Vancouver. We pursued them to Cache Creek and then down the Thompson and Fraser canyons until we met a group of police from the Lower Mainland who followed them for the remainder of their ride.

That ride was thirty-five years ago. They have not ridden into the Cariboo since.

Where the Rubber Meets the Road

I saw something on the evening news recently that summed up much of what has changed in the art of policing between my day and the present. The local Victoria television news team had been travelling near Courtenay when they saw a police car following an erratic driver along the main Island Highway. The police car was displaying its emergency lights so the television crew immediately swung in behind the low-speed pursuit and began to film it.

At first glance I was quite convinced that the driver of the pursued vehicle was either drunk or under the influence of drugs. There is always the possibility, though, that the driver may be in some medical crisis, which means there may be an added urgency to end the pursuit for the safety of the driver as well as the public. This chase, however, carried on for a considerable distance and time with the police vehicle leaving a very large gap between it and the offender. No attempt was made by the driver of the police car to go alongside the suspect and signal him to stop, in spite of the fact that the pursuit was moving along a double-laned roadway with wide shoulders on both sides.

Finally, the erratic driver chose to pull over to the extreme right and stop. The police car did likewise, leaving a distance of fifty yards or more between the cars. Neither of the drivers moved to get out for about thirty seconds. Finally the suspect driver lurched out of his car, obviously in a drunken rage, and staggered back toward the police car yelling. Just as he reached the cruiser, the officer got out and stood behind the open driver's side door, looking terrified. The drunk challenged the police officer, and when he got no response, began to kick the door. Each kick jolted the officer, who appeared to be holding the door so the drunk could get a better kick at it. He kicked the door many times and must have caused considerable damage, but there was no attempt by the officer to put a stop to this vandalism. The drunk, tiring from all his exertion, slowed and finally stopped, but there was still no action from the officer except to keep holding the door.

The drunk then weaved his way back to his car, got in and drove away just as a second police car arrived on the scene. Now we had the drunk leading a small parade with two police cars and the television crew.

The television did not show the end of this farce. The commentator stated that the drunk ran out of gasoline a short distance down the highway.

I was disgusted.

That the drunk was allowed to again arm himself with his vehicle and go hurtling along a public highway defies comprehension.

This kind of performance by a police officer is, sadly, not a rare occurrence. Many of today's police officers are so determined to avoid physical encounters that similar spectacles are common. Fear and lack of physical strength now frequently allow a minor incident to escalate into ugly encounters in which some drunk gets kicked in the nuts, pepper sprayed, or Tasered.

When I joined the Force in 1962, there was a heavy emphasis on physical fitness and physical endurance, both of which seem to have diminished in recent times. We learned to march as a unit. We learned to shovel horse manure and how to deal with those large animals who knew every trick in the book. We often heard that the outside of a horse was good for the inside of a man, and I can attest to the fact that each one of us became very familiar with the outside of a horse. During all this horse experience, we learned that the bluff and bluster by a very large opponent was just something that had to be dealt with, and that it had to be dealt with by you alone. Our horses knew in an instant if their bluffing had succeeded and they took full advantage of that knowledge. We learned that the only way to deal with them effectively was to take charge at the outset by using a firm voice and a steady hand. As we began our experience in the policing field, we soon learned that a firm voice and a steady hand were equally effective in dealing with people. Today that lesson seems to have been lost, and the police force is worse off for it. This may seem a minor point, but I believe it is symptomatic of a deeper problem.

Our modern society has progressed to the point where all people who rise to a position of power and influence have been through several years of university, where they have been made to understand that everyone is basically good and has predominantly good things in mind, regardless of what they may be engaged in at any given moment. They have been fitted with politically-correct rose-coloured glasses and sent forth to make the world a better place. They sit in their air-conditioned offices and formulate laws, policies, regulations and administrative rules, with abundant input from lawyers but without any basic understanding of conditions as they actually exist out in the real world where the rubber meets the road.

Much of what is wrong with our legal system can be put down to the influence of lawyers. Lawyers are in a group all to themselves. Ninety-nine percent of them give the rest a bad name. They are intelligent and capable people, highly educated and aware of every minute detail of their paper world. They vigorously apply these paper realities to criminal and civil court arguments for their great financial gain. They know how to play the justice game and how to manipulate the public into believing that anyone may someday find themselves before the court for some trumped-up violation. The television-educated public is all too willing to accept this fallacy, in spite of the fact that a very small percentage will ever find themselves charged with an offence. These things combine to make the members of the bar a very wealthy group.

The conflict in their position is that the system, in its present state of dysfunction, is so lucrative to them that they must fight to keep it as it is. Any legislative attempt to change the legal system is heavily influenced by lawyers. The guiding principle in their minds is that law that is not lucrative for lawyers is bad law. The purpose, practicality, or function of the law is secondary.

Today's police forces are clearly showing the effects of their new educated but inexperienced leaders. Street-educated cops who roll with the punches and dish out as good as they get have not got a snowball's chance in hell of advancement beyond their current assigned level. The exams and assessments for promotion are all formulated by the behind-the-scenes folks with rose-coloured glasses. Success in these tests comes not from the knowledge and expertise gained through experience on the street, but from the ability to remember and recite buzz-phrases taught at university.

There is no doubt that the wordsmith and the policy expert are very necessary parts of the picture we see today. My concern is the exclusion of street-level understanding and expertise, without which it is impossible to achieve some balance between the way things are and the way we would like things to be.

The Royal Canadian Mounted Police enjoyed a grand reputation in the minds of the public for the first hundred years of its existence. This respect and admiration came not from copious quantities of policy and administration manuals but from face-to-face contact with people on a daily basis. People did not really believe that every case would be solved, but they appreciated attention to their concerns and the time they were given when they made a request of their police. The benefit was mutual, because when you were out on the street getting to know your community and its people the way I knew some of the people I write about here, you invariably discovered practical solutions to problems that the authors of police manuals never imagined.

Today the police have less time for the basics of policing; their time is so absorbed in administration and computer data entry that they have lost their way. There are detachments with well over a hundred regular members in uniform and a considerable number of civilian employees to police a small city. These detachments will frequently have only five or six uniformed officers on the street for a twelve-hour shift. I do not think we need another policy book or another convoluted computer program to tell us that this is very wrong: just go out on the street and ask a few citizens.

Times have changed. I feel fortunate to have served with the Royal Canadian Mounted Police when I did; but I am also grateful that I got out when I did.